Translating for the Community

D0139677

TRANSLATION, INTERPRETING AND SOCIAL JUSTICE IN A GLOBALISED WORLD

Series Editors: Philipp Angermeyer, *York University, Canada* and Katrijn Maryns, *Ghent University, Belgium*

Translation, Interpreting and Social Justice in a Globalised World is an international series that welcomes authored monographs and edited collections that address translation and interpreting in settings of diversity, globalisation, migration and asylum. Books in the series will discuss how translation and interpreting practices (or their absence) may advance or hinder social justice. A key aim of the series is to encourage dialogue between scholars and professionals working in translation and interpreting studies and those working in other linguistic disciplines, such as sociolinguistics and linguistic anthropology. Books in the series will cover both translation and interpreting services provided by state and corporate entities, as well as informal, community-based translation and interpreting. We welcome proposals covering any combinations of languages (including Sign languages) and from a wide variety of geographical contexts. A guiding aim of the series is to empower those who may be disadvantaged by their lack of access to majority or official languages, and as such proposals which bridge the gap between theoretical and practical domains are particularly encouraged.

Topics which may be addressed by books in the series include (but are not limited to):

- Medical settings (including care settings and provision of public health information)
- Legal settings (law enforcement, court, prison, counselling)
- Educational settings (including community-based education)
- Asylum and migration procedures
- Access to democracy and citizenship
- Interactions with business and private-sector institutions
- The media and minority-language broadcasting and publishing
- Ethical and political considerations in translation
- Cultural translation
- Translation and language rights
- Translation and intercultural relations and conflict

Intended readership: academic and professional.

Full details of all the books in this series and of all our other publications can be found on http://www.multilingual-matters.com, or by writing to Multilingual Matters, St Nicholas House, 31–34 High Street, Bristol BS1 2AW, UK.

TRANSLATION, INTERPRETING AND SOCIAL JUSTICE IN A
GLOBALISED WORLD: 2

Translating for the Community

Edited by
Mustapha Taibi

MULTILINGUAL MATTERS
Bristol • Blue Ridge Summit

DOI 10.21832/TAIBI9139

Library of Congress Cataloging in Publication Data
A catalogue record for this book is available from the Library of Congress.
Names: Taibi, Mustapha, editor.
Title: Translating for the Community/Edited by Mustapha Taibi.
Description: Bristol, UK; Blue Ridge Summit, PA: Multilingual Matters, [2018] |
Series: Translation, Interpreting and Social Justice in a Globalised World 2 | Includes
    bibliographical references and index.
Identifiers: LCCN 2017028958| ISBN 9781783099139 (hardcover : acid-free paper) |
    ISBN 9781783099122 (softcover : acid-free paper) | ISBN 9781783099160 (Kindle)
Subjects: LCSH: Public service interpreting. | Translating and interpreting—Social aspects.
    | Intercultural communication.
Classification: LCC P306.947.T726 2017 | DDC 418/.02—dc23 LC record available at
https://lccn.loc.gov/2017028958

British Library Cataloguing in Publication Data
A catalogue entry for this book is available from the British Library.

ISBN-13: 978-1-78309-913-9 (hbk)
ISBN-13: 978-1-78309-912-2 (pbk)

Multilingual Matters
UK: St Nicholas House, 31–34 High Street, Bristol BS1 2AW, UK.
USA: NBN, Blue Ridge Summit, PA, USA.

Website: www.multilingual-matters.com
Twitter: Multi_Ling_Mat
Facebook: https://www.facebook.com/multilingualmatters
Blog: www.channelviewpublications.wordpress.com

The policy of Multilingual Matters/Channel View Publications is to use papers that are
natural, renewable and recyclable products, made from wood grown in sustainable for-
ests. In the manufacturing process of our books, and to further support our policy, preference is given to printers that have FSC and PEFC Chain of Custody certification. The FSC
and/or PEFC logos will appear on those books where full certification has been granted
to the printer concerned.

Typeset by Nova Techset Private Limited, Bengaluru and Chennai, India.
Printed and bound in the UK by Short Run Press Ltd.
Printed and bound in the US by Edwards Brothers Malloy, Inc.

Contents

Contributors

Mustapha Taibi is an Associate Professor in interpreting and translation at Western Sydney University, the leader of the International Community Translation Research Group and Editor-in-Chief of the journal *Translation & Interpreting*. From 2011 to 2015 he was Director of Academic Programmes, Languages, TESOL, Interpreting and Translation. His main research interests are community interpreting and community translation. His most recent publications are *Community Translation*, co-authored with Uldis Ozolins (2016, Bloomsbury) and *New Insights into Arabic Translation and Interpreting* (2016, Multilingual Matters). He also served on the NSW Regional Advisory Committee of the National Accreditation Authority for Translators and Interpreters (NAATI) from 2008 to 2015.

Dorothy Kelly is a Professor of Translation at the University of Granada (Spain), where she is also Vice Rector for International Relations and Development Cooperation. Her main research interests are translator training, directionality in translation and intercultural competence, interests she has combined over the years with intense international activity, coordinating international mobility and joint degree programmes, as well as studies into the impact of mobility on intercultural competence and the learning environment. She is founding editor of the *Interpreter and Translator Trainer*, the only indexed journal devoted specifically to translator education, and consultant editor of the *Translation Practices Explained* series. She was a member of the European Masters' in Translation Expert Group appointed by the Directorate General for Translation at the European Commission.

Alicia Rueda-Acedo is an Associate Professor of Spanish and Translation at the University of Texas at Arlington, where she created and currently directs the Spanish Translation and Interpreting programme. She received her PhD in Hispanic Languages and Literatures from the University of California, Santa Barbara, and holds a BA in Journalism from the University of Seville and a BA in Translation and Interpreting from the University of Granada. She is a Sworn Translator and Interpreter, certified by the Spanish Ministry of Foreign Affairs. Alicia has worked as a freelance translator and as a journalist and translator trainee at the European Parliament in Brussels.

She is the Community Outreach Coordinator for the Department of Modern Languages and the recipient of the College of Liberal Arts Outstanding Teaching Award in 2014. She was inducted to the UTA Academy of Distinguished Teachers in 2015, and named Professor of the Year for 2016 on behalf of the Arlington Sunrise Rotary Club. Alicia has published widely on 20th and 21st century Transatlantic Literature, and her new research interest combines the fields of community translation and service learning.

Harold M. Lesch is an Associate Professor and coordinator of the post-graduate diploma in translation and interpreting at Stellenbosch University, South Africa. He holds a DLitt qualification in translation. With a dissertation on community translation in South Africa, his research focuses on both translation and interpreting. He has published a number of essays, monographs and delivered papers, nationally as well as internationally in his field of expertise. Furthermore, he has experience as a simultaneous interpreter at the national parliament and the Western Cape Legislature, among others. He also established a training and research programme in interpreting and played a leading role in establishing the interpreting service on the campus.

Ignacio García is an Adjunct Professor at the School of Humanities and Communication Arts, Western Sydney University. Until very recently he was Academic Course Adviser for the Interpreting and Translation programme, and taught translation (English-Spanish) and translation technologies. He has published in academic and professional journals on translation memory, translation memory and machine translation integration, post-editing, and uses of machine translation for language learning and to assist communication with speakers of other languages. He has also taught and published on Spanish and Latin American studies. The theme of his current research is translation and social media.

Brooke Townsley (MA, RPSI, FCIOL) is a Senior Lecturer in public service interpreting and translation in the School of Health and Education, Middlesex University. He worked as a legal interpreter and translator with English and Turkish in the Criminal and Civil justice systems before joining the university in 2000, having lectured in legal interpreting and translation at Goldsmiths College and South Bank University. Between 2006 and 2011, he was Chair of the National Register of Public Service Interpreters (NRPSI) and a member of the Council of the Chartered Institute of Linguists (CIOL), of which he was Vice Chair between 2009 and 2011. He is a Fellow of the Chartered Institute of Linguists and is External Examiner for the Leeds Metropolitan University Vocational Certificate in Interpreting.

Leong Ko is a Senior Lecturer in Chinese translation and interpreting and Programme Convenor of the Master of Arts in Chinese Translation and Interpreting (MACTI). He is also a NAATI Advanced Translator and practising translator and interpreter. His research interest covers translation and interpreting studies and pedagogy of translation and interpreting. He has published extensively (books, book chapters and refereed journal papers) in these areas. He has also served as a reviewer and editor for a number of international journals.

Carmen Valero Garcés is Professor of Translation and Interpreting at the University of Alcalá (Madrid). She is Director of the Public Service Translation and Interpreting Training Programme, Coordinator of the FITISPos Research Group and founding member of the COMUNICA Group, an inter-university network for research in Public Service Translation and Interpreting in Spain. She has collaborated with the EU Directorate General for Translation in her capacity as an academic expert, and participated in several research projects. She has published several books and a large number of papers and book chapters on translation, interpreting, linguistics and cultural studies.

Raquel Lázaro Gutiérrez is a lecturer and Deputy Director of the Public Service Translation and Interpreting Training Programme at the University of Alcalá, (Spain). Some of her publications are:

2011: Nuevas tecnologías en la enseñanza virtual de la traducción e interpretación especializadas: herramientas de comunicación y comunidades de práctica, in *La creación de espacios comunes de aprendizaje: Experiencias de innovación*, pp. 147–160 Alcalá de Henares: Servicio de Publicaciones de la Universidad de Alcalá.

2011: Experiencias compartidas: impacto de las nuevas tecnologías en la enseñanza de traducción e interpretación, in *La creación de espacios comunes de aprendizaje: Experiencias de innovación*, pp. 147–160 Alcalá de Henares: Servicio de Publicaciones de la Universidad de Alcalá.

2011: Assessing Digital Literacy in Translation Students, in Valero Garcés, C. *et al.* (eds) *Traducción e interpretación en los servicios públicos en un mundo INTERcoNEcTado*. Alcalá de Henares: Servicio de Publicaciones de la Universidad de Alcalá.

Jean Burke (BSW, DipEd, MSW, PhD) is a Senior Lecturer in social work, Australian Catholic University and is a freelance Paraprofessional Swahili Translator and Interpreter. Jean worked in Tanzania 1992–2003 as a social worker, HIV educator and researcher. She has worked in research for nearly 20 years, mainly in the areas of HIV, gender and health, stigma, social work in Africa and community development. Her research interests and published papers include media analysis of human rights issues, AIDS metaphors and albinism, cross-cultural and bilingual practice, and community translation and interpreting in Swahili. Jean is on the editorial board of an African Studies journal.

Acknowledgements

I would like to thank Prof Gerhard Budin (Centre for Translation Studies, University of Vienna) for accepting to write the foreword for this edited volume. I would also like to thank the following scholars for their assistance in the review of individual chapters:

Prof Jeremy Munday (Leeds University, UK)
Prof Gerhard Budin (University of Vienna, Austria)
Prof Said Faiq (American University of Sharjah, UAE)
Prof Deborah Cao (Griffith University, Australia)
A/Prof Ineke Crezee (Auckland University of Technology, New Zealand)
A/Prof Jan-Louis Kruger (Macquarie University, Australia)
A/Prof Clare Sullivan (University of Louisville, USA)
Dr Erika Gonzalez (RMIT University, Australia)
Dr Xiangdong Liu (Western Sydney University, Australia)
Dr Kenny Wang (Western Sydney University, Australia)
Dr Sue-Ann Harding (Queen's University Belfast, UK)
Dr Tarek Shamma (Hamad Bin Khalifa University, Qatar)
Dr Stephen Doherty (University of New South Wales, Australia)

My sincere thanks also go to the anonymous reviewers who reviewed the entire volume for Multilingual Matters.

Mustapha Taibi
Sydney, 17 July 2017

Foreword

With this new volume on the topic of community translation, its editor Mustapha Taibi provides us with a new milestone in the research into an increasingly global activity that has developed as a response to communicative requirements in societies all over the world where social inequalities can be avoided or at least reduced by overcoming language barriers. While community interpreting has become a mainstream topic both in translation studies and in society at large, community translation is still a neglected topic in research, in education and, above all, in public administration in most countries. Mustapha Taibi has become one of the most influential, if not already *the* leading researcher in our discipline on the topic of community translation. In this book he managed to present, in addition to his own chapter, other important authors with their views and conceptions of community translation as well as with interesting reports on case studies from different parts of the world. It is interesting to note that variations and differences in how we perceive and shape the concept of community translation are openly addressed in several chapters of this book. Since the chapters cover a broad spectrum of perspectives including education and training, quality assurance, societal factors, and reports on case studies and concrete projects in Spain, the United Kingdom, South Africa and Australia, this book will serve as an important resource and as a reference handbook on the topic of community translation and will contribute to a mainstreaming effect in this regard.

Professor Gerhard Budin
Centre for Translation Studies
University of Vienna

Introduction

Mustapha Taibi

Community translation, the written language service that facilitates communication between public services and speakers of minority or marginalised languages, is still in its early stages of development. This applies to this area as a professional activity, teaching domain and research interest. In terms of research and scholarly literature, not much has been written. This volume therefore comes as an attempt to promote interest in this field of study and to draw the attention of researchers, trainers and public institutions to the significance of this communication service, the need for collaborative efforts to improve its quality, and the special practical and theoretical questions it poses. The book is a further step on a road hopefully leading to a prominent position for community translation on the agenda of translation studies scholars, public service leaders and local communities. It comes as a continuation of previous milestones such as the creation of the International Community Translation Research Group in 2013, the organisation of the International Conference on Community Translation in 2014 (University of Western Sydney) and the publication of Taibi and Ozolins' book *Community Translation* in 2016.

Community translators deal with a variety of text types and genres in a variety of national and local contexts. The texts to be translated are generally produced or commissioned by national, regional or local authorities, but they may also come from non-governmental organisations, ethnic groups, or other (individual or collective) social agents. Situations requiring the work of community translators are, naturally, characterised by bilingualism or multilingualism, whether this is the result of political, demographic or sociolinguistic developments deeply rooted in history, or more recent migratory population movements. What are often common denominators among different local situations are (1) a socio-economic gap between the dominant social group and minority groups needing community translations, (2) a linguistic and terminological gap between the mainstream language and minority languages and (3) a significant and challenging diversity within the target audience itself. Individually or together, these considerations raise a number of questions for the translators themselves, for trainers and researchers, and for the public authorities that need to address this diversity and ensure social equity.

For community translators, for instance, the three challenges together (socio-educational gaps, sociolinguistic diversity within the target community and language imparity) pose serious questions as to their ethical and professional role, the approach(es) they need to adopt when translating for such communities and the limits of their translator intervention. For public authorities and training providers, language diversity, which in many cases manifests itself in large numbers of relatively small language communities, poses challenges in terms of funding, continuity and outreach of services and viability of training initiatives. The cost and budgetary constraints themselves lead to questions such as the extent to which machine translation and collaborative volunteer translation may provide solutions or, conversely, have a negative impact on quality and professionalism.

These and other thorny issues are discussed in this edited volume from theoretical and practical perspectives and from different geographical, socio-political and linguistic backgrounds. Written by authors who are or have been translation practitioners, teachers and researchers, the chapters of the book offer rich insight into the practice of community translation, its challenges, and the ensuing societal issues and theoretical considerations for translation scholarship. Some themes, such as the distinctive features of community translation, translation accessibility, translation quality and the challenges of literacy levels run through the entire volume, which makes the sequence in which the contributions are to be read quite flexible. However, in deciding the final order, an attempt has been made to place the more 'universal' chapters first, followed by the more 'local' ones, although these too address issues common to community translation in different parts of the world through local or language-specific case studies and examples.

The volume opens with a chapter on quality assurance, where the editor puts forward a quality framework for community translation. Taibi starts from the premise – frequently recurring in this volume – that the ultimate aim of community translation is to empower disempowered social groups through equitable access to public service information, and that translations in this domain need to be tailored to the needs and specific linguistic and socio-educational peculiarities of the target readership. Taibi considers this a central or overarching consideration in the multi-faceted and multi-stage quality framework put forward for community translation in the first chapter. Within this set of guiding principles, quality of community translations is understood as a shared responsibility and the outcome of societal and professional contributions before, during and after the actual translation action. While community translators are expected to ensure acceptable quality standards through an appropriate translation approach and observance of basic professional requirements such as language appropriateness or translation checking, other stakeholders (e.g. policymakers, public institutions, and universities) also need to

play an active role by ensuring other elements of quality such as support-
ive policies, appropriate recruitment processes and adequate training
opportunities.

Chapter 2, by Dorothy Kelly, addresses community translator training,
one of the key elements for optimal translation quality and professional
status. Drawing upon her expertise in curriculum design and educational
leadership, Kelly offers a number of recommendations to improve the situation of training in community translation and, ultimately, the quality of
written language services made available to disadvantaged social groups. The
author notes that community translation suffers from lack of specific training programmes, as a result of its own low profile as well as logistical challenges such as the vast number of languages and the shortage of appropriate
teaching staff. Within this context, Kelly notes, the upside is that the overlap
between the competences of community translators and those of generalist
translators makes it feasible to cater for community translation education
within existing translation programmes and provide complementary specialised modules. As would be expected of the author of the *Handbook for
Translator Trainers*, Kelly stresses the importance of 'meaningful curricular
design', which is informed by a careful analysis and mapping of societal
needs, professional expectations and the social and organisational environment of the planned training.

In Chapter 3, Alicia Rueda-Acedo takes us to the practicalities of training
and offers an insightful report and reflection on how universities and other
education providers can create links with other societal stakeholders and
provide meaningful and contextualised training opportunities for would-be
(community) translators. The author describes a partnership between the
University of Texas at Arlington and *Proyecto Inmigrante*, a non-government
organisation, which allows students to engage in community translation for
Spanish-speaking migrants. The chapter highlights the positive impact of
service-learning and community translation on trainees and community
members alike. Echoing Kelly's recommendation that internships in social
services and relevant non-governmental bodies can provide a useful complement for generalist translation programmes, Rueda-Acedo emphasises the
important role service-learning placements play in preparing students for
both the professional market and civic engagement.

Harold Lesch (Chapter 4) sets out from the central argument of his previous work, which consists of an understanding of community translation as
a language service that aims to provide community members with a means
to inform and empower themselves and is, therefore, required to place the
social and linguistic needs of these people at the top of priorities. Strongly
arguing that 'community translation is a means to an end', the author under-
stands that quality of community translation is mainly a question of appropriateness and accessibility. For these targets to be achieved, he argues,
community translators need to abide by a number of norms that are specific

to community translation. Starting from a brief discussion of translation norms (e.g. Chesterman and Toury), he puts forward a set of norms that are based on a functional approach taking translations as meaningful acts conducive to effective communication, and the central idea that community translations are expected to reach target community readers through simplified language, explication, and accessible text organisation.

In Chapter 5 Ignacio García discusses the two main senses in which the term 'community translation' is currently used in the literature and practice: professional public service translation, as in this volume, vs volunteer or crowd-sourced translation for online communities. Instead of drawing them apart, he puts forward an ambitious and probably controversial proposal to somehow bring them together. Acknowledging that using the services of amateurs may have a negative impact on community translation as a profession, García argues that translation *for* the community (by professionals) and translation *by* the community (amateur members) need not be mutually exclusive. Rather, they could complement each other if a distinction is made between high-stake situations/translations, where the expertise of professional translators is indispensable, and non-critical ones, where fast and effective communication can be guaranteed through community translation 2.0 without much risk.

Brooke Townsley (Chapter 6) reports the findings of a small-scale study aiming to explore the situation of community translation in the United Kingdom through surveying the views of a few language service providers. Townsley notes that, although the role of community translation in ensuring equitable access to public services is often acknowledged in public discourse, the activity is also under attack, mainly for budgetary reasons. The views of the agencies the author interviewed also point to a less-than-desirable state of the art for community translation: it is perceived as of less importance than community interpreting, the volume of translations is decreasing, literacy levels are a challenge for some communities at least, appropriate education and qualifications are not given the importance they deserve, and the working conditions and volume of work available do not offer incentives to undertake training either.

Valero-Garcés and Lázaro-Gutiérrez contribute with a chapter (Chapter 7) on a unique and rarely investigated translation setting: prisons. They describe a project conducted in collaboration with the Spanish Directorate General for Penitentiaries, whose aims were to explore and analyse the measures taken to facilitate communication between Spanish prison personnel and inmates who did not have a good command of Spanish, and to contribute with other initiatives to improve communication between the two parties. The setting described in this chapter epitomises the nature of communicative situations requiring language services for migrants and language minorities (power relationships, unfamiliar institutional processes and discourses, language barrier, etc.), but in this case the needs are even direr, as the users are doubly disempowered and, what is more, physically confined and isolated.

The last two chapters are from Australia, one of the pioneer countries in community interpreting and translation, but, as mentioned earlier, the issues addressed through this national prism are quite common elsewhere. In one of these contributions (Chapter 8), Leong Ko actually observes that the localism usually associated with community translation may not always be the case, as original texts may be generated in or brought from other countries, and community translations may have international destinations. Through an extensive set of examples of English-Chinese translations, Ko offers an overview of the characteristics and challenges of community translation and the types of text translated in Australia. He concludes that, although community translation may cross national borders, the texts handled in this area of professional practice tend to be 'localised, context-specific and culture-specific', which poses serious challenges for translators who are not conversant with the local culture and institutional language.

In the last chapter Jean Burke provides rich statistical data to describe and discuss the sociolinguistic profile of Swahili as a minority language in Australia and the implications of this sociolinguistic diversity of Swahili speakers for community translation. Language variation in this context becomes a serious challenge for translators and public services. Written translation is usually associated with the standard variety of the language in question (in this case Swahili, but this also applies to other languages such as Arabic), but this High variety may not be accessible to all the target community members for reasons pertaining to geographical variation and literacy levels.

1 Quality Assurance in Community Translation

Mustapha Taibi

1. Introduction

Translation and interpreting literature abounds with references to quality and effectiveness (e.g. Drugan, 2013; Hale *et al.*, 2009; House, 1977; Moser-Mercer, 1996; Williams, 2004). However, the notion of quality in these language services is far from consensual. Understandably, each translation theory or approach defines quality differently and places more emphasis on some criteria than others. In this regard, two broad areas of literature can be identified: one academic, the other professionally oriented (Taibi & Ozolins, 2016: 108–110). The first aims to establish criteria and standards based on an academic or theoretical understanding of translation and a linguistic and textual comparison of texts. Through these criteria, target texts can be compared to source texts and a quality rating can be determined. Examples of authors representing this area of literature are House (1977, 1997, 2001, 2013 and 2015) Brunette (2000) and Depraetere (2011), whose main interest is theoretical and related to translation critique, and Petersen (1996) and Hague *et al.* (2011), who are more concerned with pedagogic applications of quality, i.e. translation learning, assessment and feedback to assist and facilitate development of translation skills. The other area of translation quality literature focuses more on professional production processes, i.e. translation as a process of service provision and project management (Drugan, 2013; Dunne, 2011; Orsted, 2001; Samuelsson-Brown, 2006). As some authors have indicated (e.g. Drugan, 2013; Lauscher, 2000; see also Townsley in this volume), there is a perceived gap between these two strands of translation quality. However, they – in principle – should inform and complement each other: translation quality cannot be understood in depth without a sound theoretical understanding of translation and the features of effective translation, on the one hand, and adequate knowledge of professional processes and industrial relations that operate on the ground, on the other.

Starting from this premise of interdependence and complementariness, in this chapter translation quality assurance is addressed in a specific and special subfield of translation, community translation, also known as public service translation. The first question that the title of the chapter (quality assurance in community translation) is likely to trigger is whether translation standards and quality assurance processes vary from one field of translation to another, i.e. whether community translation needs to have quality criteria and processes that are different from those applied in other fields of translation. The answer to this question is that, although the core of translation theories, assessment criteria, professional standards and quality assurance processes may apply to different types and settings of translation, each type and setting might require different or more specific considerations and applications, or might need quality processes and evaluations to place more emphasis on some aspects than others.

What distinguishes community translation from other types and domains of translation is that its main mission is to empower local communities and give their members voice and access to information, services and participation (Lesch, 1999 and this volume; Taibi, 2011; Taibi & Ozolins, 2016). Because community translation is intended to empower disempowered social groups by enabling them to have equitable access to public service information and to participation in their society, this overarching mission needs to be an essential consideration in understanding and applying quality standards in this subfield of translation and social services. Although many of the established criteria (e.g. accuracy, appropriateness, readability) and processes (e.g. selection of personnel, revision and editing) of quality assurance in translation are relevant and applicable to community translation, the nature of the latter and the specificity of the public it serves make it necessary to highlight a number of specific considerations, which go from translator recruitment to processing of text contents and treatment of the translation process itself.

Quality assurance in community translation is multi-faceted and, as in other fields, involves a number of stages, actors and actions (adequate training, appropriate recruitment processes, assessment and processing of source texts, production processes, consultation with target communities, etc.). However, as stated above, the nature of this language service gives a particular nuance to all these aspects. In the following sections I start with a brief discussion of some of the main quality issues in translation in general and, subsequently, propose a comprehensive framework for quality assurance in community translation, which encompasses not only the translation phase but also the phases preceding and following it, and not only the work of translators but also the role of other stakeholders.

2. Translation Quality

In an attempt to offer an all-encompassing definition for translation quality, Koby *et al.* (2014) provide both a broader definition and a narrower one.

- A quality translation demonstrates accuracy and fluency required for the audience and purpose and complies with all other specifications negotiated between the requester and provider, taking into account end user needs. (2014: 416)
- A high-quality translation is one in which the message embodied in the source text is transferred completely into the target text, including denotation, connotation, nuance and style, and the target text is written in the target language using correct grammar and word order, to produce a culturally appropriate text that, in most cases, reads as if originally written by a native speaker of the target language for readers in the target culture. (2014: 416–417)

Although quite comprehensive, well thought out and seemingly encapsulating decades-long knowledge advances in translation studies, these definitions illustrate how any aspect of translation quality may be controversial. Questions that may arise include: (1) Why are only accuracy and fluency included in the broad definition?; (2) How can the needs of end users be determined and accommodated?; (3) What happens if the requester's specifications clash with the end user's needs, as understood by the translator or another stakeholder? Is the style or register of the original an aspect that must always be mirrored, regardless what the communicative situation is?

Concern for quality in translation dates back centuries (e.g. in the case of religious and literary texts) or, at least, decades (e.g. for pragmatic or instrumental texts), as Williams (2004: xiii) observes. However, as the same author notes, although there is general agreement that translations must meet quality standards, there are disparities of views on the notions of quality, acceptability and the criteria to determine them (Williams, 2004: xiv). A number of approaches, models and quality standards have been put forward, both in translation studies (academia) and the translation industry (professional practice). Yet, none of them is able to claim applicability across text types and genres or a level of clarity and detail as to rule out assessor subjectivity.

A prominent example of the approaches in this area is the work of House (1977, 1997, 2001, 2013 and 2015), who over decades has developed a well-argued functional basis for translation quality assessment. House argues that, for the quality of a translation to be assessed appropriately, some key parameters need to be scrutinised to construct a profile of the source text and then compare it to the target text. These parameters are basically Halliday's ideational, interpersonal and textual metafunctions and their corresponding discourse descriptors: field, tenor and mode. Field 'refers to the nature of the social action that is taking place' (House, 1997: 108), that is the subject area or content the text covers. Tenor 'refers to who is taking part, to the nature of the participants, the addresser and the addressees, and the relationship between them in terms of social power and social distance...' (House, 1997: 108–109). Mode denotes the channel of communication (e.g. spoken vs written, as well as combinations such as written to be spoken, etc.) and the extent to which interlocutors are allowed to participate. For House, a quality translation is one that is recognisable as equivalent in terms of ideational and interpersonal meanings (field and tenor) and takes into consideration the means of communication and the level and type of participation (mode). House's parameters also include genre, a key aspect that assists in constructing text profiles and distinguishing one text from another. Although the register categories (field, tenor and mode) are useful in describing the relationship between text and context, the notion of genre serves as a means to situating texts in their deeper and broader intertextual context, i.e. in the class of text with which they have something in common, and the '"macro-context" of the linguistic and cultural community in which the text is embedded' (House, 2015: 64). Once a source text profile has been established using these textual and intertextual criteria, the quality of the target text can be assessed in light of and by comparison with this profile.

Another influential contribution to understanding and assessing translation quality is Skopos Theory (Reiss & Vermeer, 1984; Vermeer, 1989), which no longer seeks equivalence as much as it does adequacy or appropriateness. The theory presents translation as a purposeful action whose ultimate goal is adequacy between a translation and its *Skopos*, i.e. the intended function of the text in its new context of use. While linguistic and pragmatic models of translation have focused on equivalence for decades, Skopos Theory 'dethrones' the source text and considers it as a mere 'offer of information'. As such, what counts most is not fidelity to the original text, but the internal coherence of the *translatum* (target text). The 'coherence rule' in this theory establishes that the target text must be coherent with the situation of its audience (Reiss & Vermeer, 1984: 113). In other words, it needs to make sense and be sufficiently coherent in its new context of use, and be in line with the expectations and background knowledge of the intended audience. As Nord (1997: 29) notes, the *Skopos* rule allows translators to determine what is best for a given text and communicative situation: whether a formally faithful translation or a free version of the original text, or any position between the two is deemed situationally appropriate. Indeed, Reiss and Vermeer (1984) do not consider that a 'faithful and complete' reflection of the source text is the only valid translational option; rather, any other rendering, including summary translation, free translation or adaptation could be acceptable if appropriate and effective in a given context. In terms of quality assessment, Skopos Theory broadens the scope and understanding of translation and offers key criteria that may assist in determining quality, including translation brief, text function, adaptation to target audience and internal coherence. However, as House (2015: 11) notes, the theory falls short in terms of explicitness and operationalisation, which makes it of little use for the practice of translation quality assessment.

On the other hand, quality standards and assessment practices which have gone a long way towards explicitness, detail and operationalisation have been criticised for being too microtextual and focusing mainly on error analysis at sentence or sub-sentence level (Williams, 2004: 3–9). In Australia, for instance, the translation assessment standards of the National Accreditation Authority for Translators and Interpreters (NAATI), applicable in both its own certification testing and NAATI-approved training courses, are based on point deduction for mostly accuracy and language errors. Candidates sitting for the Professional Translator level are expected to translate two 250-word texts and obtain a minimum mark of 70/100. Examiners are provided with guidelines and examples of errors and the number of points to be deducted for each error depending on its weight (Turner et al., 2010: 14). NAATI also provides a list of recommended symbols to be used when marking translations. This is intended to ensure consistency among assessors and feedback clarity for candidates. Errors are classified 'in terms of accuracy, quality of language and technique' (Turner et al., 2010: 14). Accuracy and language appropriateness are dominant, though, as errors are further categorised as 'general errors' (serious mistranslations or major omissions), 'isolated errors affecting accuracy' (e.g. mistranslation of a given word, unjustified addition, wrong word order, grammatical error, etc.) or 'isolated errors not affecting accuracy' (e.g. unidiomatic word choice, superfluous lexical items, spelling, etc.).

Although the NAATI model dates back earlier, the adoption of quantifiable error types characterised a shift towards more 'objective' translation quality assessment in different parts of the world in the last half of the 1990s and the beginning of the 21st century (Lommel et al., 2014: 457). This came as globalisation was becoming a buzzword, compliance with ISO quality standards was gaining ground as a performance indicator in industries, and translation was coming of age as a language industry (Williams, 2004: xiv). Probably the most recent development in this shift is the Multidimensional Quality Metrics (MQM) system (Lommel et al., 2014, 2015), which was developed as part of a European Union-funded project and aims to offer an industry-wide acceptable framework within which all types of translation can be evaluated as 'objectively' as feasible. The framework does not put forward a one-solution-fits-all approach, but offers a comprehensive list of over a hundred translation and production issue types, from which stakeholders can choose the most relevant to the assessment exercise at hand (Lommel et al., 2014, 2015). The issue types included in MQM fall under well-known translation dimensions such as accuracy, fluency, style and terminology, but also cover aspects that are relatively new, at least in terms of labelling, such as design (i.e. format or presentation of a text), internationalisation (i.e. work on the source content to make it ready for translation or localisation), locale convention (i.e. the extent to which texts are formally compliant with the conventions of the target locale) and verity (i.e. the extent to which the text content is suitable for the target readership and locale) (Lommel *et al.*, 2015). One of the advantages of this quality assessment framework is its flexibility, as it offers users the possibility to customise their metric according to their needs, choosing for instance to conduct a holistic (broad) or an analytic (detailed) assessment of translations, or selecting some parameters rather than others, depending on assessment goals, the time available or other factors (Lommel *et al.*, 2015).

Translation quality standards that are based on industrial quality assurance such as ISO 9000 are attempts to cater for the need for precise, objective, quantifiable and widely accepted translation assessment tools. However, as Williams (2004: xvii) comments, translation is a complex and heterogeneous intellectual product, not a standardised or replicable industrial item, and as a result of this, translation quality assessment continues to be a challenging and controversial area. Among other pending issues, notions such as accuracy, fidelity or mistranslation continue to be debatable; quantification of errors with a view to forming an overall judgement of a translation is questionable; assessors do not agree on what constitutes a major or a minor translation error; and there is no consensus either on whose perspective and interests (translator as an expert, commissioner, end user, etc.) are to be given priority in our understanding and assessment of quality (Drugan, 2013: 38). Within this context, in the following sections a general framework is put forward for quality in community translation, not in the sense of an assessment model or standard, but in the form of general guidelines that would be helpful to follow before, during and after translation for a local community.

3. Quality Assurance in Community Translation

As observed elsewhere (Fraser, 1993; Taibi, 2011; Taibi & Ozolins, 2016), community translation is still far from professionalisation and adequate quality standards in many parts of the world. Because the end users are often disempowered people who speak minority languages, and also as a result of budgetary constraints in public services, it is often the case that *ad hoc* measures are adopted, if at all, to cater for the communication needs of these community members; and there are not appropriate quality assurance measures in place to ensure a suitable and effective translation product. For this to happen, appropriate action is required at a number of levels, which are summarised in Table 1.1 and explained in the subsequent paragraphs.

Table 1.1 A multidimensional framework for quality in community translation

1. Societal level
i. Policymaking
ii. Training
2. Inter-professional level
i. Selection of translators
ii. Preparation of source texts
iii. Briefing translators
3. Translation stage
i. Overarching mission (empowerment)
ii. Functionalist approach
iii. Language appropriateness
iv. Consultation with the community
v. Translation checking
4. Post-translation stage
i. Translation checking
ii. Community feedback

3.1 Policymaking

The first step towards offering community translation services and ensuring they meet quality standards is recognition of a societal problem, that there are social groups that do not have (an appropriate level of) access to information, participation and services due to language barriers. The socio-political regime and government policies relating to language rights and the concomitant issues of social justice and human rights determine the extent to which community translation services are made available (Taibi & Ozolins, 2016: 19). Community translation requires public funding, and without favourable policymaking, such financial support cannot be guaranteed. In turn, without sufficient funding, translations are more likely to be assigned – if commissioned at all – to non-qualified volunteers. Similarly, policies that demonstrate awareness of the social and communicative needs of language minorities are more likely to contribute to quality by ensuring appropriate training, the aspect that is addressed in the following section.

3.2 Training

For anybody to offer a quality product or service in a given profession or practice – whether manual or intellectual – they need to be adequately trained. However, although efforts have been made towards professionalisation of translation, it is indisputable that access to this activity is still loose and many practitioners have had no specific training (Dimitrova, 2005: 2; Pym *et al.*, 2013: 12). In community translation in particular this is much more so for a number of reasons, including availability, viability and affordability of training courses. Specific training in community translation is very scarce around the globe (Kelly, this volume; Taibi, 2011; Taibi & Ozolins, 2016). Some of the reasons contributing to this state of affairs include: (1) the fact that community translation itself has been neglected in the translation studies literature; (2) the lack of employment opportunities in this sector due to unfavourable government policies or insufficient interest among private companies; (3) the language diversity and demographics that characterise communities where community translation is needed: each language community is often so small that it is unable to ensure viability for training programmes; and (4) the lack of qualified trainers who have minority community languages as languages of specialisation. However, if there is sufficient recognition and support at the societal level (mainly government and the education sector, but also private companies), solutions can be found. For instance, to address viability challenges, community translation courses may be designed for mixed language groups instead of language-specific streams. Similarly, to overcome the shortage of language-specific trainers in some communities, a combination of qualified trainers without language-specific expertise and translation practitioners or linguists from the relevant community could offer a way out.

Kelly (this volume) concludes that the most sustainable way to offer training in community translation is for tertiary education providers to design a combination of generalist translation programmes and short intensive courses or optional modules on community translation. Kelly believes that the skills required for community translation coincide to a great extent with those expected of a general translator. Accordingly, they can be covered in existing generalist training programmes and complemented with modules that specifically address the specific needs and features of community translation. Taibi (2011: 221) argues that existing generalist translation programmes in different countries may offer an adequate foundation for future community translators, as they normally cover essential aspects such as translation skills, intercultural communication, text types and audience expectations. Taibi then continues to suggest that training offerings that are specifically focused on community translation settings and the needs of the local community would be a better option. Graham (2012: 28) seems to agree: 'applied translation courses develop a range of skills that are relevant to any context, including PST [public service translation]. However, PST still requires knowledge of public service institutions and practices (e.g., police, councils, hospitals) and academics report that these are rarely taught as part of a translation programme'.

3.3 Selection of translators

As pointed out in the previous section, a significant portion of the manpower working in translation in general and community translation in particular has not undertaken specific training in the field. Some countries have accreditation or certification systems in place, which can guarantee a level of translation competence, but many do not, which leaves translation work accessible to people from different educational backgrounds and with diverse levels of expertise. This makes it even more crucial for translation quality that public services and translation agencies undertake informed and systematic selection of personnel, both at the time of recruitment for contract or permanent employment and when assigning a given translation task. Selection of translators is included under the inter-professional level in Table 1.1 above, as it does not fall within the translator's own quality assurance phase, but pertains to the relationship between translators and other professionals who need their services (e.g. local governments, healthcare organisations, environment agencies, translation agencies, etc.).

In situations requiring community translation, public services and translation agencies often find themselves torn between quality standards, on one hand, and, on the other, budgetary considerations and availability of qualified translators in the relevant working languages. The latter is a serious issue, especially in countries that continue to receive migrants with an ever-expanding range of linguistic and cultural backgrounds (e.g. the United States, the United Kingdom, Australia or Germany). In the case of what is sometimes referred to as 'emerging languages', i.e. minority languages emerging in a given country or state in terms of interpreting and translation demand as a result of new population movement trends, interpreting and translation needs are immediate but qualified translators and interpreters are less likely to be available. The mediators available – often students, highly literate people from other professions, or paraprofessional translators – may have no training in translation and limited understanding of professional translation ethics, quality standards and protocols. A possible solution could be to seek the services of qualified translators in other parts of the world, including the countries of origin of the migrant population in question. As a result of advances in electronic communication, international commissioning of translations is already a fact of translation professional practice. However, as has become established in this volume and elsewhere (e.g. Taibi & Ozolins, 2016), community translation is a localised exercise: although some textual contents may be general or universal enough to allow recruitment from a wider international pool of translators, a considerable portion of texts translated for the community requires knowledge of the local context and institutions (e.g. school system, welfare benefits, legal system, etc.).

Not all service providers and translation agencies worldwide will find optimal conditions for quality (i.e. appropriate funding, qualifications, professional certification, sufficient experience, relevant expertise, etc.). However, while each stakeholder is working towards better quality, it is important for translation commissioners and intermediaries to take measures to ensure the best quality possible with the resources available and within the constraints of each local community. In Australia, public services generally employ NAATI-accredited translators. The New South Wales Multicultural Health Communication Service, for instance, advises: 'It is strongly suggested that except in unusual circumstances, such as with new or emerging languages, a National Accreditation Authority for Translators and Interpreters (NAATI) Accredited Health translator be used (...) Choosing native speakers, no matter how language proficient they may be can lead to inaccuracies' (NSW Multicultural Health Communication Service, 2014: 3). Another example, from the United Kingdom this time, is the Sussex Interpreting Services, a charitable organisation based in Brighton, which aims to empower minority communities by offering interpreting and translation and other services. The company makes public its criteria for selection of translators and the measures they take to ensure quality. In the first place, they employ community translators who are members of:

- The Institute of Translation and Interpreting, a professional organisation which promotes quality in these two fields;
- The Chartered Institute of Linguists, the UK-based body which serves the interests of linguists worldwide, and provides a number of accredited qualifications;

And/or

- Community translators who have undertaken the Open College Network accredited Community Translation course;

And/or

- Community translators who hold a Diploma or Degree in Translation.

When candidates meeting the above criteria are not available, the service 'will approach a translator who has considerable experience working in the field of translation and, wherever possible, who has completed a CIESK (Community Interpreting Essential Skills and Knowledge) program' (Sussex Interpreting Services, 2012). Further quality assurance measures include proofreading documents translated into English, spot-checking translated work on a monthly basis and taking proofreader feedback into consideration in future allocation of work (Sussex Interpreting Services, 2012).

3.4 Preparation of source texts

The second quality requirement that applies at the inter-professional level is work on original texts to make them more suitable for effective translation. This is an interface where public service staff and translators can cooperate to produce multilingual resources of better quality. Materials handled by community translators often contain complex institutional information, procedures and advice, while the target readership in minority communities significantly differs from the mainstream community in terms of cultural and educational background and knowledge of institutional systems. Public service texts that need translating are often written with a mono-cultural audience in mind and with assumptions of shared knowledge that are far above what can be found on the ground. This is why it is very important for drafters of such texts to be aware that their texts will be used by some end users, but also be processed as raw material (to be translated) for further use by other members of the community. In some pioneering countries, this is already happening. The Multicultural Health Communication Service (NSW, Australia), mentioned above, has Guidelines for the Production of Multilingual Resources, where, among other practical recommendations, producers of multilingual healthcare information are advised they 'must ensure that the text is written in clear, cohesive, unambiguous, plain English, avoiding medical or specialist health jargon or acronyms. Specifically, writers may consider writing in the active voice, minimising the use of pronouns, using short sentences, and providing definitions for any technical terms' (NSW Multicultural Health Communication Service, 2014: 3). This is not to suggest that community translators would not be able to comprehend and adapt complex texts; on the contrary, professionals adopting a functionalist approach that captures the essence of community translation (see Sections 3.6 and 3.7 below) would know how to adjust a source text to the needs and expectations of their target readership, but a streamlined original would make the process even smoother. It would also be proactively effective, especially in the event of the source text falling in the hands of a translator who believes that their role is to mirror the structures, lexical choices and clarity level of the source text regardless what the translation context is.

3.5 Briefing translators

With functionalist approaches to translation, such as Skopos Theory mentioned in Section 2 above, the notion of translation brief has become an essential aspect in the translation process and the contractual relationship between translator and client. A brief refers to the information and instructions provided by the commissioner to the translator as to the translation's purpose, target readership, context of use, medium and other particulars (Gentzler, 2001: 73). Although translators often complain about lack of instructions or, at best, scanty briefs (Koby & Baer, 2003: 222), it is generally agreed that the clearer the assignment and the more detailed and relevant the information about the translation task, the easier it is for translators to choose the most appropriate translation strategies. Koby *et al.*'s (2014: 416) definition of translation quality in Section 2 above stresses the importance of compliance 'with all other specifications negotiated between the requester and provider, taking into account end user needs'. For the community translation context, in particular, this statement offers some keywords that are fundamental to quality: specifications, negotiation, requester, provider and end user. Translation brief is often understood as instructions coming from the initiator, requester or client, who is usually the party who commissions and pays for a translation. In community translation, at least, there is often a need for the translation specifications to be negotiated between requester and translator, taking into account the needs and expectations of the end users. This is because (1) the requester (in many cases a public service) may not necessarily have as much cultural and sociolinguistic knowledge about the target readership as the translator; and (2) community translators are also bound by the ethical expectation to empower end users (often members of minority groups) and take their interests and perspectives into consideration (see Section 3.6).

One of the essential aspects of quality where inter-professional cooperation can make a difference relates to the translation approach to be used and the extent to which the target readership, as a pivotal stakeholder, needs to be accommodated. This is a central issue in community translation: translators often face the dilemma of whether to comply with the expectation of accuracy in terms of content and register, or satisfy the need for translations that are communicative and effective on the ground. Inter-professional discussion of these aspects, in light of the cultural and socio-educational background of the community of end users, can assist in determining how the objectives of accuracy and communicability can be attained in a non-mutually exclusive fashion. Another aspect, which is also closely linked to the previous point and to quality, concerns the format or medium of communication. Professional discussions between translation commissioners and community translators may lead to alternative communication media (e.g. audio-visual adaptations) replacing the traditional printed translation in some specific cases. Communities of end users vary in terms of literacy levels and communicative channel preferences. Therefore, by negotiating the translation brief with public service commissioners, community translators can play a more active role in quality assurance (Taibi & Ozolins, 2016: 49, 71). Where the relationship between translation requester and provider is mediated by agencies, it is important for the latter to play that active role, seeking informative and detailed specifications from the client, consulting with the translator(s) regarding the assignment and any related issues, and liaising between the two parties to ensure the final product is up to the expectations of both commissioner and the community of users.

3.6 Overarching mission (empowerment)

As is argued in this volume (e.g. Lesch, García, Taibi), central to community translation is the empowerment of local communities and facilitation of people's access to information and participation. This objective constitutes an overarching mission, general framework, or macro-skopos by which community translators need to be guided. Within this framework, professionals may then consider other aspects such as translation brief (micro-skopos), text type and so on. Taibi and Ozolins (2016: 76) visually portray the process of community translation as a filtering arrow or pipe going from source text to target text through, first, the overarching mission of community translation (community empowerment) and, subsequently, a number of filters or considerations, including translation brief, text type, textual norms, audience, medium, technical requirements, etc. By placing their translation action in this context, with community empowerment as a foregrounded goal, community translators demonstrate their awareness of their role as social agents and of the social ramifications of their translatorial actions beyond processing of individual sentences and texts.

The relevance of this macro-skopos to translation quality lies in the fact that, without due attention to it, community translators may produce translations that meet many of the quality standards or the client's specifications, but fail to achieve the *raison d'être* of their activity, namely empowering the communities they serve. Following Koby *et al.*'s (2014: 416–417) narrower definition of quality above, translators may abide by the translation brief or their own assumptions regarding quality and translator role, and produce a target text which accurately reflects the denotative, connotative and interpersonal features of the original text, and lives up to the grammatical and stylistic norms of the target standard language. Yet, this by no means guarantees an appropriate quality standard in the eyes of the end users, who may need a more accessible text, a translation in a specific sociolinguistic variety, a combination of text and visual illustrations, and so on and so forth. Translation quality is relative and, as Lesch (this volume) asserts, translating texts for the community without foregrounding societal factors, the ultimate objectives of community translation, and the audience's expectations of appropriateness and accessibility will only result in a non-communicative translation that is void of real value.

3.7 Functionalist approach

Closely tied to the generic skopos or overarching mission outlined in the previous section is the issue of translation approach. Given the nature of community translation, a functionalist approach would seem to be the most appropriate. As mentioned earlier in this chapter, a functionalist approach (e.g. Skopos Theory) takes into consideration the communicative situation of the target text, i.e. the translation brief, the intended function of the translation (in our case both the macro-skopos of community translation and the micro-skopos of a particular text), the expectations of the target readership and so on. Based on these elements, the translator can choose a more or less free approach to translation, and – in consultation with the relevant stakeholders – determine the most appropriate form of translation or transcreation in each situation (e.g. summary translation, adaptation or version, or a transcreated product in a more creative format). A functionalist approach also distinguishes between text types and, therefore, allows the (community) translator to take informed decisions case by case. In contexts requiring community translation, texts to be translated may be produced by different social agents, including public institutions, non-government organisations, local community leaders, and individual citizens or residents (Taibi, 2011: 214). This creates an overwhelming richness and diversity of text types, formats and discourses (e.g. personal statements, official documents, press releases, government letters, informative flyers, school invitations, relief appeals, etc.), for which only a functionalist understanding of translation – coupled with an empowerment mission – can offer appropriate guiding principles.

3.8 Language appropriateness

As in any other field of translation, community translations must meet the quality standards relating to target language grammar and stylistic conventions. To use Koby *et al.*'s (2014: 416–417) words again, a quality target text demonstrates use of 'correct grammar and word order' and 'in most cases, reads as if originally written by a native speaker of the target language'. This is probably the first level of translation quality assessment that is identified, not only by experts but also by the general public. Failure to comply with the linguistic conventions of the target community – be it at the level of spelling, lexical choices, structures or idiomaticity – would suggest poor quality even before comparing a target text with its corresponding source text.

In the particular case of community translation, language appropriateness is not only – or not necessarily – a matter of compliance with the standard rules of a target written language. As was pointed out above, communities may have different literacy levels, preferences and needs. Within the same society, there may be social groups for whom language appropriateness is not synonymous with compliance with the mainstream language norms (i.e. standard or dominant language). Language appropriateness in such cases would be closer in sense to language variety appropriate for understanding and accessibility, rather than to conformity with grammatical and stylistic norms. In Arabic, a diglossic language, texts are written in a standard variety that only highly educated people are able to understand and produce. Accordingly, in some Arabic-speaking communities in Europe, for instance, translations into regional dialects of Arabic may be more appropriate and effective than texts in Standard Arabic, with complex structures and specialised terminology, which not many end users understand. In South Africa, Walker *et al.* (1995) note that, with the process of democratisation and social change in the country, African languages were made official, and public authorities started efforts to communicate with local communities in their own languages, including in those situations where literacy is limited and the languages in question have not developed terminology to match scientific and institutional English. In this context, the authors observe, translators have opted for incorporating loan words in their translations, paraphrasing or replacing specialised terms with more general lexical items in African languages. Within these constraints, language appropriateness is not the use (or creation) of standard equivalents that would reflect the register of the original, but a focus on communication effectiveness through a language variety (or code-mixing) that ensures grassroots levels are reached. Like quality, language appropriateness is relative.

3.9 Consultation with the community

This element is included under the translation phase in Table 1.1 above, but it applies to the inter-professional level as well. Consulting the relevant community is something that needs to be done by both the producers of community texts (e.g. public services, private organisations) and the translators of such materials. Services producing resources for the community need to ascertain, among other things, whether similar resources are already available, whether the planned flyer or booklet contains any culturally sensitive issues, or whether print material is the most suitable way to communicate with the target audience (NSW Multicultural Health Communication Service, 2014: 1). During the translation process, community translators need to consult members of the community of users whenever they face specific challenges (e.g. cultural issues, language varieties, etc.) or have uncertainties about the extent to which some of their translation choices are accessible. This type of consultation is different from community feedback in Point 3.11 and does not need to be done in a systematic or organised manner.

3.10 Translation checking

As can be seen in Table 1.1 above, translation checking has been included under both the translation stage and the post-translation stage. During translation, checking is to be undertaken by the translator him/herself; after a translation is completed, it needs to be checked or proofread by another participant in the quality assurance process (e.g. peer translator, copy editor, proofreader, etc.). By checking their own translations, professional translators can detect apparently insignificant typos (e.g. grammatical words such as 'not', spelling of homophones, inconsistencies in names and numbers) or passages they may have inadvertently omitted. By having a double-checking step in place, public services, private organisations or translation agencies can avoid serious damage to their reputations and to third parties. Taibi and Qadi (2016) cite a number of clearly unacceptable Arabic-English translations provided to Muslim pilgrims by Saudi public services. These generally literal and ungrammatical renderings could have been detected by any reader with an advanced command of English, let alone a professional translator or proofreader.

3.11 Community feedback

User feedback is now an integral part of quality assurance in industrial production and service provision. Community translation should be no exception; especially due to the real-life impact this type of translation has in terms of social inclusion, equity, participation and change. Drugan (2013: 40) acknowledges that seeking the feedback of a group of informants or a committee of experts would have a positive outcome, but she notes that this is rarely possible due to factors such as deadline and budget. Another potential impediment is that professional translators are sensitive towards feedback coming from people who are not translation experts. However, community feedback on translations does not have to be – and, for logistical reasons cannot be – a step in the production line of every translation. Especially in those cases where community translations are managed by a service or agency, a system may be put in place to enable periodic community feedback on sample translations or a one-off community consultation on parts of larger translation projects. Community leaders, focus groups or randomly selected readers may be able to make a significant contribution to translation quality, or at least draw the agency's attention to issues that may have gone unnoticed. As in research projects, it is important for groups of participants in community feedback to be as representative of the target population as possible. Community leaders may have higher socio-educational levels than the average community reader, so a focus group consisting of such individuals only may not be the best option. Similarly, the group of informants needs to reflect the linguistic diversity of the target community of users. For instance, in the case of translation into Spanish, speakers of both peninsular and South American varieties need to be consulted, unless the target readership is known to come from only one regional background.

4. Conclusion

Translation quality has been debatable for decades, if not centuries, and although translator educators, translators, translation agencies, translation scholars and users generally agree that translations need to demonstrate appropriate quality standards, not everybody agrees what exactly translation quality consists of and how it can be assessed. A number of theoretical and practical contributions have been made in this area but, given the complex nature of translation and the many stakeholders involved, it is difficult to find a translation quality model that is relevant to and easily operational in all translation subfields and communicative situations. However, the accumulation of wisdom in scholarship and professional practice over the years has led to the identification of key elements to quality that may be debatable in their specifics but can hardly be disputed in terms of their overall value, validity and contribution to quality. These include the purpose of translation, the type of text, the nature and expectations of the target readership, and language appropriateness.

These are some of the key elements proposed in this chapter as part of a set of guiding principles for quality assurance in a specific subfield of translation, namely community or public service translation. The core arguments in this quality framework are:

(1) Translation quality is multi-faceted, needs to be addressed at different stages (before, during and after the actual translation process) and must involve the different stakeholders in community translation (e.g. institutions providing training, public services working on original materials and consulting language experts, translators and translation agencies consulting and negotiating with commissioners, community members providing advice and feedback on translations, etc.).
(2) Community translation has a distinctive feature and mission, which consists of empowering disempowered language communities and, therefore, this needs to be seen as a macro-*skopos* and a fundamental criterion of quality.

References

Brunette, L. (2000) Towards a terminology for translation quality assessment: A comparison of TQA practices. *The Translator* 6 (2), 169–182.
Depraetere, I. (ed.) (2011) *Perspectives on Translation Quality*. Berlin: Mouton de Gruyter.
Dimitrova, B.E. (2005) *Expertise and Explicitation in the Translation Process*. Amsterdam and Philadelphia: John Benjamins.
Drugan, J. (2013) *Quality in Professional Translation*. London: Bloomsbury.
Dunne, K.J. (2011) From vicious to virtuous cycle: Customer-focused translation quality management using ISO 9001 principles and Agile methodologies. In K.J. Dunne and E.S. Dunne (eds) *Translation and Localization Project Management. The Art of the Possible* (pp. 153–188). Amsterdam and Philadelphia: John Benjamins.

Fraser, J. (1993) Public accounts: Using verbal protocols to investigate community translation. *Applied Linguistics* 14 (4), 325–343.

Gentzler, E. (2001) *Contemporary Translation Theories*. Clevedon: Multilingual Matters.

Graham, A.M. (2012) Training provision for public service interpreting and translation
in England'. See https://www.llas.ac.uk/news/6673 (accessed 7 March 2016).

Hague, D., Melby, A. and Zheng, W. (2011) Surveying translation quality assessment: A
specification approach. *The Interpreter and Translator Trainer* 5 (2), 243–267.

Hale, S., Ozolins, U. and Stern, L. (2009) *The Critical Link 5: Quality in Interpreting – A
Shared Responsibility*. Amsterdam and Philadelphia: John Benjamins.

House, J. (1977) *A Model for Translation Quality Assessment*. Tübingen: Gunter Narr.

House, J. (1997) *Translation Quality Assessment: A Model Revisited*. Tübingen: Gunter Narr
Verlag.

House, J. (2001) Translation quality assessment: Linguistic description versus social evaluation. *Meta* 46 (2), 243–257.

House, J. (2013) Quality in translation studies. In C. Millán and F. Bartrina (eds) *Routledge
Handbook of Translation Studies* (pp. 534–547). London: Routledge.

House, J. (2015) *Translation Quality Assessment: Past and Present*. London and New York:
Routledge.

Koby, G.S., Fields, P., Hague, D., Lommel, A. and Melby, A. (2014) Defining translation
quality. *Tradumatica* 12, 413–420.

Koby, G.S. and Baer, B.J. (2003) Task-based instruction and the new technology. In B.J.
Baer and G.S. Koby (eds) *Beyond the Ivory Tower: Rethinking Translation Pedagogy* (pp.
211–228). Amsterdam and Philadelphia: John Benjamins.

Lauscher, S. (2000) Translation quality assessment: Where can theory and practice meet?
The Translator 6 (2), 149–168.

Lesch, H.M. (1999) Community translation: Right or privilege? In M. Erasmus (ed.)
Liaison Interpreting in the Community (pp. 90–98). Pretoria: Van Schaik.

Lommel, A., Burchardt, A. and Uszkoreit, H. (2015) Multidimensional Quality Metrics
(MQM) definition. See http://www.qt21.eu/mqm-definition/definition-2015-12-30.
html (accessed 7 March 2016).

Lommel, A., Uszkoreit, H. and Burchardt, A. (2014) Multidimensional Quality Metrics
(MQM): A framework for declaring and describing translation quality metrics.
Tradumatica 12, 455–463.

Moser-Mercer, B. (1996) Quality in interpreting: Some methodological issues. *The
Interpreters' Newsletter* 7, 43–56.

Nord, C. (1997) *Translating as a Purposeful Activity: Functionalist Approaches Explained*.
Manchester: St Jerome.

NSW Multicultural Health Communication Service (2014) Guidelines for the production of
multilingual resources. See http://www.mhcs.health.nsw.gov.au/services/translation/
pdf/updateguidelines.pdf (accessed 7 March 2016).

Orsted, J. (2001) Quality and efficiency: Incompatible elements in translation practice.
Meta 46 (2), 438–447. See http://www.erudit.org/revue/meta/2001/v46/n2/003766ar.
pdf (accessed 7 March 2016).

Petersen, M. (1996) Translation and quality management: Some implications for the
theory, practice and teaching of translation. *Hermes* 16, 201–220. See http://down
load1.hermes.asb.dk/archive/download/H16_09.pdf (accessed 7 March 2016).

Pym, A., Grin, F., Sfreddo, C. and Chan, A.L.J. (2013) *Status of the Translation Profession in
the European Union*. London: Anthem Press.

Reiss, K. and Vermeer H.J. (1984) *Grundlegung einer allgemeinen Translationstheorie*.
Tübingen: Niemeyer.

Samuelsson-Brown, G. (2006) *Managing Translation Services*. Clevedon: Multilingual
Matters.

Sussex Interpreting Services (2012) *Quality Assured Community Translation Service*. See http://www.sussexinterpreting.org.uk/docs/Quality%20Assured%20Community%20Translation%20reviewed%20July%202012.pdf (accessed 7 March 2016).

Taibi, M. (2011) Public service translation. In K. Malmkjær and K. Windle (eds) *The Oxford Handbook of Translation Studies* (pp. 214–227). Oxford: Oxford University Press.

Taibi, M. and Ozolins, U. (2016) *Community Translation*. London: Bloomsbury.

Taibi, M. and Qadi, A. (2016) Translating for pilgrims in Saudi Arabia: A matter of quality. In M. Taibi (ed.) *New Insights into Arabic Translation and Interpreting* (pp. 47–68). Bristol: Multilingual Matters.

Turner, B., Lai, M. and Huang, N. (2010) Error deduction and descriptors – a comparison of two methods of translation test assessment. *Translation & Interpreting* 2 (1), 11–23.

Vermeer, H. (1989) *Skopos und Translationsauftrag – Aufsätze*. Heidelberg: Universität.

Walker, A.K., Kruger, A. and Andrews, I.C. (1995) Translation as transformation: A process of linguistic and cultural adaptation. *South African Journal of Linguistics, Supplement* 26, 99–115.

Williams, M. (2004) *Translation Quality Assessment: An Argumentation-Centred Approach*. Ottawa: University of Ottawa Press.

2   Education for Community Translation: Thirteen Key Ideas

Dorothy Kelly

1. Introduction

It is generally accepted that community interpreting (CI) or public service interpreting has become consolidated over recent years as a specialised area of professional activity and a specialism within Interpreting Studies. Community translation (CT) or public service translation, however, remains the poor sister, is much less present in both the professional world and academia, is under-researched and under-taught.

In this chapter, my immediate aim is to offer reflections and recommendations to enhance university provision of education for professional CT in the broadest sense. It is to be noted that this does not necessarily imply the provision of full, specialised degree or even diploma programmes. Of course, beyond that immediate aim, there are others which are by no means secondary: to promote research in the area and, ultimately, to dignify translation provision for migrant communities of all kinds around the world. I shall address the issues surrounding the training of community translators by approaching them from a series of key ideas, which have turned out coincidentally to be 13 in number. They describe the current situation and analyse it in the light of societal needs and of community translation as a profession; in the light of the nature of higher education provision today, of curricular design, of trainer competence, and of innovative approaches to teaching and learning.

2. Education for Community Translation

2.1 There is little specific educational provision in CT on offer in general around the world at university-level today

This first key idea may be corroborated by any internet search. Indeed, the first results of a search with 'community translation' as a keyword will have no relation to community translation in the sense in which we are using it in this volume, but rather to on-line and digital communities of practice in translation, linked to phenomena such as fan-subbing, a polysemy the discipline will doubtless resolve with time. Once we actually come upon community translation in the sense in which it is used in this volume, we find that specific programmes or even specific modules on more general programmes are few and far between. An interesting exception is that of the Master's degree in Intercultural Communication, and Public Service Interpreting and Translation at the University of Alcalá in Spain. But on the whole the situation at our universities is that community translation, where it is recognised at all, is subsumed under module categories and titles such as legal or medical translation. In Graham's very complete and detailed study (2012) of training provision for public service interpreting and translation in England (with some mention of programmes in the remaining three nations of the UK), she finds no specific provision for CT at any of the many universities offering training in translating and interpreting.

2.2 There is greater awareness and presence of CI as a specialized field of interpreting than of CT as a specialised field of translation

Drawing again on Graham's study on England, we can once again confirm the initial idea that CT is the poor sister in the general area of community language services. Although her study addresses training provision for public service interpreting and translation, it is devoted almost entirely to CI. This is again reflected in any bibliographical data search: community interpreting has over the years established itself as a niche area in interpreting studies and many institutions now offer modules, or even full programmes in CI. The field has its own international conference series (Critical Link, since 1995), and there have been numerous monographs and journal articles devoted to the subject. Recently, the *Interpreter and Translator Trainer*, the only indexed journal devoted entirely to training of translators and interpreters, published a special issue on the training of dialogue interpreters (Davitti & Pasquandrea, 2014). Professional interpreter associations identify CI as a specialist area and activity, although there is still much to be done to promote and protect the profession. But CT lags far behind in all respects: training, research, professional status, social awareness and recognition. And one has the impression it is often an afterthought, or add-on to its much more consolidated elder sibling.

Recent initiatives such as the First International Conference on Community Translation at the University of Western Sydney (UWS) in September 2014, attended by academic and professional participants from around the world, the establishment of an international research group devoted to the field (http://communitytranslation.net), or the monograph by Taibi and Ozolins (2016), are thus extremely welcome and will undoubtedly slowly begin to put CT on the map.

2.3 There is, however, more scope for general translator education courses and programmes to offer training in CT than for interpreter education courses to offer training in CI

From these seemingly pessimistic first thoughts, I would now like to introduce an element of optimism for CT, and posit that even if there is little specific provision, there is considerable room for CT on general translator education programmes. These tend to last longer than their counterparts in interpreting, if only because there is more provision at undergraduate level. They also tend to be organised in a two-tier structure whereby basic competences are first developed in language, intercultural and instrumental areas, before continuing to practical experience with a number of specialised areas, such as legal, scientific or technical translation. Interpreter training provision, on the contrary, tends to be structured around modes of interpreting (consecutive – only sometimes dialogue – then simultaneous), where the ultimate aim is becoming proficient in conference interpreting. There is little room on these programmes for variety in kinds of professional interpreting, leading to the need for separate CI courses, with the attendant difficulties to which I shall return below. However, in translator education provision, there is room for greater variety in offer especially through optional modules, in response to the enormous diversification of translation-related professions over the past 15 or 20 years. Furthermore, I believe that CT competence coincides in great measure with general translator competence, rendering it much simpler to incorporate elements of the skills required in a transversal manner on existing education programmes. Such an approach has the further advantage of extending awareness of the specificities of CT to a greater number of potential future practitioners, rather than limiting it to a group of initiated enthusiasts, as is the case of bespoke programmes.

2.4 As in all educational programmes, there is a need to agree on learning outcomes necessary for professional activity (often termed competences), analyse them in the social and institutional context in which training is needed, and apply this analysis to curricular design

In earlier work (e.g. Kelly, 2005), I have called for a systematic and aligned approach to the process of curriculum design. My approach is cited here as a starting point for further reflection:

Systematic approaches to curricular design take as their starting point the institutional and social context in which training is to take place, and from there establish their objectives or intended outcomes with input from the professional sector for which students are to be trained, from

society at large and from the academic disciplines involved; careful attention is paid to the resources available, and to the profile of the participants involved: students and teaching staff. Teaching and learning
activities are designed with a view to attaining the learning outcomes
desired, are carefully sequenced and coordinated with each other and
with assessment. Assessment includes not only evaluation of the [...]
attainment of the learning outcomes established for the programme, but
also the functioning of the programme itself, with a view to identifying
areas for improvement. The final stage thus closes the circle, in that it
consists of incorporating into programme content, organization and
activities that innovation and improvement identified as necessary by
the evaluation process. (Kelly, 2005: 2–3)

The establishment of clear learning outcomes (competences) as an essential
basis for education provision is interestingly taken up by Graham (2012).
Perhaps paradoxically, since it is a starting point, she formulates it as her final
recommendation:

Recommendation 10: Discuss and agree an overview of the training
requirements to be adopted for the profession.

Many believe that the lack of a national minimum standard for interpreter and translator training hampers both the image and the status of
the professions. While there are independently produced, government-
funded, National Occupational Standards, used by the National Registers
as a benchmark for entry requirement and professional performance, the
research shows that these are not adopted across the board as a minimum standard for interpreting or translation. The higher education community should explore ways to use the National Occupational Standards
as a benchmark for vocational training programmes and feed into future
reviews of the National Occupational Standards. (Graham, 2012: 54)

Although Graham's position perhaps subordinates excessively the universities' role only to that of the profession(s), the central idea that these two,
often distanced, communities should cooperate on standards is more than
valid. And even more to the point, the need for clearly expressed outcomes,
which should be linked to societal demand, including professional bench-
marking, has been a major pillar of translator education for many decades,
and is now central to competence-based curricular design around the world,
including the much-maligned and largely misunderstood Bologna process
in Europe.
    In the next two sections, I shall explore these issues in greater detail from
the perspective of translator competence models as a basis for curricular
design, and how these are already, or could easily be, incorporated into CT
training provision.

2.5 CT competence can be understood in the light of general translator competence descriptions

For the purposes of this chapter, I shall use the term 'competence' in the sense and for the purpose for which it is currently used widely in higher education, and subscribe to the definition used by the International Tuning Academy: 'Competences represent a dynamic combination of knowledge, understanding, skills and abilities.' (http://www.unideusto.org/tuningeu/competences.html).

There are several well-established descriptions or models of translation competence available in our discipline, among them: PACTE (2005), Kelly (1999, 2002 and 2005), or Gambier (2009), the latter developed by an international expert group within the framework of the Directorate General for Translation's European Master's in Translation project (EMT) at the European Commission. All three have been developed for the purpose of designing, enhancing or researching the acquisition of professional translator competence. It is not surprising, therefore, that there should be quite some degree of coincidence amongst them. Indeed, the divergences are either terminological (e.g. PACTE's 'bilingual competence' vs Kelly's 'communicative and textual competence' vs EMT's 'language competence'), or arise from the way in which each model groups lower-level competences into larger categories (EMT's and Kelly's 'intercultural competence' and 'thematic competence' vs PACTE's 'extra-linguistic competence'). For the purposes of this chapter, I shall use my own model (Kelly, 1999, 2002 and 2005), in the conviction that similar conclusions could be reached with either of the two others mentioned above. Let us take each of the seven areas of competence described in Kelly (2005: 32–33) and comment briefly on their importance in CT professional practice, and therefore education.

> *Communicative and textual competence in at least two languages and cultures. Active and passive skills in the two languages involved, together with awareness of textuality and discourse, and textual and discourse conventions in the cultures involved.*

There can be no doubt of the importance of communicative competence in CT. Key to this competence for CT is the ability to adapt any text to its intended reader, an essential tenet of functionalist approaches to translation and often known as 'audience design' (see for example Nord (2006 [1991]) and Mason (2000)). The intended reader in CT has a much more varied level of language ability than in other kinds of translation (Taibi, 2011); in some cases, the reader is unable to read and understand simple texts in their own language, something which the professional translator must inevitably take into account, making use of a wide range of strategies including non-verbal communication.

Cultural and intercultural competence. Not only encyclopaedic knowledge of history, geography, institutions and so on of the cultures involved (including the translators' or students' own), but also and more particularly values, myths, perceptions, beliefs, behaviours and textual representations of these. Awareness of issues of intercultural communication and translation as a special form thereof.

Again, there can be no doubt about the extreme importance of cultural, but especially intercultural, competence for CT. In CT practice, intercultural distance tends to be greater than in the majority of professional translation work, and is particularly central as the areas in which CT is required directly affect the readers' personal lives: health, safety, civic rights, etc. Many general translator education programmes limit their approach to cultural and intercultural competence to declarative knowledge about B and C language societies and nations. Such an approach is reductionist and unlikely to help foster the intercultural expertise necessary to address typical CT situations of cultural distance. More innovative approaches to the development of this competence on training programme involve direct experiential learning through multicultural classrooms or internships, mobility programmes and similar opportunities, followed by reflective analysis, building on the work of specialists in intercultural communication such as Byram (1997) or intercultural communication in translation (see Katan, 2014 [1999]; or the PICT project at http://www.pictllp.eu/).

Subject area (Thematic) competence. Basic knowledge of subject areas the future translator will/may work in, to a degree sufficient to allow comprehension of source texts and access to specialized documentation to solve translation problems.

Any specialized translation requires a degree of knowledge of the subject area, at least in sufficient amount to allow meaningful documentary and terminological research. In CT the major, but not only, areas of professional practice are the health, legal and social services sectors. Professionals will require some knowledge of these, and opportunities to acquire this knowledge should be offered on education programmes, through for example taught thematic modules, online support material, or work experience. Interesting good practice exists in some institutions where students of Translation (CT in this case) are brought together in collaborative projects with students of Law, Social Work or Health Science disciplines (Way, 2003). Not only does this promote future translation professionals' thematic knowledge, but it prepares future professionals in other fields for collaboration in their professional life with translators and interpreters.

Professional and instrumental competence. Use of documentary resources of all kinds, terminological research, information management for these purposes; use of IT tools for professional practice (word-processing, desktop publishing, data

bases, Internet, email …). Basic notions for managing professional activity: con-
tracts, budgets, billing, tax; ethics, professional associations.

This area of competence differs little for CT from other professional specialisations, although of course particular attention needs to be paid to documentary sources related to the areas mentioned above; similarly, the questions of
professional and general ethics are very often more acute than in other
sectors.

Psycho-physiological or attitudinal elements. Self-concept, self-confidence, atten-
tion/concentration, memory. Initiative.

Again, this area differs little for CT from other professional specialisations,
although emphasis should probably be placed on issues of self-concept, given
the often-complex nature of interaction between sender and target reader/
receiver, and the role of the translator. Much work has been done in this field
in CI (see e.g. Baraldi & Gavioli (2012) for a recent collection of papers), and
is partly applicable to CT, although the non-face-to-face nature of much CT
work eases the pressure on translators in this respect in comparison with
their CI counterparts.

Interpersonal competence. Ability to work with other professionals involved in
the translation process (translators, revisers, documentary researchers, termi-
nologists, project managers, layout specialists), and other actors (clients, initia-
tors, authors, users, subject area experts). Team work. Negotiation skills.
Leadership skills.

Again, this area differs little from other professional sectors, although special
attention is required regarding awareness of the specific differential characteristics of the end-user (lack of local knowledge, cultural distance, degree of
literacy).

Strategic competence. Organisational and planning skills. Problem identification
and problem-solving. Monitoring, self-assessment and revision.

This area is central to translator competence, as it consists in the ability to
combine all the others for each specific translation commission. Of particular importance is the ability to identify problems in the communicative
process and thereafter potential solutions to them. For CT, this competence is similar to other professional sectors, centring on the professionals'
awareness of the complex communicative situation and their role in its
realisation.

2.6 CT competence includes special emphasis on certain areas of competence often already included on university programmes

In the light of the brief analysis in point 5 above, we can conclude that the competences required for professional CT may be covered by existing general translator education provision, but require specific emphasis on certain aspects which must be made explicit if general translation programmes are to serve the purposes of offering at least initial education in CT, of raising awareness of CT as an increasingly important professional sector, of attracting suitable young translators to the field. Let us now offer a tentative list of specific areas which must be present if a programme is to claim that it is addressing CT requirements:

Awareness of the nature of the communicative situation specific to CT: power distance, the very varied characteristics of the end-user, the sensitive nature of the context of CT communication. These issues may be addressed in introductory courses to Language, Linguistics and Translation, and reinforced in specialised modules on CT itself or, where that is not possible, on legal or medical translation.

Awareness of CT as a special form of intercultural communication: Byram's research (1997) mentioned above defines the 'intercultural speaker' as one who possesses what he calls *savoirs* (knowledges):

- intercultural communicative competence as a complex entity of intercultural relations (savoir être);
- knowledge of social groups and practices in both the target and home cultures (savoirs);
- skills of interpreting and relating (savoir comprendre);
- skills of discovery and interaction (savoir apprendre/faire);
- critical cultural awareness (savoir s'engager), which comprises abilities to evaluate perspectives, practices and products of both home and target cultures (Byram, 1997).

This approach has been further developed by the PICT project in direct application to general translator education and competence. The project (http://www.pictllp.eu/en/the-pict-project) subdivides intercultural competence into three dimensions (theoretical, textual and interpersonal), easily linked to the models of translator competence described above, and offers a framework for incorporating the development of intercultural competence into education programmes, both through more declarative approaches (specific theoretical modules) and in a more transversal way (activities for general and specialised translation modules). The subdimensions proposed by this project offer a starting point for the design of curricular intervention in this field:

Theoretical dimension

Core concepts of the theory of intercultural communication (e.g. culture, identity, representations, etc.).

Conceptual tools for analysing intercultural perspective (e.g. frameworks for cultural comparison, scales of cultural awareness etc.).

Knowledge of the cultural context of translation (e.g. differences between professional translation practices in several countries, implications for translators, etc.).

Links between intercultural communication theory and Translation Studies (e.g cultural profiling and readership analysis, cultural subjectivity and translator's personal visibility).

Textual dimension

Comparative analysis of cultural issues from source and target audiences.

Comparative analysis of texts from an intercultural perspective – lexical and syntactic features, discourse patterns, visual resonance – and the use of the analysis in the translation processes.

Recognition of problems of non-equivalence and applying strategies to address them (e.g. explicitation, omission, substitution, etc.).

Recognition and management of the impact of the translator's internalised culture and emotional reaction to elements of the source culture and text.

Interpersonal dimension

Cultural awareness and empathy manifested in social exchange (e.g. when negotiating a translation brief with a member of the source culture).

Curiosity and pro-activeness in all forms of contact with other cultures (e.g. when interacting with colleagues or clients from the source culture).

Sensitivity to affects and potential conflicts in communication (e.g. spoken, non-verbal etc.).

Social positioning (i.e. deciding whether to conform, hybridise, or deviate from the dominant social norms).

(PICT, 2012: 8–11)

Programmes wishing to include CT amongst their potential professional objectives need to adopt this kind of approach (e.g. nuancing the concepts of source and target cultures, of clients and end-users), make it explicit to their students, and reinforce certain aspects (e.g. sensitivity, social positioning).

Good use can be made of the international or intercultural classroom in this respect as a hands-on experiential learning space (see Atkinson *et al.*, 2006; Mayoral & Kelly, 1997; the International Classroom Project: the challenges of the multilingual and multicultural learning space at http://intluni.eu). Programmes also have at their disposal a wide range of informal and non-formal learning spaces which are particularly suited to the development of intercultural competence: internships in the social services, non-governmental bodies dealing with migrant population; mobility programmes (Kelly, 2008b); multicultural social and cultural activities outside the classroom.

Thematic competence in the fields of healthcare, law and social services. Many programmes already offer optional modules of this kind. Programmes wishing to incorporate CT need to ensure that the focus is not entirely on translation for the elite or for large multinational companies or organisations, but also on areas affecting migrant populations: social services, local services, healthcare. The same applies to documentary resources in pertinent fields.

Ethics. The ethical issues arising around CT are often more complex in nature than those affecting other sectors of the translation profession, and should be dealt with specifically either in general modules on translator ethics or in specific modules on CT.

General awareness of and reference to CT as an emerging professional sector. Teaching staff should be encouraged to include references to CT in modules on the profession, on documentary research, on terminology, on linguistics and on practical translation, whether it be specialised or not. In this way, CT can gradually become mainstreamed as one of many professional specialisations open to trainees.

2.7 University programmes have difficulty covering societal demand for community translators due to the range of language combinations

Thus far, we have considered general translator education provision without reference to language combinations. Yet, this is one of the major limitations affecting programmes around the world, and is particularly acute in CT. Custom, and university funding mechanisms, will have it that programmes are normally constructed around a single 'A' language and a limited number of 'B' and/or 'C' languages. Programmes in bilingual regions sometimes offer two 'A' languages (the case of Catalunya or the Basque Country in Spain), but only very few offer more than one 'A' language in other circumstances. One case is that of the Faculty of Translation and Interpreting at the University of Geneva, which, due to its very international and multilingual target student population and its direct link to numerous multilingual international organizations, offers between five and seven 'A' languages depending on the programme. As for 'B' and 'C' languages, few programmes offer more than four or five languages in all, usually major world languages, such as English,

French, Spanish and more recently Chinese. Even major languages such as Arabic or Russian are in quite short supply (and/or demand).

This offer is of course often inappropriate for CT, where the languages under demand are the languages of the migrant communities in each geographical context. Sometimes these will coincide with major world languages: the case, for example, of Spanish or Chinese in Australia or Arabic in Europe and Australia. But in the majority of cases, demand is for languages such as Urdu, Wolof or European languages such as Romanian, which are not taught in general on university programmes outside their countries or regions of origin.

It will never be the case that universities can offer all the languages demanded on mainstream translator programmes, and institutions need to look for imaginative and creative ways to cover societal needs in this regard. Given the role of English as a lingua franca and their strong drive to recruit international students, English-speaking institutions now have fairly substantial experience in offering programmes to a multilingual student body, and in the design of core non-language specific modules which are then complemented by small group tutorial work in specific language combinations. Such an approach allows some further scope for programmes, but does not always allow for the full range of demand. Another issue for CT is that demand by language combination fluctuates in response to flows of migration of different kinds, which in turn respond to geopolitical and economic situations around the world. Traditional rigid approaches to curricular design and to professional certification will not solve this issue, which requires innovative, flexible and probably collaborative approaches, involving the use of information and communication technologies for virtual provision, clear definition and differentiation of core and language-specific competences, and joint national and international efforts to cover as many combinations as possible.

Further to this must be an understanding that translator competence may be transferred from one language combination to another, and that translators educated to work in one combination should easily be able to transfer their specialist knowledge and know-how to another, provided that they have sufficient active and/or passive competence in the languages involved: that is translation is a truly transferable competence. Traditionally, translator education programmes have made little use of this concept.

2.8 University programmes have difficulty addressing societal demand for professional community translators in relation to the direction in which they work

Another major issue for education programmes in many contexts is that of directionality. Western translation theory and practice has it, in general, that translation should be carried out from a foreign language into the translator's native language, a dogma which has been diligently applied by international organisations and large translation service providers and publishers, and forms part of the professional identity (self-concept) of many translators in our societies. University departments and academics have on the whole followed suit. This is despite the fact that actual professional practice and indeed recent academic studies question the traditional axiom, to use Pokorn's words (see Kelly *et al.*, 2003; Pokorn, 2005).

In the case of CT in particular, direction of translation is a huge issue which also calls into question the golden mother-tongue rule. Let us start with what we mean by 'mother tongue' or 'native speaker'. Many CT (and CI) professionals are themselves first-, second- or third-generation members of a migrant community ('heritage speakers'), brought up bilingually, speaking their family's language at home and in the local community, their adopted country's language at school and in the wider community; most of them would be hard put to define their mother tongue as such. Indeed, research in linguistics is also fuzzy on the definition of mother tongue and/or native speaker (see e.g. Davies, 2003), rendering black and white positions unsustainable in practice.

Many universities, however, continue to adhere to the mother-tongue rule for a variety of reasons: availability of teaching staff, insecurity of existing teaching staff vis-à-vis translating into a non-mother tongue, professional status of translation into other languages, and so on. Furthermore, there is a strong tendency (inherited from language programmes) to organize programmes around language combinations and, where translation into other languages is contemplated at all, by direction. This 'never the twain shall meet' attitude often precludes a serious approach to translation into non-mother tongues, with much teaching based essentially on questions of language use and little attention paid to the actual process itself and how it differs from translation into the mother tongue. More flexible approaches to this question are also required for sound education in CT where, as we have seen, a large proportion of translations required are into the community or minority language as a service to the migrant population.

2.9 The professional status of community translators in many countries is an obstacle to full professional programmes at advanced level

Alongside the various other difficulties mentioned above, the fact that CT is not a recognised profession as such, and indeed that – with honourable exceptions such as Australia – it is hard to make a living only from working in CT, is of course a considerable obstacle to full professional education programmes being set up, as lack of student interest rapidly renders them unsustainable (see Graham, 2012). This vicious circle (lack of recognition of profession > lack of professional training > lack of recognition) is one of the major reasons for supporting CT education being situated in general translation programmes, where students can find sufficient room for meaningful development of competences if the points made above are taken into account.

Graduates of such programmes have a wide range of options available to them, and those who do make their way into professional CT will gradually serve to break the vicious circle.

2.10 University programmes have difficulty finding and/or employing appropriate teaching staff for CT courses

On top of all the difficulties already mentioned, one last problem worthy of mention is the lack of appropriate teaching staff for CT on university programmes. It is already quite an effort to find well-prepared teachers for professional translation programmes in general, as good teachers need to combine professional know-how with an academic background and peda-gogical ability: not an easy cocktail (Gouadec, 2007; Gambier & Pokorn, 2013; Kelly, 2008a). In the case of CT, the range of languages and the very small talent pool with relevant professional experience or know-how make this task even more complex in the rigid staffing systems of universities in many countries.

But all is not negative. As we have seen above, there are innovative approaches to education at university level which can help solve some of the problems outlined, and indeed enhance educational provision in general. Let us look at some of these for the remainder of this chapter.

2.11 Collaborative approaches to translator education would help to ensure range and quality of provision

In line with universities' drive towards greater social engagement and more local, national and international partnerships in general, one way of offering more complete and better education in CT is through collabora-tion with local professionals, local service providers or even local clients (see Way, 2003, for an interesting experience involving Law students and Translation students). Local professionals may participate part-time in teaching activities, or simply occasionally give talks; they may offer short internships to interested students, as may local service providers or clients. Universities in the same region can get together to pool their expertise in kinds of translation or language combinations, offering joint face-to-face or virtual modules on their programmes. Or at international level, univer-sities can exchange students or staff to ensure a broader range of specialisa-tions (including CT) or languages (see Morón (2009) for a detailed study of a multinational, multilingual triple degree programme in Europe). Creative use of ICT facilitates this kind of cooperation where physical mobility is difficult or impossible. Teachers may also pool teaching materi-als and resources which, for CT, may be difficult to obtain given the con-fidential nature of much of the subject matter (see the proposal made by Graham, 2012).

2.12 Innovative approaches to training would help to ensure range and quality of provision

More extensive use could be made of informal and non-formal learning spaces to develop CT competences. Experiences such as internships or mobility are now commonplace on university programmes, although they are often seen as a kind of extra or afterthought, rather than forming an integral part of programme design. More should be done to incorporate these elements. But, beyond these widely accepted practices, much more could be made of volunteer work, community service learning, together with the numerous occasions for multicultural contact and interaction which most modern universities offer. Student reflection on these learning experiences is a rich source of personal development (see e.g. Atkinson *et al.*, 2006; Kelly, 2008b).

2.13 Diversification of kinds of provision (and their funding) would help ensure societal needs are better met

There is a tendency when speaking of university programmes to think in terms of full degree structures: undergraduate and postgraduate programmes. And indeed, that is what we have done to some extent in this article also. But education provision for CT could (perhaps should) also take the form of shorter, less rigid programmes to complement these. For example, a student graduating in Translation in Spain with English and French as her working languages, with a mobility experience in Romania, could then take a short intensive programme in CT with Romanian as a working language to complement her general translation education. This could be offered either in Spain or in Romania, in a collaborative format to make the most of existing resources and specialised staff. A learning-outcomes or competence-based approach to education facilitates this kind of incremental approach to provision, where each student's prior learning is recognised and the end result may be reached by following a variety of pathways.

3. By Way of Conclusion

Underlying these thirteen key ideas lie several major principles, on which I should like to recap by way of conclusion. Meaningful curricular design must be based on detailed analysis of societal and professional needs and adapted to the social and institutional context in which it is to be implemented. In order for this to take place, a learning-outcomes approach is more pertinent and flexible than a content-based approach. It is essential for education programmes of all kinds to be sensitive to innovative approaches and non-traditional learning spaces, and to incorporate both into their design.

Despite an increasingly competitive higher education environment, the best programmes will be those incorporating a higher degree of collaboration with other universities, with professionals and with service providers, as it is extremely unlikely that one single university will be able to provide the wide range of languages, teacher expertise and learning opportunities required for a sound grounding in CT, or indeed in many other specialised fields of translation. In the light of all the above, it is probably the case that the most sustainable approach to university education provision in CT is a carefully planned combination of generalist translation programmes at undergraduate and postgraduate level with provision of short intensive specialist courses.

References

Atkinson, D., Morón, M. and Kelly, D. (2006) *Teaching in the Multicultural Classroom at University: The TEMCU Project.* Granada: Atrio.

Baraldi, C. and Gavioli, L. (eds) (2012) *Coordinating Participation in Dialogue Interpreting.* Amsterdam and Philadelphia: John Benjamins.

Byram, M. (1997) *Teaching and Assessing Intercultural Communicative Competence.* Clevedon: Multilingual Matters.

Davies, A. (2003) *The Native Speaker: Myth and Reality.* Clevedon: Multilingual Matters.

Davitti, E. and Pasquandrea, S. (eds) (2014) *Dialogue Interpreting in Practice: Bridging the Gap Between Empirical Research and Interpreter Education.* Special Issue of *Interpreter and Translator Trainer* 8 (3), 329–335.

Gambier, Y. (dir.) (2009) Competences for professional translators, experts in multilingual and multimedia communication. See http://ec.europa.eu/dgs/translation/programmes/emt/key_documents/emt_competences_translators_en.pdf (accessed 15 December 2015).

Gambier, Y. and Pokorn, N. (2013) The EMT translator trainer profile competences of the trainer in translation. Presented at an OPTIMALE Training session, Tallinn.

Gouadec, D. (2007) *Translation as a Profession.* Amsterdam and Philadelphia: John Benjamins.

Graham, A.M. (2012) *Training Provision for Public Service Interpreting and Translation in England: PSIT Report – Routes into Languages.* Southampton: Routes into Languages.

Katan, D. (2014 [1999]) *Translating Cultures: An Introduction for Translators, Interpreters and Mediators.* Manchester: St Jerome/Abingdon: Routledge.

Kelly, D. (1999) *Proyecto Docente.* Unpublished Teaching Project: Universidad de Granada.

Kelly, D. (2002) Un modelo de competencia traductora: Bases para el diseño curricular. *Puentes. Hacia nuevas investigaciones en la mediación intercultural* 1, 9–20.

Kelly, D. (2005) *A Handbook for Translator Trainers: A Guide to Reflective Practice.* Manchester: St. Jerome.

Kelly, D. (2008a) Training the trainers: Towards a description of translator trainer competence and training needs analysis, *TTR: Traduction, Terminologie, Redaction* 21 (1), 99–125.

Kelly, D. (2008b) Student mobility programmes as a learning experience: The development and assessment of specific translation and transferable generic competences in study abroad contexts. In J. Kearns (ed.) *Translator and Interpreter Training: Ideas, Methods and Debates* (pp. 66–87). London: Continuum.

Kelly, D., Martin, A., Nobs, M.-L., Sánchez, D. and Way, C. (eds) (2003) *La Direccionalidad en Traducción e Interpretación. Perspectivas Teóricas, Profesionales y Didácticas.* Granada: Atrio.

Mason, I. (2000) Audience design in translating, *The Translator* 6 (1), 1–22.

Mayoral Asensio, R. and Kelly, D. (1997) Implications of multilingualism in the European Union: Translator training in Spain. In M. Labrum (ed.) *The Changing Scene in World Languages* ATA Scholarly Monograph Series Vol. IX (pp. 19–34). Amsterdam and Philadelphia: John Benjamins.

Morón, M. (2009) *Percepciones sobre las Aportaciones de la Movilidad a la Formación de Traductores: la Experiencia del Programa LAE (Lenguas Aplicadas Europa)*. Granada. Universidad de Granada.

Nord, C. (2006 [1991]) *Text Analysis in Translation. Theory, Methodology, and Didactic Application of a Model for Translation-Oriented Text Analysis*. Amsterdam: Brill/Rodopi.

PACTE (2005) Investigating translation competence: Conceptual and methodological issues. *Meta* 50 (2), 609–619.

PICT (2012) Intercultural Competence Curriculum Framework. See http://www.pictllp. eu/download/curriculum/PICT-CURRICULUM_ENGLISH.pdf (accessed 28 June 2017).

Pokorn, N. (2005) *Challenging the Traditional Axioms: Translation into a Non-Mother Tongue*. Amsterdam and Philadelphia: John Benjamins.

Taibi, M. (2011) Public service translation. In K. Malmkjær and K. Windle (eds) *The Oxford Handbook of Translation Studies* (pp. 214–227). Oxford: Oxford University Press.

Taibi, M. and Ozolins, U. (2016) *Community Translation*. London and New York: Bloomsbury.

Way, C. (2003) Traducción y derecho: Iniciativas para desarrollar la colaboración interdisciplinar. *Puentes* 2, 15–26.

Websites cited

International Community Translation Research Group: http://communitytranslation. net/

International Tuning Academy: http://www.unideusto.org/tuningeu/competences.html

Promoting Intercultural Competence in Translators (PICT) project: http://www. pictllp.eu/

Challenges of the multilingual and multicultural learning space (International Classroom Project): http://intluni.eu

3 From the Classroom to the Job Market: Integrating Service-Learning and Community Translation in a Legal Translation Course

Alicia Rueda-Acedo

1. Introduction: Service-Learning in the Translation Curriculum

During the Spring semester of 2014, a service-learning component was incorporated for the first time in SPAN 4341: Business and Legal Translation, a course offered at the University of Texas at Arlington. As defined by the National Service-Learning Clearinghouse (2016), '[s]ervice-learning is a teaching and learning strategy that integrates meaningful community service with instruction and reflection to enrich the learning experience, teach civic responsibility, and strengthen communities.' Students enrolled in SPAN 4341 translate a minimum of 25 hours for *Proyecto Inmigrante*, a non-profit organization 'dedicated to ensure that injustices against the immigration population community are not committed in the Dallas-Ft. Worth area and its surrounding counties' (*Proyecto Inmigrante*, 2016).

1.1 The translation curriculum at the University of Texas at Arlington

SPAN 4341 has been exclusively taught by the author since the Spring of 2006 as part of the Certificate in Spanish Translation, which she created at the undergraduate level. The Certificate consists of three core translation courses: Introduction to Translation, Business and Legal Translation, and Medical, Scientific and Technical Translation.[1]

The Certificate program responds to the dramatic demand in the Dallas–Fort Worth area, as in the rest of the United States, for professionals with a command of both Spanish and English who are capable of effectively translating from Spanish into English and vice versa. Forty million people speak Spanish in the United States (U.S. Census Bureau, 2016), the second largest Spanish speaking country after Mexico. There are more Spanish speakers in Texas – almost 7 million people (*Texas Tribune*, 2015) – than in countries such as Nicaragua, Puerto Rico, Uruguay, Costa Rica or Panama. Just in the Dallas–Fort Worth-Arlington area there are more than 1.7 million Hispanics, i.e. 27.9% of a total population of over 6 million people (Pew Research Center, 2010). Responding to this local demand, the Certificate in Spanish Translation was the first one of its kind in North Texas and it is a program oriented towards community translation and service-learning.

From the beginning, students majoring in Spanish and in other fields such as Business, Nursing, Social Work, Criminal Justice or Communication showed a great interest in this program consisting of a total number of 15 units: six units of prerequisites, and nine units of translation core courses. In order to enroll in the first translation course, students need to complete the following prerequisites: Advanced Spanish for Heritage Speakers or Advanced Spanish Grammar (depending whether they are Spanish heritage speakers or not), and Composition Through Literature. Once they have passed these courses with a grade of B or better, they become eligible to enroll in SPAN 3340: Introduction to Translation, an introductory class to the basic principles of translation theory, history and practice. Provided they pass SPAN 3340 with a minimum grade of B, they can concurrently undertake SPAN 4341: Business and Legal Translation, and SPAN 4342: Medical, Scientific, and Technical Translation the next semester. The last two translation classes are advanced upper-division courses opened to seniors and graduate students with a focus on scientific, technical, medical, economic and legal texts. To receive the Certificate, students are also required to pass an Exit Examination, a comprehensive exam on translation where students are tested on different translation problems and text types. The exam consists of translating two different texts, one from Spanish into English and another one from English into Spanish.

2. Teaching Methodology for Service-Learning and Community Translation Purposes

2.1 SPAN 4341: Learning outcomes and contents

The main five learning outcomes described in the course syllabus are:

(1) Demonstrate the ability to identify text communicative functions and follow translation assignments.

(2) Demonstrate the ability to analyze original texts for translation and examine the conventions of the text and genre.
(3) Demonstrate the ability to differentiate types of texts, tools, language and strategies for specialized translation.
(4) Demonstrate the ability to compare and use parallel texts and reference works.
(5) Demonstrate the ability to translate key terms and phrases in the fields of business and law.

Regarding service-learning and community translation, these are the learning outcomes and activities for SPAN 4341:

(1) Practice legal translation in class and outside class.
(2) Demonstrate the ability to provide professional translations at *Proyecto Inmigrante*.
(3) Gain professional and work experience at *Proyecto Inmigrante*, Inc.
(4) Demonstrate an understanding of the Hispanic immigrant community needs in terms of immigration-related issues.

In SPAN 4341, among other things, students learn about the job application process within the US and in other Spanish-speaking countries. They learn how to write a résumé and a job application letter in English and Spanish following the linguistic, stylistic, format and cultural aspects pertaining to each language and community. As part of this activity, students are required to make an appointment at the UTA Career Development Center in order to receive feedback on their résumés and cover letters. This activity is not only beneficial for senior students who are about to graduate and are getting ready for the job market in the US, but also for those looking for professional opportunities abroad.

Upon completion of this course, students are expected to be able to translate professionally the following documents from Spanish to English and vice versa: (a) certifications of vital records (birth, death and marriage certificates); (b) criminal records; (c) official letters; (d) bank account applications; (e) rental agreements; (f) academic transcripts and diplomas and (g) job application and recommendation letters, etc.

Birth certificates, marriage licenses and certificates, divorce decrees, death certificates and criminal records are the kinds of texts students translate the most at *Proyecto Inmigrante*. In order to implement service-learning and community translation into SPAN 4341, and after consulting with the supervisors at the non-profit organization, the first five weeks of the semester are dedicated to teaching legal translation and the actual translation of the following documents:

(1) Birth Certificates from: Chihuahua, Mexico; San Salvador, El Salvador; and Austin, Texas.

(2) Marriage Certificates from Cacaopera, El Salvador; and Santa Barbara, California.
(3) Municipal Letters from Ovejas, San Diego de la Unión, Guanajuato, Mexico.
(4) Certificates of Good Conduct from Chalchihuites, Mexico.
(5) Death Certificate from Guanajuato, Mexico.
(6) Samples of letters of petitioners and applicants.

2.2 Classroom instruction

Considering that the translations students will undertake at *Proyecto Inmigrante* are goal-oriented and have a clear purpose, the following methodology is employed in SPAN 4341. Students analyze original texts for translation and examine the conventions of the text and genre in order to identify texts' communicative function and typology (Reiss, 1971, 2000). Then, students follow a translation assignment or commission – 'the instruction, given by oneself or by someone else, to carry out a given action – here: to translate' (Vermeer, 2000: 229), and become familiar with the *skopos* theory (Reiss & Vermeer, 2013; Vermeer, 1996), the purpose of the translation and its ultimate reader.

Students are expected to complete translations and reading assignments on a daily basis and are given a daily participation grade. Homework assignments require students to find parallel texts and prepare a first draft of the translation. Through discourse analysis, their versions are compared in class and they discuss alternative translation options and solutions. Finally, they provide a final version of each translation. The final grade is based on attendance and participation, homework (weekly translation preparation), two translation projects or exams, one oral group presentation of a translation project and a final translation project/exam. In the three Certificate courses students deepen their knowledge of translation theory and build and consolidate their skills in translation. The author has created blogs and used Blackboard© for the three translation courses and they turned out as invaluable pedagogic instruments where several resources are included, such as parallel texts, online dictionaries and thesauri, as well as other practical information related to class instruction.

One of the aims of SPAN 4341 consists in equipping students with the knowledge and skills necessary to translate the texts they will be handling at *Proyecto Inmigrante*. Students also study the administrative texts they will encounter the most in their professional careers as legal translators because '[a]lthough greater attention has been paid to the translation of legislation in the past, much of legal translators' work is concerned with the much more mundane world of administrative documents' (Way, 2016: 1013). Administrative documents facilitate communication between government administrations and citizens and are key components of immigration cases. Administrative texts are also official documents that 'include the spectrum of documents that relate to immigrants' or temporary residents' identity, status, qualifications and histories in various ways' (Taibi & Ozolins, 2016: 77). Directive and referential functions of language are predominant in these kinds of texts that belong to the field of legal translation. As Way points out, '[l]egal translation is the label given to the translation of not only legislative texts and international treaties but court documents and administrative, commercial, and financial texts' (2016: 1013).

When teaching the translation of these legal documents, the characteristics of legal language are analyzed, allowing students to learn how legal language develops and evolves in a particular context and culture within a country or region, and how legal concepts vary not only from one language to another, but also between legal systems that share the same language (Soriano Barabino, 2002: 53). It is important for students to understand when translating legal documents that Spanish-speaking countries have a civil law system based on Roman Law and the Napoleonic code, whereas most English-speaking countries have a common law system based on case law and the doctrine of judicial precedent. Students need to be aware of the existing difficulties and challenges when translating between two systems due to a lack of equivalence between legal forms (Borja Albi, 2000: 9). Then, attention is paid in class to general characteristics of legal texts, analyzing in particular textual, linguistic, communicative, pragmatic and semiotic aspects.

The concept of functional equivalence described by Nida as 'the closest natural equivalent to the source-language message' (1964: 166) is pedagogically useful when teaching vital records certificates, the most common kinds of texts students are expected to translate at *Proyecto Inmigrante*. Although it is a shaky concept at best, as Mayoral Asensio has extensively argued, the lack of equivalence between legal systems forces the translator to look for a functional equivalent, a concept that fulfils the same role in the target culture and text (2002: 12). Mayoral Asensio further explains that this type of equivalence is mainly used when the target reader is not familiarized with the foreign legal system (2002: 12). Nevertheless, birth, death and marriage certificates are what Borja Albi considers 'fossilized texts' because they present a conventional, fixed and stereotyped form (2000: 8). With the exception of marriage licenses, these documents always present information that is the same in both languages and legal systems. Taibi and Ozolins highlight that '[r]epresenting the original fairly and accurately and always striving for equivalence is the leitmotif of translation of official documents. The facts as presented in the original must be rendered accurately' and 'equivalence can be shown in both form and content' (2016: 91). Soriano Barabino has also explored the relevance of functional equivalence when applied to legal translation, highlighting that it is necessary to look for the functional equivalents that different legal systems have in common (2002: 54). This situation occurs, for instance, with documents such as marriage licenses and marriage certificates that can be issued on the same document in the United States where couples need to obtain a license that authorizes them to get married. When translating these documents into Spanish, translators face the reality that marriage licenses do not exist in the majority of Spanish-speaking countries, where only marriage certificates are issued. In this case, Mayoral Asensio's (2002: 13) recommendation of focusing mainly on translation problems and then combining different translation strategies results in an efficient approach to translating these kinds of documents.

Teaching legal translation poses many other difficulties given that '[l]egal translation students frequently have little or no grounding in the field of law' and they are required 'to translate texts that are completely alien to their prior experience and social practices' (Way, 2016: 1019). Legal translation students encounter two main difficulties: an obsession with words and terminology and lack of vital experience (Way, 2016: 1020) in a field 'which perhaps requires the culture-bridging skills of the translator more so than other fields of specialized translation' (Way, 2016: 1019). According to Way, these problematic aspects of legal translation that trainees usually face can be addressed in the classroom in two different ways: following a discourse analysis approach to translation, and focusing on 'decision making as a pillar of the translation process' (2016: 1021). In this discourse analysis model 'students are guided through a step-by step procedure that first situates the text within social processes and social events.' (2016: 1022). Once the text is located within the 'discursive practice (production, distribution, consumption), students become familiar with the internalized social structures and conventions governing the text' (Way, 2016: 1022). This model works particularly well when translating birth, death and marriage certificates, as they are highly 'fossilized texts' (Borja Albi, 2000: 8). In SPAN 4341, students translate original certificates from Mexico and Central America as the majority of *Proyecto Inmigrante* clients originate from these regions. Although they are not expected to translate from English into Spanish during their placement at the non-profit organization, in class students are assigned vital records from the United States so that they familiarize themselves with the language and conventions of US documents and have the opportunity to practice translation into Spanish. This allows them to be more prepared to work in this direction in their future professional career. After students undertake textual analysis, specific translation problems concerning words and terminology, and legal aspects that students do not fully understand are addressed in class. Identifying translation problems (such as cultural references, proper names and context-specific information) and seeking solutions seems to be one of the best ways to approach legal translation (Mayoral Asensio, 2002: 13). It is only then that the discourse analysis approach is 'applied in the target language and target culture to discover whether parallel discursive and social practices exist, thereby leading to parallel or similar texts. Only then does the translation process proper begin' (Way, 2016: 1021).

After completion of this stage of classroom instruction, parallel documents are analyzed. Students are asked to find these documents, and this is usually a very easy task for them to complete, not only because the internet provides them with countless resources, but also because most of the students in this course are from Mexican-American or Latin American origins and are happy to share their own certificates. It is emphasized in class that the purpose of studying these parallel texts is '[t]o help understand how the source document needs to be organized in terms of formatting and categories that will be clear to the institutional reader in the host society' (Taibi & Ozolins, 2016: 92).

Apart from analyzing and translating different vital records certificates in order to fully understand how these documents operate, Civil Registry and other related websites from Mexico, Central America and the United States are visited in class in order to compare the services they provide and to download relevant forms. These are very helpful preparatory activities for students undertaking this kind of translation. A practical example assigned to students is the translation of a marriage certificate from Cacaopera, El Salvador, which does not have the standardized format for this kind of vital records and consists of an entire narrative paragraph, rather than the more usual format used in Spanish-speaking countries, including particulars such as groom and bride, date of marriage, etc. The need to find vital records from the US – parallel texts in the target language – for the purpose of re-verbalization (Reiss, 2000) is particularly important because at the non-profit organization students translate into English. At the same time, students in SPAN 4341 are given the opportunity to complete extract translations when working at *Proyecto Inmigrante*, where in order to translate birth, death and marriage certificates, they fill out a template with the most relevant information, which they need to extract from the original: name, place, date and time of birth/marriage/death, witnesses, country of registration, certificate number, book, volume, etc. Using this template helps students to identify text type and *skopos* (Vermeer, 1996), and the characteristics of their final commissioner (Vermeer, 2000), US Citizenship and Immigration Services (USCIS). It is very common in the case of community translation that host institutions use templates or extract translations 'to bring order and/or efficiency to a still often complex practice' (Taibi & Ozolins, 2016: 5). At the same time, 'predictability and repetitiveness' (Taibi & Ozolins, 2016: 78) are also characteristics of these kinds of documents, making the use of a template very suitable to translate them. Moreover, 'there may be information in the original that is superfluous to the requirements of the template, which tends not to be a problem' (Taibi & Ozolins, 2016: 87). This is the case of information such as witnesses, and more detailed data regarding age, nationality or occupation of the parents that appears in the majority of birth certificates from Hispanic countries and is not provided in US birth certificates. The same can be applied to the translation of formal expressions present, for instance, in Mexican vital records certificates such as the following:

> En el nombre del estado libre y soberano de _____, como oficial del Registro Civil, certifico y hago constar que en los archivos que obran en esta oficialía del Registro Civil, se encuentra asentada un acta de nacimiento en la cual se contienen los siguientes datos.

> [In the name of the free and sovereign state of _____, and as official of the Civil Registry, I certify that in this Office of the Civil Registry there is a birth certificate that contains the following information].

These formulaic expressions are not included in the template used by *Proyecto Inmigrante*, but are translated by SPAN 4341 students in class. The same happens with the information regarding grandparents, witnesses, etc. that is not relevant for USCIS. Using a template and undertaking the full translation of the same document in class reinforces the idea that there is never only one way to undertake a specific translation (Mayoral Asensio, 2002: 9), allowing students to experience firsthand that a legal text can be translated in different ways depending on its purpose and translation assignment (Mayoral Asensio, 2002: 9).

When in class, students follow the translation assignment or commission of translating for a 'real' client. The author plays the role of her students' client (playing the role of different commissioners) and their payment (grade) depends on the quality of their translations. Students are given 24 to 48 hours to turn in their translations, replicating the deadlines that translators are usually required to meet for these kinds of texts. The intention is to simulate what students will be doing at *Proyecto Inmigrante* and as professional translators once they graduate. Students have to conduct research at home and turn in the first version of their translation to be analyzed and corrected in class. After classroom discussion, clarification and feedback, they submit an amended version of their translations. They then bring their third version to class, and it is reviewed anonymously by a classmate who pays attention to language and style (such as punctuation, spelling, grammar, etc.), terminology, accuracy, content and format. The student in charge of the revision proposes corrections and changes, alternative terminology and discourse and stylistic amendments, following the recommendations proposed in Way's (2009: 136–137) 'Evaluation Sheet.' Finally, the teacher reviews their translation and provides further feedback and comments, which students can incorporate into their final version.

3. From Classroom to Practice: Translating for the Hispanic Immigrant Community in the Dallas–Fort Worth Area

3.1 *Proyecto Inmigrante*: A community translation and service-learning project

Before incorporating this service-learning component into SPAN 4341: Business and Legal Translation, a partnership with *Proyecto Inmigrante* was established in the autumn of 2013. Services offered by *Proyecto Inmigrante* include the following: Applications for Citizenship, Deferred Action for Childhood Arrivals (DACA), Employment Authorization (EAD card), Provisional Waivers, Waivers, Adjustment of Status (AOS), Consular Processing (CP), Family Petitions, National Visa Center Process (NVC), FBI Record, Fiancé(e) Visas, Resident Card Renewal, Removal of Conditional Status, Temporary Protection Status (TPS) and Translations. The three principles that define the mission statement of *Proyecto Inmigrante* (2016) are Serve, Inform and Assist the immigrant community:

> We will work to the best of our abilities to help our clients become permanent residents or citizens of the United States [...] We are strongly committed to doing everything legally and ethically possible to prevent our clients from suffering any unnecessary immigration hardship.

This partnership was established thanks to Mr Danilo Douglas Interiaro, Chief Executive Officer of *Proyecto Inmigrante*, a UTA graduate and one of the author's former students. In a three-year period, a total of 71 students collaborated with *Proyecto Inmigrante*, translating documents related to US Citizenship and Immigration Services (USCIS), translating a total of 2049 hours, over 1000 documents, and impacting hundreds of people's lives. The following table shows student numbers per cohort and total number of service hours completed by each group of students in the periods indicated:

Semester	Number of participating students	Service-learning hours completed
Spring 2014	26 out of 31	884
Spring 2015	18 out of 18	495
Spring 2016	27 out of 30	670

SPAN 4341 is described in the syllabus as a service-learning course. At the beginning of the semester, students are offered the option of either taking an exam, or completing service-learning hours with *Proyecto Inmigrante*. Both options have the same weighting towards their final grade, a total of 25%. Collaborating with *Proyecto Inmigrante* involves 25 hours of translation work, receiving a positive evaluation from the non-profit organization, submitting a final reflective essay about the student's service-learning experience and participating in four oral discussions about the service-learning experience throughout the semester. There are also spontaneous reflective conversations during class instruction as students are encouraged to share their experience at *Proyecto Inmigrante* when applicable to class discussion. The importance of reflective activities in translation pedagogy[2] has been emphasized as an important tool to help students 'become aware, reflective and resourceful practitioners' (Crezee, 2016: 30). By participating in in-class discussions, reflecting on their own work as translators and writing about their experience while participating in a service-learning course, students are guided in this direction.

This service-learning component provides a unique situated learning experience that allows students to participate in a 'community of practice,' learning by immersion and not just by internalizing knowledge (Lave & Wenger, 1991). By joining a 'community of practice,' students acquire the 'practices and ways of thinking of these communities by being involved in their professional activities' (Kiraly, 2005: 1105). Enríquez-Raído and González-Davies further explain that:

> Situated Learning is generally understood as a context-dependent approach to translator and interpreter training under which learners are exposed to real-life and/or highly simulated work environments and tasks, both inside and outside the classroom [...] Ultimately, Situated Learning seeks to enhance learners' capacity to think and act like professionals. (2016: 1)

In order to achieve this goal, SPAN 4341 students translate in a real-life work environment when collaborating with *Proyecto Inmigrante*. At the non-profit organization, they translate an ample variety of documents related to the Waiver and Provisional Waivers Departments. Working in different departments involves undertaking different types of translation. Every semester, 5–7 of the best students in the class are recommended to collaborate in the Provisional Waivers Department. These students work directly with clients, being supervised at the beginning, and conducting interviews themselves after the initial training. These students are in charge of translating statements and letters of petitioner and applicant (beneficiary), provisional waiver letters (pardon letters)[3] and status of USCIS requests. The remaining students work for the Waiver Department translating the following documents: birth certificates, marriage licenses and certificates, divorce decrees, death certificates, criminal records, newspaper articles, municipality letters and statements from clients' native country, and letters of recommendation from clients' family, friends and employers. Other kinds of documents translated by SPAN 4341 students include *Proyecto Inmigrante*'s website, job descriptions, local news from Mexico, certificates of good conduct, receipts, grocery lists, rental agreements, school documents, utility bills, medical records and prescriptions. Although these documents do not strictly belong to the field of law, they can have important legal implications (Borja Albi, 2016), considering that any human activity can be involved in a legal process at any time (Mayoral Asensio, 2002: 10). Students gain knowledge on how to translate all these documents in the three translation courses that integrate the Certificate in Spanish Translation. As can be easily appreciated, students undertake the translation of different documents related to immigration, gaining extensive experience in the field. All students' translations undertaken at *Proyecto Inmigrante* are certified and validated by the Waiver and Provisional Waiver Departments Coordinators.

3.2 Integrating community translation and service-learning

In *Community Translation*, Taibi and Ozolins review several definitions of what is also known as public service translation, an emerging 'subfield of translation studies' (2016: 8). They also specify that it is a term used in two different ways: (1) as 'translation *for* the community' undertaken by professional translators and (2) as 'translation *by* the community for the community,' referring to the translation undertaken by volunteers (2016: 8) in online communities (2016: 10). For the authors, community translation falls under the first definition, and it is also the one that applies to the translation undertaken by SPAN 4341 students when collaborating with *Proyecto Inmigrante*. Taibi broadly defines community translation as the translation of:

> Texts generated by the larger community (society) or by smaller communities (linguistic or ethnic communities within the larger society, local communities, religious groups, etc.) in order to ensure communication with all citizens [and residents] and permit their participation and, therefore, empowerment. (Taibi, 2011: 214–15)

In the case of SPAN 4341 students, they translate to empower prospective residents and citizens, members of a smaller community, allowing their communication with immigration services: 'While much of community translation is translation from the host languages into minority languages, in the translation of official documents a large part may be translation of documents in other languages into the host country's official language' (Taibi & Ozolins, 2016: 5), as is the case for *Proyecto Inmigrante*'s clients. After reviewing several definitions of this type of translation (García, 2014; Gouadec, 2007; International Conference on Community Translation, 2014;

Niska, 2002; O'Hagan, 2011; Pym, 2011), Taibi and Ozolins conclude that community translation:

> bridges the communicative gap between public services and those citizens or residents who do not speak mainstream language, and thereby improves relations and cohabitation between different social groups; facilitates information flow between mainstream/established community members and less powerful, minority or newcomer members; and provides opportunities for the latter to improve their socio-economic position and participate more effectively in their (new) community. (2016: 11)

This last statement in particular applies to the kind of service students in SPAN 4341 provide to *Proyecto Inmigrante's* clients, as their translations empower the immigrant community in the Dallas–Fort Worth area. For Taibi and Ozolins, community translation has three main features: power imbalance, language (im)parity and audience diversity (2016: 11). It also has 'an overarching mission or role: empowering the social groups for whom translations are provided, and enabling them to have full access to public service information and to participate actively in the different realms of the society where they live' (2016: 65), a goal that service-learning also seeks to achieve. They emphasize that 'community translation is still in its infancy as a subfield of translation studies and as an area of translation practice' (2016: 17) partly because 'disempowered users of translation such as migrants, refugees and members of ethnic and linguistic minorities' (2016: 17–18) are the main 'clients' for this kind of translation. In this context, integrating a service-learning component in a legal translation course results in an extraordinary tool to overcome this situation and help the above-mentioned groups in need of legal translation, a 'field where translators' work may have an immediate impact, affecting people's lives directly' (Way, 2016: 1017).

Service-learning is without a doubt a significant way to affect people's lives. In the different definitions provided for the term in the literature, the features that stand out are community engagement, civic responsibility, reflection and academic learning. Bringle and Hatcher provide a definition that encompasses all of the above:

> We consider service-learning to be a course-based, credit-bearing educational experience in which students (a) participate in an organized service activity that meets identified community needs and (b) reflect on the service activity in such a way as to gain further understanding of the course content, a broader appreciation of the discipline, and an enhanced sense of civic responsibility. (1995: 112)

It is important to highlight that service-learning represents a significant component of the syllabus, teaching activities and assignments, and the grade students obtain in a certain course: '[t]his is in contrast to co-curricular and extracurricular service, from which learning may occur, but for which there is no formal evaluation and documentation of academic learning' (Bringle & Hatcher, 1995: 112).

The association between service-learning and translation may appear obvious, but the literature linking the two is limited (Bugel, 2013; Faszer-McMahon, 2013; Lizardi Rivera, 1999; Shaw & Robertson, 2009). However, the impact of service-learning on Spanish language learners has received more attention, as Hellebrandt and Varona (1999), for example, clearly indicate. As Barreneche and Ramos-Flores (2013: 224) point out:

> Although measuring the positive linguistic outcomes from service-learning can be problematic, there has been plenty of documentation of an increase in the level of confidence that students gain in speaking the language as a result of these experiences. (Hellebrandt & Varona, 1999; Hellebrandt et al., 2004; Wurr & Hellebrandt, 2007)

These two authors also highlight that 'surveys indicate that students who participate in a service-learning experience tend to want to continue language study and they feel more confident because of perceived gains in their Spanish abilities (Hale, 1999)' (Barreneche & Ramos-Flores, 2013: 224). Also, as Faszer-McMahon highlights, there are several other studies that indicate 'Spanish programs at the college level have proven particularly active in the burgeoning field (Abbott & Lear, 2010; Barreneche, 2011; Caldwell, 2007; Grabois, 2007: 164; Hellebrandt & Varona, 1999; Nelson & Scott, 2008; Pellettieri, 2011; Weldon & Trautmann, 2003; Zapata, 2011)' (252). The connection between service-learning and translation and its impact outside the classroom has been observed by Bugel:

> as Baker (2011 [1992]: 4) points out, most aspects of life and interaction between members of different speech communities relate to translation, given the production of intragroup and intergroup meaning. Thus, familiarizing students with translation through service-learning is an endeavour that quite naturally extends beyond the four walls of a classroom or a university campus to reach the community. (2013: 371)

In their reflective essays and evaluations, UTA students continuously comment on how collaborating with *Proyecto Inmigrante* has impacted their career choices.

3.3 Reinforcing the connection between course content and service-learning

In his study 'on the application of social constructivism to Translator Education,' Kiraly (2000: 1102) demonstrates that:

a migration from classroom activities as exercises to pieces of work would entail radical changes in students' relationships to their instructors, their fellow students, and the professional community, as well as in their understanding of the learning and teaching process and their own self-concept as developing professionals. (2005: 1102–1103)

In their reflective essays,[4] students commonly refer to the valuable professional experience they gain and their willingness to participate in these kinds of active learning initiatives if provided: 'If you were to ask me if I would do it again, I would. I think it's a great experience for future translators especially if they have no experience because it helps them see how it is to work for a company as a translator.'

Another essential aspect of bringing professional experience into the classroom is providing students with the opportunity to experiment first-hand how professional translators work in the business industry. Needless to say, students receive professional work experience before graduating, being able to add a significant line to their résumés before entering the job market:

I was able to apply hands on in a professional setting the things I've been learning in school these past few years. [...] My service had a great impact in my life, I went into *Proyecto Inmigrante* as a volunteer and ended up with a full time job there right out of college. I couldn't be more grateful for the opportunity that was given to me.

Service-learning students value and are grateful for these kinds of opportunities that enable at the same time better relationships with instructors (Bugel, 2013: 370; Kiraly, 2005: 1103; Pak, 2007: 38):

It was a great opportunity that [the tutor] organized for us to practice our translation skills in a real-life setting. I think if more professors put together experiences like this for their students, they would have a much easier time transitioning from the life of academia to life in the professional world. There are limits to what can be done in a classroom setting, and universities often lack accessible options for hands-on experience for students while still studying.

Transitioning from the classroom to a professional setting is usually a challenge that students face as they lack translation competence. Different models of translation competence have been proposed[5] in order to develop objectives and learning outcomes for the translation curriculum (Way, 2009: 132). Kelly points out that translation competence is the 'macrocompetence that comprises the different capacities, skills, knowledge and even attitudes that professional translators possess and which are involved in translation as an expert activity' (2002: 14–15). Providing students with the opportunity to work at a professional setting through service-learning improves their translation competence understood as 'the ability to transition from a classroom community of practice to a professional community of practice through Situated Learning' (Enríquez-Raído & González-Davies, 2016: 2). And this is precisely one of the aims of this service-learning collaboration, to align classroom learning and course objectives with the experience students have at *Proyecto Inmigrante*. For Kiraly, '1) translator competence emerges as the result of the collaborative completion of authentic translation work, and 2) by observing translators, both non-professional and professional, in the socially-situated praxis of authentic translation work' (2005: 1101). This is exactly the context students are provided at *Proyecto Inmigrante*, where they 'develop their capability to function as professional translators in the real world outside of the academic ivory tower' (Kiraly, 2005: 1101).

Students have reflected in their essays that they improved significantly in three sub-competencies of translation competence: psycho-physiological or attitudinal competence, interpersonal competence, and strategic competence (Kelly, 2010):

(1) 'Psycho-physiological or attitudinal competence' involves '[s]elf-concept, self-confidence, attention/concentration, memory, initiative' (Kelly, 2010: 90). Examples from relevant student reflections include the following:
   – 'Before volunteering at *Proyecto Inmigrante*, I did not know exactly what a translator would do in a professional setting on a daily basis. Volunteering enhanced my translating ability because of the variety of documents that had to be translated in a timely fashion. It helped me become less nervous and to believe in myself and my work.'
   – 'With all the experience of translating and the professionalism of *Proyecto Inmigrante*, I will only continue to enhance my translation skills and further develop my usefulness in the workplace.'

(2) 'Interpersonal competence' encompasses the '[a]bility to work with other professionals involved in translation process [...] and other actors (clients, initiators, authors, users, subject area experts). Team work. Negotiation skills. Leadership skills' (Kelly, 2010: 90). In relation to this subcompetence, students stated:
   – 'I lacked the knowledge of knowing the importance of my skills and that I could use my skills to help others in need.'
   – 'Because of this experience I was able to make lots of connections and know my classmates better as well since we worked together and helped each other.'

(3) 'Strategic competence' involves '[o]rganizational and planning skills. Problem identification and problem-solving. Monitoring, self-assessment

and revision.' (Kelly, 2010: 90). The following testimonials show the impact of service-learning on this subcompetence:

– 'The fact that I was translating for real life situations brought a lot of complications to me since I was still learning about certain documents in class. However, I was still able to consult my professor about the problems that I had during the translations and she would help me.'

– 'Now once I apply for a job I have some of the tools that will help me excel in the working field. I have firsthand experience of the expectations that companies require and how much work is put into projects.'

– 'The students that were unsure of certain translation they would first do research, ask their classmates, then ask Proyecto staff.'

Collaborating with *Proyecto Inmigrante* provides students with better skills for the decision-making process, as they have stated in their reflective essays and was observed in their overall classroom performance when translating these kinds of texts. It also reduces students' levels of anxiety and strengthens their self-esteem and motivation as translators, modifying the way they perceive their own abilities and improving their confidence. In order to take full advantage of this service-learning component and to help students improve the aspects mentioned above such as self-esteem, competence, motivation and confidence, it is very important to provide support and guidance to students, reinforcing the connection between class instruction and the tasks they undertake at the community partner location:

A good thing about this experience was that it covered a lot of the topics that I was learning in class, so I was able to apply my knowledge right away. It was like doing homework, but I was actually doing work for a company [...] I think that all the help that was provided made this experience more enjoyable, being able to consult your professor or being helped by the people that worked a that place every day made things go smoother.

Also, dedicating class time to reflect and share their service-learning experience allows students to understand its importance not only academically, but also in their professional and personal lives. At the same time, they can appreciate in a real-time manner how course content and professional work relate to each other:

Although, it wasn't part of the service-learning I was also able to get a little insight on the immigration laws and able to learn more about the process and options an applicant has. The professors always said it in class, but it wasn't until I experienced it that I understood that the beauty of translating is that in order to do a good job you have to become a little specialist in the field you're trying to translate.

Service-learning opportunities also help students realize whether translation is the field they want to work in and to decide whether they have chosen the right career path: 'Prior to this class and opportunity, translation was just a set of classes to fill the gaps in my schedule, now I view it as a very plausible career choice.'

The combination of engaging in-class learning activities with the 25-hour translation work experience they obtain at *Proyecto Inmigrante*, is an invaluable way to train students for the job market. As has been highlighted by Way (2016: 1019–1020), a lack of vital experience is one of the challenges legal translation students face. Providing a service-learning component in a legal translation course is an invaluable tool to fill this gap as 'only real praxis inside and outside the classroom can bring a complex profession alive' (Kiraly, 2005: 1103), and this is exactly the way many students perceive it:

> Indeed it was worthwhile investment. It was significant because I was able to use what I have learned in class to apply it in real life, helping real people who are in desperate need of the attention and care they deserve. The experience was not comparable to being able to speak Spanish in the classroom, in a restaurant, or with fellow Hispanic friends.

4. Outcome of the Project: Community Translation and the Impact of Service-Learning on Students and Community Partners and Members

At the beginning of each Spring semester, *Proyecto Inmigrante* staff give a presentation to SPAN 4341 students in class to introduce themselves, their organization and their clients: low-income immigrants. In order to strengthen the links between classroom instruction and service-learning, *Proyecto Inmigrante* staff outline their expectations regarding this partnership, the existing translation needs in the community, and the importance of the service provided by volunteer translation trainees. In this presentation, students also learn how to translate vital record certificates according to the guidelines of the non-profit organization, using the above-mentioned template. At the end of the semester, *Proyecto Inmigrante* staff visit the class again to thank students for their participation in this service-learning project. The tutor gives students a letter of acknowledgment and they also receive a certificate of completion from *Proyecto Inmigrante*. A social event is also organized where students, their tutor and *Proyecto Inmigrante* staff celebrate the completion of activities and share their experiences. This aspect is very important, as highlighted by Jenkins and Sheehey, who propose '[t]he checklist [that] delineates the four-stage service-learning process: (a) preparation, (b) implementation, (c) assessment/reflection, and (d) demonstration/celebration.' (2011: 52). In the words of *Proyecto Inmigrante's* staff:

Proyecto enjoyed this collaboration as many things were accomplished. Not only did the students have the opportunity to translate official documents and obtain experience, but also our agency received help in an area that was much needed. Many students had a willing heart to participate and attempted their best to help. It gave the opportunity to see the necessity in the immigrant's community. Also, many extended their vocabulary and worked with others.

At the assessment/reflection stage, students in SPAN 4341 were also required to write the above-mentioned reflective essay and were invited to complete two questionnaires voluntarily. A pre-questionnaire was designed to measure students' expectations before collaborating in a service-learning course, and a post-questionnaire to evaluate their actual experience and the impact that collaborating with *Proyecto Inmigrante* had in their personal, academic, and professional lives. The first time SPAN 4341 was taught with a service-learning component back in Spring 2014, a questionnaire was distributed at the end of the semester only. At a later stage, it was considered that a pre- and post- questionnaire was required in order to compile comprehensive data regarding participant satisfaction. In order to better accommodate this service-learning, new situated learning experiences and student-centered activities were implemented, and the teaching approach was modified when needed. This modification involved coordinating students' participation and schedules at the non-profit organization, constant communication with students and *Proyecto Inmigrante* staff, teaching the types of legal texts students would be translating during their placement and coordinating reflective activities and *Proyecto Inmigrante's* staff in-class presentations.

The number of respondents who took the surveys each semester is as follows:

	Pre-questionnaire number of respondents	Post-questionnaire number of respondents
Spring 2014		26
Spring 2015	14	13
Spring 2016	25	21

Students' responses, examples of which are given below, offer a glimpse into how they perceive this experience before and after participating in a service-learning course. Students were given a five point-rating scale (from strongly disagree to strongly agree: 1–5). The following presents the percentage of respondents that agreed to each item (respondents who chose a 4 or 5).

A growing number of students throughout the three academic years agreed at the end of the semester that service-learning would have an impact on their academic and career choices (Spring 2014: 88.46%; Spring 2015: 100%; Spring 2016: 95%). They were also very satisfied with the inclusion of service-learning in SPAN 4341 (Spring 2014: 100%; Spring 2015: 100%; Spring 2016: 95.2%). They agreed as well that collaborating with *Proyecto Inmigrante* helped them understand the relevance of the course's subject matter in their everyday life (Spring 2014: 92.30%; Spring 2015: 100%; Spring 2016: 95.23%) as they have also stated in their reflective essays:

- 'This opportunity, I believe, has made me a better translator because it put me in the middle of real-life scenarios.'
- 'Now once I apply for a job I have some of the tools that will help me excel in the working field. I have firsthand experience of the expectations that companies require and how much work is put into projects.'

Moreover, the percentage of students who agreed that they had gained valuable experience for their résumé and experienced personal satisfaction by helping others was also very high (Spring 2015: 100%; Spring 2016: 95.23%). In their own words:

- 'Working for *Proyecto Inmigrante* was an incredible experience and very rewarding. At *Proyecto Inmigrante* I was able to use my translating abilities in a real-life setting. I did not do an internship while in school so having this service-learning also gave me something to add to my resume.'
- 'This service-learning opportunity really broadened my perspective of the real world. I gained experience in an environment which I am glad to list on my resume. At *Proyecto Inmigrante* I got my first taste of what translating professionally in an office feels like, along with a prime opportunity to aid thousands of immigrants in our community.'

In terms of time investment, the author wanted to measure the impact that collaborating with *Proyecto Inmigrante* would have in students' academic and personal lives. The percentage of students who agreed on having less time for their schoolwork (Spring 2015: 38.46%; Spring 2016: 57.14%) and their work (Spring 2015: 53.84%; Spring 2016: 9.5%) was not significantly high. When asked if they had less time to spend with their family and friends, students agreed that this was not an issue (Spring 2015: 53.84%; Spring 2016: 0%).

It is interesting to compare their expectations about service-learning and how their opinions changed in a positive way after completing their collaboration with *Proyecto Inmigrante*[6] at the end of the semester:

Q: My contribution to the community will make a real difference	Pre-questionnaire	Post-questionnaire
Spring 2015	92.85%	100%
Spring 2016	84%	95.23%

Q: Without community service, today's disadvantaged citizens have no hope	Pre-questionnaire	Post-questionnaire
Spring 2015	78.57%	100%
Spring 2016	64%	76.19%

Q: I want to do this service-learning activity	Pre-questionnaire	Post-questionnaire
Spring 2015	92.85%	100%
Spring 2016	96%	100%

Overall, the majority of students were satisfied about helping community members and all of them agreed they would repeat an experience like this. As many of them expressed it in their reflective essays:

— 'What I found most important was the simple act of lending some assistance to another human being. Sometimes that is the most powerful act that any person, citizen or non-citizen, can do in life.'
— 'Doing the service-learning at *Proyecto Inmigrante* particularly was very significant for me; it was an environment where I felt I could relate to not only the professionals working there but the people they would help as well. Coming from a family with immigrants it made me want to do the best I could to help the people coming in.'

In terms of instruction and supervision, students agreed that the texts translated in class were appropriate and helped them to translate better while collaborating with *Proyecto Inmigrante* (Spring 2014: 96.15%; Spring 2015: 100%; Spring 2016: 100%). One student commented: 'With this experience students are able to apply what they learned in the classroom to their work, work in a professional environment, and see the impact they are making in their community.' They also agreed that the supervision from *Proyecto Inmigrante* staff while on site was appropriate (Spring 2014: 76.92%; Spring 2015: 92.30%; Spring 2016: 90.47%), and that communication between the non-profit organization, the instructor, and themselves was appropriate as well (Spring 2014: 88.46%; Spring 2015: 100%; Spring 2016: 95.23%). It is also very interesting to highlight that the majority of the participants would recommend this course to other students because of its service-learning component (Spring 2014: 92.30%;

Spring 2015: 100%; Spring 2016: 100%. This question could be answered with either Yes or No):

- 'This experience made me grow as a translator, and as a person too, I highly recommend it.'
- 'I would recommend service-learning to anyone who has the opportunity to do it, it's a great experience and it could result in a possible job in the future[7].'

5. Conclusions: Benefits of Integrating Community Translation and Service-Learning into the Curriculum

As Taibi and Ozolins emphasize, community translation 'has little presence in the curriculum' (2016: 23) around the world, probably due to how translation is traditionally taught in fields of specialization or within generalist programs (2016: 23–24). They recommend students in programs oriented towards community translation should be exposed to 'community texts,' be able to understand 'local communities and public service settings, and develop the specific translation and intercultural communication skills they will need when translating for public services or local communities.' (2016: 25).

The author would add that, whenever possible, students should not only be exposed to these kinds of texts, but actually translate them for the members of their local communities to better develop the translation skills required to undertake community translation. This way, they learn how community translation empowers members of a smaller community in need for translation services. Concurrently, bringing professional experience into the classroom through service-learning provides students with the opportunity to experiment firsthand how professional translators work in the industry and obtain professional work experience before graduating. It also helps students to decide whether a career in translation is suitable for them.

Service-learning is an extraordinary tool when combined with community translation, as instructors teach in class the texts to be translated at the non-profit organizations, the students understand firsthand the relevance of local communities and public service settings, and develop intercultural communication skills and civic responsibility at once. At the same time, 'translation and service-learning complement each other and engage the parties involved in partnership, providing a sound basis for the development of long-term multilingual and multicultural community projects' (Bugel, 2013: 369). For these reasons, when teaching community translation, service-learning is a significant component in translator education.

Among other benefits of integrating service-learning, Bugel points out that '[t]he possibility of teaching service-learning translation courses has come to replace the artificiality with real clients with tangible needs' (2013: 369). Gaining professional experience and readiness for the job market, self-confidence and translation competence, together with civic responsibility and active citizenship (Eyler & Giles, 1999: 157) complement other obvious benefits such as the impact that service-learning and community translation has on the community and the university.

Teaching community translation and incorporating this service-learning component into SPAN 4341 required a significant improvement and innovation in the manner in which the author traditionally taught this course, and it also required modifications in the way the translation of legal texts is commonly taught. Nevertheless, the experience has been very rewarding for everybody involved, has helped develop better relationships between tutor and students, and has had a significant impact on students' training and professional careers as well as on the target communities.

Notes

(1) These three courses are now part of the new Bachelor of Arts in Spanish Translation and Interpreting offered by UTA. The first promotion of students in this program graduated in Spring 16. In Fall 15, the first group of students obtained the new Certificate in Spanish Interpreting. All translation and interpreting programs at UTA are oriented towards community translation and interpreting.

(2) Crezee summarizes the work of scholars who have studied the relevance of reflective activities in translation training: Bernadini, 2004; Mossop, 1999, 2000; Luján Mora, 2006; Cleary et al., 2015 (Crezee, 2016: 30).

(3) According to USCIS (2016), the provisional waiver process allows 'certain individuals who are family members of U.S. citizens and lawful permanent residents (LPRs), and who are statutorily eligible for immigrant visas, to more easily navigate the immigration process. The provisional waiver process promotes family unity by reducing the time that eligible individuals are separated from their family members while they complete immigration processing abroad.'

(4) All the following quotes come from different reflective essays that students submit at the end of the semester. Every single comment is from a different student in the Spring 2014, 2015 and 2016 offerings.

(5) Among others, different competence models can be found in: Ammann, 1990; Campbell, 1998; Delisle, 1980 and 1992; Gile, 1995; Hatim and Mason, 1997; Hurtado Albir, 1995, 1996 and 2007; Kiraly, 1995; Wilss, 1976; Krings, 1986; Neubert, 1994 and 2000; Nord, 1991 and 1992; PACTE, 1998, 2000–2003 and 2005; Kelly, 1999, 2002 and 2005; Risku, 1998; Roberts, 1984; Way, 2002 and 2009.

(6) The questions included in the post-questionnaire were formulated in the past tense.

(7) Since 2014, a total number of 5 students have been hired by *Proyecto Inmigrante* after completing their service-learning at the non-profit organization.

References

Abbott, A. and Lear, D. (2010) The connections goal area in Spanish community service-learning: Possibilities and limitations. *Foreign Language Annals* 43, 231–245.

Ammann, M. (1990) *Grundlagen der modernen Translationstheorie – Ein Leitfaden für Studieren*. Heidelberg: Universität.

Baker, M. (2011) *In Other Words: A Coursebook on Translation.* Abingdon, Oxon: Routledge.

Barreneche, G.I. (2011) Language learners as teachers: Integrating service-learning and the advanced language course. *Hispania* 94 (1), 103–120

Barreneche, G.I. and Ramos-Flores, H. (2013) Integrated or isolated experiences? Considering the role of service-learning in the Spanish language curriculum. *Hispania* 96 (2), 215–228.

Bernadini, S. (2004) Corpus-aided language pedagogy for translator education. In K. Malmkjaer (ed.) *Translation in Undergraduate Degree Programmes* (pp. 17–30). Amsterdam: John Benjamins.

Borja Albi, A. (2000) *El texto jurídico inglés y su traducción al español.* Barcelona: Ariel.

Borja Albi, A. (2016) 'La traducción jurídica: Didáctica y aspectos textuales'. *Aproximaciones a la traducción, Centro Virtual Cervantes* http://cvc.cervantes.es/lengua/aproximaciones/borja.htm (accessed 8 July 2016).

Bringle, R.G. and Hatcher, J.A. (1995) A Service-learning curriculum for faculty. *Michigan Journal of Community Service Learning* 2 (1), 112–122.

Bugel, T. (2013) Translation as a multilingual and multicultural mirror framed by service-learning. *Hispania* 96 (2), 369–382.

Caldwell, W. (2007) Taking Spanish outside the box: A model for integrating service learning into foreign language study. *Foreign Language Annals* 40, 463–469.

Campbell, S. (1998) *Translation into the Second Language.* London: Longman.

Cleary Y., Flammia M., Minacori P. and Slattery D.M. (2015) Global virtual teams create and translate technical documentation: Communication strategies, challenges and recommendations, *2015 IEEE International Professional Communication Conference (IPCC)* (pp.1–10) Limerick. http://ieeexplore.ieee.org/stamp/stamp.jsp?tp=&arnumber=7235802&isnumber=7235772

Crezee, I. (2016) The benefits of reflective blogs in language-neutral translator education. *FitisPos International Journal of Public Service Interpreting and Translation* 3, 28–41. http://www3.uah.es/fitispos_ij/OJS/ojs-2.4.5/index.php/fitispos/article/view/93/123

Delisle, J. (1980) *L'analyse du discours comme méthode de traduction: Initiation à la traduction française de textes pragmatiques anglais, théorie et pratique.* Ottawa: Presses de l'Université d'Ottawa.

Delisle, J. (1992) Les manuels de traduction: Essai de classification. *TTR: Traduction, Terminologie, Redaction* 5 (1), 17–48.

Enríquez-Raído, V. and González-Davies, M. (2016) Situated learning in translator and interpreter training: Bridging research and good practice. *The Interpreter and Translator Trainer* 10 (1), 1–11.

Eyler, J. and Giles, D.E. Jr. (1999) *Where's the Learning in Service-Learning?* San Francisco: Jossey-Bass.

Faszer-McMahon, D. (2013) Social networking, microlending, and translation in the Spanish service-learning classroom. *Hispania* 96 (2), 252–263.

García, I. (2014) Volunteers and public service translation. Paper presented at International Conference on Community Translation, University of Western Sydney, 11–13 September, 2014.

Gile, D. (1995) *Basic Concepts and Models for Interpreter and Translator Training.* Amsterdam: John Benjamins.

Gouadec, D. (2007) *Translation as a Profession.* Amsterdam: John Benjamins.

Grabois, H. (2007). Service-learning throughout the Spanish curriculum: An inclusive and expansive theory driven model. In A. Wurr and J. Hellebrandt (eds) *Learning the Language of Global Citizenship: Service-Learning in Applied Linguistics* (pp. 164–189). Bolton, MA: Anker.

Hatim, B. and Mason, I. (1997) *The Translator as Communicator.* London: Routledge.

Hale, A. (1999) Service-learning and Spanish: A Missing link. In J. Hellebrandt and L.T. Varona (eds) *Construyendo Puentes = Building Bridges: Concepts and Models for Service-Learning in Spanish* (pp. 9–25). Washington, DC: American Association for Higher Education.

Hellebrandt, J. and Varona L.T. (1999) *Construyendo Puentes = Building Bridges: Concepts and Models for Service-Learning in Spanish*. Washington, DC: American Association for Higher Education.

Hellebrandt, J., Arries J. and Varona L.T. (2004) *Juntos: Community Partnerships in Spanish and Portuguese*. Boston: Thomson/Heinle.

Hurtado Albir, A. (1995) La didáctica de la traducción. Evolución y estado actual. In P. Fernández Nistal and J. M. Bravo Gozalo (eds) *Perspectivas de la Traducción Inglés/ Español. Tercer Curso Superior de Traducción* (pp. 49–74). Valladolid: Instituto de Ciencias de la Educación.

Hurtado Albir, A. (1996) La enseñanza de la traducción directa 'general'. In A. Hurtado Albir (ed.) *La Enseñanza de la Traducción* (pp. 31–56). Castellón de la Plana: Universitat Jaume I.

Hurtado Albir, A. (2007) Competence-based curriculum design for training translators. *The Interpreter and Translator Trainer* 1 (2), 163–195.

International Conference on Community Translation (2014) University of Western Sydney, 11–13 September, 2014. https://www.westernsydney.edu.au/community translation

Jenkins, A. and Sheehey, P. (2011) A checklist for implementing service-learning in higher education. *Journal of Community Engagement and Scholarship* 4 (2), 52–60.

Kelly, D. (2002) Un modelo de competencia traductora: Bases para el diseño curricular. *Puentes. Hacia nuevas investigaciones en la mediación intercultural* 1, 9–29.

Kelly, D. (2005) *A Handbook for Translation Trainers: A Guide to Reflective Practice*. Manchester: St. Jerome.

Kelly, D. (2010) Curriculum. In Y. Gambier and L. Doorslaer (eds) *Handbook of Translation Studies: Vol. 1* (pp. 87–93). Amsterdam: John Benjamins.

Kiraly, D.C. (1995) *Pathways to Translation: Pedagogy and Process*. Kent, Ohio: Kent State University Press.

Kiraly, D.C. (2000) *A Social Constructivist Approach to Translator Education: Empowerment from Theory to Practice*. Manchester: St. Jerome.

Kiraly, D.C. (2005) Project-based learning: A case for situated translation. *Meta: Journal des Traducteurs/Meta: Translators' Journal* 50 (4), 1098–1111.

Krings, H.P. (1986) *Was in den Köpfen von Übersetzern vorgeht. Eine empirische Untersuchung zur Struktur des Übersetzungprozesses an fortgeschrittenen Französischlernern*. Tübingen: Narr.

Lave, J. and Wenger, E. (1991) *Situated Learning. Legitimate Peripheral Participation*. Cambridge: Cambridge University Press.

Lizardi-Rivera, C. (1999) Learning the basics of Spanish translation: Articulating a balance between theory and practice through community service. In J. Hellebrandt and L.T. Varona (eds) *Construyendo Puentes = Building Bridges: Concepts and Models for Service-Learning in Spanish* (pp. 107–121). Washington, DC: American Association for Higher Education.

Luján-Mora, S. (2006) A survey of use of weblogs in education. *Proceedings of the 4th International Conference on Multimedia and Information and Communication Technologies in Education (m-ICTE 2006)* (pp. 255–259). Seville: Formatex.

Mayoral Asensio, R. (2002) ¿Cómo se hace la traducción jurídica? *Puentes* (2), 9–14.

Mossop, B. (1999) What should be taught at translation school? In A. Pym, J. Fallada, J. Ramón Biau and J. Orestein (eds) *Innovation and E-Learning in Translator Training* (pp. 20–22). Tarragona: Universitat Rovira i Virgili.

Mossop, B. (2000) The workplace procedures of professional translators. In A. Chesterman, N. Gallardo San Salvador and Y. Gambier (eds) *Translation in Context* (pp. 39–48). Amsterdam: Benjamins.

National Service-Learning Clearinghouse https://gsn.nylc.org/clearinghouse (accessed 12 November 2016).

Nelson, A. and Scott, J. (2008) Applied Spanish in the university curriculum: A successful model for community-based service-learning. *Hispania* 91 (2), 446–460.

Neubert, A. (1994) Competence in translation: A complex skill, how to study and how to teach it. In M. Snell-Hornby, F. Pöchhacker and Kaindl (eds) *Translation Studies: An Interdiscipline* (pp. 411–420), Amsterdam: John Benjamins.

Neubert, A. (2000) Competence in language, in languages, and in translation. In C. Schäffner and B. Adab (eds) *Developing Translation Competence* (pp. 3–18). Amsterdam: John Benjamins.

Nida, E.A. (1964) *Toward a Science of Translating.* Leiden: E.J. Brill.

Niska, H. (2002) Community interpreter training: Past, present, future. In G. Garzone and M. Viezzi (eds) *Interpreting in the 21st Century: Challenges and Opportunities* (pp. 133–144). Amsterdam: John Benjamins.

Nord, C. (1991) *Text Analysis in Translation: Theory, Methodology, and Didactic Application of a Model for Translation-Oriented Text Analysis.* Amsterdam: Rodopi.

Nord, C. (1992) Text analysis in translator training. In C. Dollerup and A. Loddegaard (eds) *Training Talent and Experience. Papers from the First Language International Conference, Elsinore, Denmark, 1991* (pp. 39–48). Amsterdam: Benjamins.

O'Hagan, M. (2011) Introduction: Community translation as a social activity and its possible consequences in the advent of Web 2.0 and beyond. *Linguistica Antverpiensia: Special Issue on Translation as Social Activity* 10, 11–23.

PACTE (1998a) La competencia traductora y su aprendizaje: Objetivos, hipótesis y metodología de un proyecto de investigación, Poster presented in the *IV Congrés Internacional sobre Traducció*, Universitat Autònoma de Barcelona, Barcelona.

PACTE (1998b) Procesos de aprendizaje y evaluación en la adquisición de la competencia traductora, Paper presented in the *EST Congress*, EST/Universidad de Granada, Granada.

PACTE (1998c) Der Erwerb der translatorischen Kompetenz. Das Forschungsprojekt PACTE, Poster presented in *Modelle der Übersetzung – Grundlagen für Methodik, Bewertung Computermodellierung*, Saarbrücken.

PACTE (2000) Acquiring translation competence: Hypotheses and methodological problems in a research project. In A. Beeby, D. Ensinger and M. Presas (eds) *Investigating Translation* (pp. 99–106). Amsterdam: John Benjamins.

PACTE (2001) La competencia traductora y su adquisición. *Quaderns, Revista de Traducció* 6, 39–45.

PACTE (2002) Una investigación empírico-experimental sobre la adquisición de la competencia traductora. In A. Alcina Caudet and S. Gamero Pérez (eds) *La Traducción Científico-Técnica y la Terminología en la Sociedad de la Información* (pp. 125–138). Castellón de la Plana: Publicaciones de la Universitat Jaume I.

PACTE (2003) Building a translation competence model. In F. Alves (ed.) *Triangulating Translation: Perspectives in Process Oriented Research* (pp. 43–69). Amsterdam: John Benjamins.

PACTE (2005) Primeros resultados de un experimento sobre la Competencia Traductora. In *Actas del II Congreso Internacional de la AIETI (Asociación Ibérica de Estudios de Traducción e Interpretación). Información y documentación* (pp. 573–587). Madrid: Publicaciones de la Universidad Pontificia Comillas.

Pak, C. (2007) The service-learning classroom and motivational strategies for learning Spanish: Discoveries from two interdisciplinary community-centered seminars. In

A.J. Wurr and J. Hellebrandt (eds) *Learning the Language of Global Citizenship: Service-Learning in Applied Linguistics* (pp. 32–57). Bolton, Mass: Anker Publisher.

Pellettieri, J. (2011) Measuring language-related outcomes of community-based learning in intermediate Spanish courses. *Hispania* 94 (2), 285–302.

Pew Research Center (2010) 'Hispanic population in select U.S. metropolitan areas, 2010'. http://www.pewhispanic.org/hispanic-population-in-select-u-s-metropolitan-areas/ (accessed 12 November 2016).

Proyecto Inmigrante, Inc. (2016) Mission statement. http://www.proyectoinmigrante.org/ (accessed 12 July 2016).

Pym, A. (2011) Translation research terms: A tentative glossary for moments of perplexity and dispute. *Translation Research Projects* 3, 75–110. http://isg.urv.es/publicity/isg/publications/trp_3_2011/pym.pdf

Reiss, K. (1971) *Möglichkeiten und Grenzen der Übersetzungskritik: Kategorien und Kriterien für eine sachgerechte Beurteilung von Übersetzungen*. München: M. Hueber.

Reiss, K. (2000) Type, kind and individuality of text, decision making in translation. In L. Venuti (ed.) *The Translation Studies Reader* (pp. 160–171). London: Routledge.

Reiss, K. and Vermeer, H.J. (2013) *Towards a General Theory of Translational Action: Skopos Theory Explained*. Manchester: St. Jerome.

Risku, H. (1998) *Translatorische Kompetenz*. Stuttgart, Stauffenburg Verlag.

Roberts, R.P. (1984) Competence du nouveau diploma en traduction. *Traduction et Qualité de Langue. Actes du Colloque Societé des traducteurs du Québec, Conseil de la langue fraçaise* (pp. 172–184). Québec: Diteur Officiel du Québec.

Shaw, S. and Robertson, L. (2009) Service-learning: Recentering the deaf community in interpreter education. *American Annals of the Deaf* 154 (3), 277–283.

Soriano Barabino, G. (2002) Incongruencia terminológica y equivalencia funcional en traducción juridica: la guarda de menores en España e Inglaterra y el País de Gales. *Puentes: Hacia nuevas investigaciones en la mediación intercultural* 2, 53–60.

Taibi, M. and Ozolins, U. (2016) *Community Translation*. London and New York: Bloomsbury.

Taibi, M. (2011) Public service translation. In K. Malmkjaer and K. Windle (eds) *The Oxford Handbook of Translation Studies* (pp. 214–227). Oxford: Oxford University Press.

Texas Tribune. (2015) 'As Texas grows, more languages are spoken at home', *Texas Tribune*. https://www.texastribune.org/2015/11/26/languages-spoken-texas-homes/ (accessed 12 November 2016).

U.S. Census Bureau (2016) 'FFF: Hispanic heritage month 2016'. http://www.census.gov/newsroom/facts-for-features/2016/cb16-ff16.html (accessed 12 November 2016).

U.S. Citizenship and Immigration Services (2016) 'USCIS to allow additional applicants for provisional waiver process'. https://www.uscis.gov/news/news-releases/uscis-allow-additional-applicants-provisional-waiver-process (accessed 12 November 2016).

Vermeer, H. (1996) *A Skopos Theory of Translation: (Some Arguments for and Against)*. Heidelberg: Textcon Text Verlag.

Vermeer, H. (2000) *Skopos* and commission in translational action. In L. Venuti (ed.) *The Translation Studies Reader* (pp. 221–232). London: Routledge.

Way, C. (2009) Bringing professional practices into translation classrooms. In I. Kemble (ed.) *The Changing Face of Translation: Proceedings of the Eighth Annual Portsmouth Translation Conference Held on 8 November 2008* (pp. 131–142). Portsmouth: University of Portsmouth.

Way, C. (2014) Structuring a legal translation course: A framework for decision-making in legal translator training. In L. Chen, K. Kui Sin and A. Wagner (eds) *The Ashgate Handbook of Legal Translation* (pp. 135–152). Farmham: Ashgate.

Way, C. (2016) The challenges and opportunities of legal translation and translator training in the 21st century. *International Journal of Communication* 10, 1009–1029.

Weldon, A. and Trautmann, G. (2003) Spanish and service-learning: Pedagogy and praxis. *Hispania* 86 (3), 574–585.

Wilss, W. (1976) Perspectives and limitations of a didactic framework for the teaching of translation. In R.W. Brislin (ed.) *Translation Applications and Research* (pp. 117–137). New York: Gardner.

Wurr, A.J. and Hellebrandt, J. (2007) *Learning the Language of Global Citizenship: Service-Learning in Applied Linguistics*. Bolton, Mass: Anker Publisher.

Zapata, G. (2011) The effects of community service learning projects on L2 learners' cultural understanding. *Hispania* 94 (1), 86–102.

4 From Practice to Theory: Societal Factors as a Norm Governing Principle for Community Translation

Harold Lesch

1. Introduction

It is often falsely believed that the notion of community translation has developed around technological platforms forming a social network, where volunteer translators become a typically unspecified interest group who works together towards a common goal. In the recent past, there has been an increase in social networking on the internet, and in the process translation activities have also become a social activity undertaken by internet users. These individuals collaborate as a 'virtual community', i.e. a group of people who interact through online resources (Rheingold, 2000). Recently, this too has been identified as community translation. This chapter, however, takes as its premise that the notion of community translation is not a new one and does not necessarily have its origin in the worldwide technological platform. It focuses on community translation as a language service usually offered to a local community that is characterised by multilingualism, multiculturalism and a number of socio-economic gaps.

The initial point of departure, for community translators, is that the original concern with the quality of translation is replaced by a concern with the appropriacy and accessibility of the target text (Cluver, 1992; Fraser, 1990; Meintjes, 1992). Translation becomes a means to an end; providing communities with the means to inform and skill themselves and putting their needs on the agenda, making effective communication with the reader the only valid measure of its success. Such an approach takes societal factors into consideration. For translation practice to be a teleological activity, it is pointed out that translators in heterogeneous societies should take the target audience into account. Otherwise, the translation will be a mere symbolic gesture, empty of value, and will therefore not communicate the intended message.

This chapter puts forward a reflection on community translation in relation to societal issues (with reference to the South African context), that is the accessibility of the translated text, and aims to propose norms for this practice. As an offshoot of this chapter, empirical studies can also be undertaken to ascertain whether these norms, as developed in relation to the societal issues, are relevant for public service and crowd-sourced translation for the virtual community.

Fraser's (1990: 81–82) argument below is taken as a point of departure for developing norms:

> Precepts, propositions and stock-in-trade are all useful tools for a translator but only in so far as they are determined by the *purpose* for which the translation is made and the *people* for whom it is being made. The problem with the way in which both translation and translation theory are taught … is that translation is assumed as an end in itself rather than a means to an end. No light is shed on *why* a translation is being made as the result that the techniques are taught in a pragmatic vacuum, whereas in fact the purpose and destination of a translation should always be made explicit …

The objectives of this chapter are: (i) to set a basis and consider a typology for community translation; (ii) to marry translation theory and community translation practice with reference to the South African language context; and (iii) to propose norms for the practice of community translation as embedded in translation theory. To achieve this, the chapter is divided as follows: first, a rationale for the study – contextualised in terms of translation variation theory – is presented; subsequently, community translation is classified into different types; and finally, the norms that are linked to the relevant translation theory are outlined.

2. The Rationale

Most of the research on language barriers originates in developed countries that experience an influx of people from less affluent parts of the world. These immigrants encounter new challenges relating to language and culture; for instance, in their communication with public services (hence 'public service translation', an alternative term for 'community translation'). In South Africa, major communication problems are not encountered by immigrants, but by fellow citizens. English and Afrikaans have been the dominant languages of public services and business and were the only official languages in the country until 1994, whereas the majority of South

African nationals speak African languages (e.g. Ndebele, Sotho, Northern Sotho, Swazi, Tsonga, Tswana, Venda, Xhosa or Zulu). With the democratisation process of the mid-1990s, these local languages were recognised and made official, and considerable efforts have since been made to translate government and public service information into them. The question arises, though, whether it is excusable that, in a country that has been focusing so much on the rights of the individual since the dawn of democracy in 1994, citizens in many instances do not receive the necessary service delivery (e.g. health care) in a language they understand. Community translation as an avenue for effective communication bridges the communicative gap between public services and those citizens or residents who do not speak the mainstream language and thereby improves relations and cohabitation between different social groups; facilitates the flow of information between mainstream community members and less powerful (linguistic) minority members; and provides opportunities for the latter to improve their socio-economic position and participate more effectively in their community (Taibi & Ozolins, 2016: 11).

Intercultural communication by nature is a complex activity and in a multilingual society like South Africa, it is bound to surface as a challenge. The services of a language intermediary are often considered to break the impasse in this communication process. The communication problem between the service provider and the client is often not simply a matter of language, but also of societal factors, of which both the community interpreter or translator and the commissioner of the assignment should be aware in order to play a constructive role in effective communication. To render a source text in multilingual and multicultural societies like South Africa brings forth its own difficulties, and translators in these societies must consider the diversity of the target audiences. Diversity in this case is not only a question of linguistic or ethnic background, but also – and most importantly – level of education. The statistics from the 2011 census (Census in Brief, 2011) show a significant gap between White South Africans and Black and Coloured citizens (see Table 4.1, Table 4.2 and Figure 4.1).

If the community is defined in terms of level of education, we find a community of 25.4% of the total South African population aged 20 years or over who had no schooling or completed primary schooling only. The percentage rises to 59.2% when the range of low educational levels includes from 'no schooling' to 'some secondary schooling' (see Table 4.2). It is against the backdrop of the above statistics that the need for plain language came to the fore, especially during the 1990s, within the South African context. This was at a stage in our political history when human rights were placed at the forefront in the constitution. Needless to say, in a democratic society it is of utmost importance to inform the average citizen of their basic rights and responsibilities and to do so in an understandable language. Indeed, Sullivan (2001: 97) explicitly points out that '[t]he purpose of [for instance] drafting

Table 4.1 Distribution of persons aged 20 years and older by highest level of education and by province

Level of education	WC	EC	NC	FS	KZN	NW	GP	HP	LP	SA
No schooling	102,242	375,754	76,861	115,380	621,199	248,516	301,311	325,540	499,073	2,665,874
Some Primary	401,362	653,118	116,115	262,576	784,305	353,753	612,990	271,726	334,189	3,790,134
Completed Primary	208,798	223,075	43,111	86,950	240,411	111,439	277,528	96,770	125,813	1,413,895
Some Secondary	1,430,909	1,300,491	236,956	563,698	1,802,050	697,908	2,714,950	726,904	1,007,709	10,481,577
Grade 12/Std 10	1,055,442	707,524	154,008	435,291	1,784,358	529,121	2,832,448	670,343	645,578	8,814,113
Higher	539,827	310,872	50,765	158,799	537,664	162,815	1,492,322	223,579	273,469	3,750,112
Other	18,304	8815	1746	4762	16,097	5258	45,418	6270	6918	113,586
Total	3,756,884	3,579,649	679,562	1,627,455	5,786,084	2,108,808	8,276,967	2,321,133	2,892,750	31,029,291

Table 4.2 Percentage distribution of persons aged 20 years and older by highest level of education completed, and by province

Level of education	WC	EC	NC	FS	KZN	NW	GP	MP	LP	SA
No schooling	2.7	10.5	11.3	7.1	10.7	11.8	3.6	14.0	17.3	8.6
Some Primary	10.7	18.2	17.1	16.1	13.6	16.8	7.4	11.7	11.6	12.2
Completed Primary	5.6	6.2	6.3	5.3	4.2	5.3	3.4	4.2	4.3	4.6
Some Secondary	38.1	36.3	34.9	34.6	31.1	33.1	32.8	31.3	34.8	33.8
Grade 12/Std 10	28.1	19.8	22.7	26.7	30.8	25.1	34.2	28.9	22.3	28.4
Higher	14.4	8.7	7.5	9.8	9.3	7.7	18.0	9.6	9.5	12.1
Other	0.5	0.2	0.3	0.3	0.3	0.2	0.5	0.3	0.2	0.4
Total	100.0	100.0	100.0	100.0	100.0	100.0	100.0	100.0	100.0	100.0

legislative texts in plain language is to enhance democracy and the rule of law by making legislation accessible to the people whose lives it affects'.

Effective communication is essential for the functioning of public service personnel on all levels, including politicians. Consequently, in the context of communication across language barriers, it is necessary to communicate easily and precisely. According to Vasalikakos (1989: 3), people should not only be made aware of their rights and privileges, but also their obligations, as failure to do so would leave them unable to communicate, participate and contribute to the social, political and cultural life of the country. At the same time, they would be deprived of the knowledge of their rights, benefits and obligations. Legal texts for instance are generally difficult to understand, and

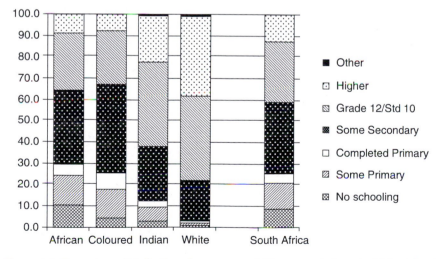

Figure 4.1 Percentage distribution of persons aged 20 years and above by highest level of education completed and by population group

this comprehension difficulty can be attributed in part to the distinct features of legal language, which are not regularly used in other discourse
domains (Cornelius, 2010: 172). The question that arises therefore is how can
ordinary people or the general reader without legal training access the information in legal or government documents? The answer to this question may
be found in the notion of text simplification, which 'aims to maximize the
comprehension of written texts through the simplification of their linguistic
structure' (Candido *et al.*, 2009: 34). According to Cornelius (2010: 172), text
simplification presupposes the existence of a source text, which is regarded
as too complex and too dense for a particular target audience. Therefore, it
needs to be altered in some way to unlock meaning and to provide access to
the information contained in such a text. Such an approach helps us to appreciate the translation of communicative texts, which opens the door for
studying the developmental impact or lack thereof on the society as a whole
(Marais, 2012: 29).

3. Translation Variation Theory

During the 1960s and 1970s translators focused on linguistics as a suitable framework for understanding translation (Schaffner, 1997: 5). This linguistic approach is grounded in correspondence between the linguistic
structures of the source text (ST) and the target text (TT). But this approach
has advanced further, as Fourie (2003: 21) confirms. The text-linguistic
approach was developed to accommodate the differences between pure linguistics and culture. Consequently, the focus changed from reproducing
meanings, words and sentences to producing complete texts. This translation approach deals with choices and decisions rather than with the methods
or mechanisms of the ST or the TT. The text-linguistic approach offers
insight into the relationship between ideas, meanings and language, as well
as into individual and cultural aspects of language and behaviour. Translation
was no longer defined as transcoding linguistic signs, but as retextualising
the ST (Schaffner, 1997: 5).

As a follow-up to the text-linguistic approach, Reiss and Vermeer (1984),
offered the *Skopostheorie* as a theory of translation. *Skopos* is the Greek word
for 'purpose', and according to this theory the *skopos* of a translation is determined by the intended function of the TT. In essence, each text is produced
for a given purpose and should serve this purpose. The translation process is
considered to be functional when it fulfils its intended communicative purpose according to the client or commissioner/initiator (Nord, 1999: 1).
Accordingly, *Skopostheorie* also became known as a functionalist approach.

Although 'translation proper', which transmutes both the content and
the form of the source text, is regarded as the first and foremost standard in
translation, various translation procedures are often followed in translation

practice. The translation brief for the translator may also vary. Translation variation as opposed to translation proper originates from the contents of the original text by using appropriate language skills (e.g. adaptations such as supplement, reduction, editing, summarisation, combination and remodelling) in light of the special needs of the target text readers to enhance effective communication.

According to Huang (2002), translation variation theory aims to explain the nature of translation variation. Translation variation is defined as an activity aimed at deriving the relevant content of the source text by using appropriate adaptations such as expansion, deletion, editing, commentary, condensation, combination and reformation against the backdrop of the needs of the TT readers under specified conditions (Jianzhong, 2000: 590). Zhonglian Huang (2002: 46–48) and Xu Jianzhong (2000: 384–397), as translated by Zhang (2007: 7–8), offer the following definitions respectively:

> Translation variation is an activity aiming at deriving the contents concerned from the original by using the appropriate adaptations such as supplement, reduction, editing, summarization, reduction, combination and remodelling in the light of the special needs of the readers [or the brief of the commissioner of the assignment – HML].

> Translation variation is a thought activity or an extra-language activity which deriving [sic] the relevant content of original content by using the appropriate adaptation ways such as explanatory, deletion, editing, commentary, condensation, combination, reformation and imitation in the light of special field readers' needs and special field conditions.

In such cases, the source text is not seen as sacred, as some translation scholars (favouring 'translation proper') tend to believe. Therefore, a new model for translation quality assessment as opposed to ST-based assessment (House, 1981) is needed for translation variation. In the case of translation variation, translators are given more freedom. Since translation with variation may not keep all the information and stylistic characteristics of the ST, it might encourage translation of various qualities – depending on the different variables. In line with the text-linguistic approach, as stated above, it aims to meet certain needs of the target readers but it may also omit important information from the ST.

The aim of translation variation is not to boast with the various forms of a target text, but to make the contents more effective by flexibly transferring the forms and ultimately enhancing communication by partly negating the ST. What translation variation affirms are the contents of the ST which meet the demands of the target readers; what it negates are the contents which fail to satisfy the needs of the target readers (Zhang, 2007: 8).

Translation variation serves the special needs of the target text readers and the commissioner as it shows that the translator has a definite purpose in mind, i.e. who the target readers are and why a certain text needs to be translated. It is a strategy to provide the target readers with the information they need. As a result, the target text might not include the form and entire content of the source text.

In accordance with the concept of instrumental translation (Nord, 1991: 73), Huang (2000: 308, cited in Zhang, 2007: 9–11) identifies various means for translation variation: addition, reduction, editing, reporting, condensation, combination and summary, and adaptation. In a nutshell, these entail the following:

Addition – the information conveyed through a translation with variation is more than that of the complete translation or the original.

Reduction – the information conveyed through a translation with variation is less than that of the complete translation or the original. Reduction refers to 'selective translation', which means selecting only the essential points of the original work to be translated (Huang, 2000: 18).

Editing – edited translation means restructuring an original work before or while translating to meet the specific requirements of the specific target readers (Huang, 2000: 100). Edited translation includes selecting, combining, generalising, adjusting the order, retelling, intra-paragraphic edited translation, inter-paragraphic edited translation, intra-chapter edited translation, inter-chapter edited translation, intra-book edited translation, and inter-book edited translation.

Reporting – to report in this context is to merge the activities of translation and reporting (Huang, 2000: 141). It means reporting the main points or parts of the ST without putting any subjective viewpoints or creating any ideas that are not mentioned in the original work. Translation by reporting requires being faithful to the original work, but not being constrained by the author's style.

Condensation – Condensed translation means using condensed words to reproduce the soul or essence of the original work (Huang, 2000: 142). One aspect of condensed translation is that the length of the original work would be greatly condensed and nearly no part of the ST will be preserved in translated versions.

Combination and summary – this refers to a combination of translation and summarising, thus a summarised translation. Summarised translation involves summarising the main points by collecting the related materials (Huang, 2000: 174). When applying summarised translation, one has to firstly confirm the topic, logically arrange all the materials, and then prepare the summarised translated version in a certain format. Usually, a summarised translation will include a preface or introduction, the main body, a conclusion, and an appendix, if necessary.

Adaptation – Adaptation translation consists of altering exotic contents, forms, or styles to accord with the domesticated perceptions (Huang, 2000: 228). It emphasises the readers' requirements and involves at least two aspects, namely adaptation of content and adaptation of form and style.

In terms of translation quality, Campbell (1998: 8), as cited by Fourie (2003: 32), considers the reader, not the translator, as central to the assessment of the quality of a translation, whereas quality assessment is concerned with the text only. Campbell emphasises that the quality of a translation reflects the translator's competence. Recently, translation scholars have confirmed that successful translation cannot be achieved without a great deal of target reader support (Jang, 2000; Lesch, 2012). Jang (2000) studied 'translation quality and the reader's response' and concluded that it is a misconception to believe that a good translation is as close, accurate, and faithful as possible to the source text. In order for a translation to become adequate, there should be interaction between the translator, the source text, and the translator's perception of the target-text readers throughout the translation process, since it is the target audience's response to the translation that determines its adequacy (Fourie, 2003: 32).

As communicators, professional translators are to produce adequate translations efficiently and effectively. In order to fulfil client expectations, they are expected to be mindful of reader variables, context, and function. A translation will be judged by the degree to which it meets the recipient's capacity to decode it. This means that it is the audience's background, not prescriptive rules, that determine the strategies for producing the best possible translation. From a functional point of view, translation is viewed as a teleological activity that emphasises the importance of the intended use of a translation in the target context.

4. Theoretical Background

From a theoretical point of view two aspects need to be clarified, namely *community* as defined within community translation and the concept of *norms*.

4.1 From 'community' to 'community translation'

As referred to in the introduction, there is certain terminological and disciplinary confusion regarding community translation. *Community* can be defined by different means (accessibility of the target text, public service translation or virtual community) that intersect within the domain. From a sociological perspective, a community is defined as a social group of any size whose members are related to one another by continued relations such as social status, role fulfilment and social networks. Otherwise, it is a large social grouping that shares a common geographical area, shared government, and often a common cultural and historical heritage (see McMillan & Chavis, 1986: 8–9). In the virtual world, *community* is defined as an online space that has:

(a)   people, who interact socially as they strive to satisfy their own needs or perform special roles, such as leading or moderating;
(b)   a shared purpose, such as an interest, need, information exchange, or service that provides a reason for the community;
(c)   policies, in the form of tacit assumptions, rituals, protocols, rules, and laws that guide people's interactions; and
(d)   computer systems to support and mediate social interaction and facilitate a sense of togetherness (Preece, 2000).

Lesch (2012: 44) takes the definition provided for 'community' in Collins Cobuild (1990: 280) as a point of departure: 'The community is all the people who live in a particular area or place; a particular group of people or part of society who are all alike in some way'. *Community* in this context refers to a geographical grouping of people but also to a specific group in society where people relate to one another in certain situations. The notions of *belonging to the group, identifying with the group* or *being part of the group* are inherent to the term. Within the South African context, the group referred to consists of working class communities with a relatively low level of education and high unemployment rates. Lesch (2012: 43–45) therefore goes further to define *community* in terms of the level of education and does not necessarily refer to a demographic community. The uneven power relationships and the advocacy role of the language mediator are paramount within this definition of the community.

The following statement by Pöchhacker (2004: 57), even though he apparently refers to community interpreting, is also applicable to community translation: 'In community-based domains, the primary parties are typically of unequal social status and highly discrepant educational backgrounds. In such situations, the induction to use "the verbal [or written] form best suited to understanding by audience" becomes a critical challenge'. The majority of professional translators in South Africa are commissioned to translate texts for what could loosely be called parallel audiences. This means that the profile of the source text reader matches that of the target reader, who is educated in the standard language.

As is the case with community interpreting, community translation aims to empower the community:

[The] starting point is a recognition that the problem of communication between these two parties is not simply a matter of language; it is equally created and compounded by the fact that they are separated by a wide gap of power. This power gap is directly related to class, race and/or culture, often gender and the differential power relations between a professional and his or her lay client. (...) So the community interpreter [translator] is more proactive: (he or she) is not only the interpreter [translator] for these clients but to represent their interests, to assess their needs and to help them obtain whatever they are entitled to. (National Language Project, 1996)

The uniqueness of community translation, as portrayed by Lesch (1999, 2005), is that the source text reader and target text reader do not necessarily belong to the same socio-economic level. The translator is then required to adapt the target text to make it accessible for the target group. In this regard, Siegrühn (1991: 33) came to the conclusion that the original concern with the quality of translation is rather replaced by a concern with the appropriateness and accessibility of the translation. Community translation is thus a means to an end, namely to equip the community with the necessary information and other means of developing their own skills (Lesch, 2012: 48–50). It is an attempt to balance the power relationship between the sender and the receiver by prioritising the needs of the community (see also Fraser (1990: 81–83) in this regard). With reference to the effectiveness of the communication process, Cluver (1992) states the following:

> [T]ranslators need to be sensitive [to] the needs of the different groups. Within any speech community there are marginalised groups who have been excluded from mainstream developments and for whom the form in which information is encoded presents a barrier [...] The task of the community translator is not only to make information available in another language (in a parallel manner) but to make it available to marginalised communities in a more assimilable format. (1992: 36)

The empowering role that the translator is expected to play is echoed by Walker *et al.* (1995: 102–105), who emphasise that a translated text does not need to be a mirror image of the original. Instead, the notion of translation needs to expand to include such reformulations and adaptations which are necessary in order to reach the lower end of the speech community. There is no doubt that when the need exists, communication will take place and translation is no exception.

According to Cornelius (2010: 172), in the case of community translation, where the reader occupies an important position, specialised terminology and standardised language are not essential. The translator has to develop strategies whereby concepts and terms from the ST that are likely to be incomprehensible in the target language (TL) are explained. In order to do this, the translator should not only possess excellent linguistic abilities, but also develop outstanding skills in adapting and reformulating texts. As any other translator, Lesch (1999: 94) confirms that the community translator is expected to have excellent knowledge of both the source language (SL) and the subject matter they are dealing with as well as the ability to manipulate the TL for a specific group to be able to use it. Nord (1992: 39) argues that what has paramount importance is the function or set of functions that the TT has in the TL, rather than the original function of the SL text, as is the case for equivalence-based translation theories.

In principle, translation is an extended communication process that makes information accessible to people who would not otherwise have access to that information. Access to information and to the exchange of information and ideas among a group of people, aim to place people in a position to make better-informed decisions, to make their own contribution and thus to participate more fully in debates relevant to their lives and societies. This is in line with the statement of Vasalikakos (1989), as mentioned earlier, regarding the rights, privileges and obligations people have in a democratic society. However, availability of translations does not always equate with access to information, as Meintjes (1992: 14–15) explains:

> This belief in the democratic thrust of translation is nevertheless dependent on how this information is made available, to whom, by whom, for what reason and so forth.
>
> (…)
>
> It is assumed that translation automatically makes a text accessible, but this is not necessarily so. *It is possible to translate a text from one language into another and for it still to remain incomprehensible to the broader mass of people, or for it to remain unacceptable, alienating. People's right to easy access to information and to participation is not provided for if the translation is inaccurate or written in such a way that it continues to be as inaccessible as the original. Translation has to be more than symbolic (…) if it is to assist the democratic process.* (Italics HML).

In the same vein Sieghrun (1992: 34) states the following:

> [T]he community translator is neither a social worker, nor an educator, nor an advocate. The community translator is aware of the power imbalances in society and chooses to mediate in order to make [target] texts accessible, instead of offering 'parallel' translations.

This practice requires certain skills from the translator. In this light, Walker *et al.* (1995: 113) make the following statement:

> For some time to come, translation in South Africa will differ radically from conventional preconceived ideas of what translation should

constitute. Translation teachers need to prepare their students adequately to meet the needs of a multilingual South Africa in their profession.

What can be deduced from the above quotations is that linguistic interaction via translation should be actively linked to identifiable needs of the community. From a translation perspective, there should be a clearly identified language benefit for the community. The notion of reciprocity comes to mind: the relationship must be mutually beneficial. This means reciprocity between those who are serviced – the community on the one side and the initiator or commissioner (Nord, 1991: 8–10) on the other. The initiator wants to inform according to democratic principles and the reader needs the information concerning privileges and obligations (e.g. voter education).

4.2 Types of community translation

The following types of community translation (CT) can be identified: parallel CT, non-parallel CT, intralingual CT, and a community approach to translation (Lesch, 2012: 47–56).

(i)   Parallel CT involves a SL community text that is aimed at a language-impoverished group as the target reader, which is translated in a similar manner for a target group that has an equivalent educational profile.
(ii) Non-parallel CT involves a source text originally written for an advanced SL target group, which needs to be translated for a language-impoverished group.
(iii) Intralingual CT takes the division between interlingual, intralingual and intersemiotic translation as a point of departure. With intralingual community translation, a ST is translated intralingually (in the same language) in the sense that it is made accessible to a broader target readership; the text is thus rewritten into a simplified version.
(iv) A community translation approach implies that although both the ST reader and the TT reader are on the same level, the initiator of the translation process (the commissioner) may request that the translator write their translation as if the target group were not parallel to the source group, and that the target text be adjusted to suit a lower target group.

If a community translation approach is followed, it would follow that the target market of the ST and that of the TT lie on parallel literacy levels. However, the request of the commissioner is that the TT should be made more accessible to the TT reader. This can be done by using short sentences, explaining difficult terms, avoiding passive constructions, ensuring that there is always an antecedent, avoiding complex sentence constructions, and so on. The brief of the commissioner contains explicit guidelines with regard to the type of text that should be compiled. In the translation brief included in the Appendix, both the ST and the TT are aimed at students undertaking a correspondence course. The same content of the ST needs to be covered in the TT, but the commissioner's request is clear that the target text should be made accessible to the TT readers: they explicitly advise the translators to use short sentences, simple language, and avoid tedious terminology, etc. In short, the expectation is that plain language should be used.

Fine (2001: 19–21) states the following with regard to plain language:

> [P]lain language (is) accessible, user-friendly, understandable and informative. It is characterised by a lucid and well-organised structure; by a clear and user-friendly lay-out and design for written materials and visuals. When spoken, it is presented with back-ups and appropriate and user-friendly tone and body language.

Eagleson (1990: 4, cited in Burns & Kim, 2011: 59) defines plain language as follows:

> In short it is the opposite of gobbledegook and of confusing and incomprehensible language. Plain English is clear, straightforward expression, using only as many words as are necessary. It is language that avoids obscurity, inflated vocabulary and convoluted sentence construction. It is not baby talk, nor is it a simplified version of the English language.

To use plain language entails that the generic reader should be able to understand the text. Within Holmes' (1988: 22) so-called mapping theory, it means that the reader should be in a position to draw a realistic mental perception *(map)* of the text. Cornelius (2010: 171), in accordance to Bhatia's (1993) notion of easification, concurs that plain language is a form of intra-lingual translation, a process during which particular interventions are brought to bear on a complex text, in order to fit the linguistic competence of a particular target audience. In this way, complicated content is unlocked and meaning mediated. The use of plain language is to decrease the cognitive processing difficulties experienced by the reader. Careful consideration must therefore be given to the linguistic features used in this alternative text.

Lesch (2005: 266–267) also made a case for the use of plain language in favour of the generic reader: different readers and listeners must be addressed in writing and speech at a level that they can understand. A plain language approach to translation for communication purposes requires text producers to consider plain language for effective communication. At the same time, it should be borne in mind that there are various degrees of 'plainness'. The communicator and translator can achieve a relative 'plainness' – a 'plainer' language that, in the eyes and ears of the audience, is more adequate than, for instance, the juridical Afrikaans version and, in terms of communication, represents an improvement of the original source text language. The concept of 'plain language' is dynamic and will vary from one group of users to another.

Translators can use two approaches: to think of a text in terms of plain language *before* translating; or to transfer a text into plain language *during* the translation process. The latter approach requires rephrasing and adaptation as part of the construction of target texts. I believe this is the better way of ensuring effective intercultural communication across power gaps.

The importance of using plain language in reader-oriented translation in national (and international) contexts similar to the South African one is further illustrated by Gile's (1995) gravitational model of linguistic availability. Gile's model of language proficiency applies to lexicon, syntax and other linguistic rules. Describing the relative availability of lexical units and linguistic rules, it represents the status of the individual's oral or written command of a language at a particular point in time and under specific circumstances. Gile's model consists of a variable and an invariable part. The latter refers to language elements that are assumedly available all the time or, at least, change very slowly. This applies to basic rules of grammar and to a small number of the most frequent words in a language. According to Gile (1995: 216), the variable part is much larger and includes dozens of rules and many thousands of words and idioms as well as metaphorical language.

It can be said that 'plain' language is close to Gile's nucleus and that its lexis and linguistic rules belong to the invariable part. This implies that it is more readily available to translators for retrieving functional equivalents for target texts. It is an advantage for readers' understanding of texts written in accessible language in that the lexis is readily available, the meaning is clear, and the structure further facilitates the comprehensibility of a text. The dynamics of Gile's gravitational model enable translators to be conscious of the availability of linguistic material in the 'active' zones of the target text readers. The underlying principle is that the more frequently words and rules are used, the stronger the centripetal effect. This means that words that are used often become more available than words or rules used less frequently.

4.3 Critique against community translation in formative years

Concerning the need for translation adaptation and abiding by the rule of loyalty to the people, the use of plain language is not without drawbacks. Several features may prove to be obstacles to communication. They include, among others, perceptual barriers that make people with different personalities, interests, education, social backgrounds, cultures, etc., understand even simple messages and everyday situations in different ways.

A translation with variation may not preserve all the characteristics with regard to content and form of its ST, but the omission of information should not be dismissed so easily, because sometimes omitted contents are necessary. Before answering whether or not a complete translation is superior to a translation with variation, we should answer another question: 'Best for whom?' Different translations of the same text are produced to fulfil the intended purposes of the TT. The relative adequacy of different translations of the same text can only be determined in terms of the extent to which each translation successfully fulfils the purpose for which it was intended.

The relative validity of each translation is measured by the degree to which the receptors are able to respond to its message in comparison with (1) the original response as intended by the author in the original audience and (2) how that audience did in fact respond. The responses can, of course, never be identical, since interlingual communication always implies some differences in cultural setting, with accompanying diversities in value systems, conceptual presuppositions, and historical antecedents. Nida (1964) considers many factors such as the purpose of the translation, the roles of both the translator and the receivers, and the cultural implications of the translation process.

An approach involving adaptation might be met with severe criticism. See the following examples as representative of the general critique:

> The primary responsibility to make texts more accessible, acceptable and suitable rests with the author, not the translator. The language use, style and register is adjusted by the author according to the target public, what he or she has in mind, in any case that is how it should be. The translator does not necessarily know who the target text is aimed at. (Le Roux, 1992: 31, translation – HML)

> I pointed out to the person asking about translating for adults with low-reading ability that they need to ensure that the original English or Afrikaans text is targeted to adults with similar ability. It is not right to expect the translator to take a text written for English university students and expect him to translate it into Sotho so that it can be understood by newly literate adults. (Hermanson, 1996: 7)

> A translator is not a creative artist or journalist – he/she relays the original text into the other language. Just as technical or just as simple as the original. (Taljaard, 1996: 9, translation – HML)

These South African language practitioners, Le Roux (1992: 31), Hermanson (1996: 7) and Taljaard (1996: 9) argue along the same lines. In contrast, I want to claim that translation is among other things, a creative and proactive activity (see Kussmaul, 1998: 118–125). Therefore, the community translator needs to have exceptional linguistic skills as well as cultural and linguistic sensitivity to respond to the differing demands of the divergent challenges. The necessary resources and skills need to be developed and should also be reflected in the training, which includes, among other aspects, the ability to interpret, rewrite, reformulate, annotate and comment (Meintjes, 1992: 18). In practice, it does not necessarily mean that the community translator is taking over the responsibility of the ST author when it comes to accessible communication. Apart from the brief of the commissioner for the translator, one can also argue that the community translator should form an integral part of the production team, from inception to final production, and not be the allegedly invisible and neutral individual behind his desk. Cooperation between the original author and the translator can also result in developing an intra-lingual translation text conforming to an accessible language. Translators, often by the nature of their experience, can be resourceful and versatile language workers and can assist in coding or evaluating the original text. In this manner, the author takes on some self-editing functions and preserves control over part of the translation process before turning to the eventual inter-lingual phase.

Such a point of departure puts more focus on the translation process than on the product. Research has shown that translation is a process in which the translator constantly has to make choices within a given social environment. From the view of the community translator, translation is not solely viewed as an inter-linguistic attempt, but as an intercultural endeavour taking place within a social setting. This social setting according to Marais (2008: 51) relates to larger social issues such as power struggles between languages and cultures, ethics and the role translators play as agents of communication. This relevancy for the society is also echoed by Taibi and Ozolins (2016: 11), who state that it is obvious that community translation is a branch of translation which is characterised by its social mission.

This proactive approach is in line with the notion that, more than anything else, translation is a teleological activity (Toury, 1980, 1985). Translators who take this view must seriously make a deliberate and consistent effort to identify their potential target audiences, since the audience does not simply decode an utterance. Rather, the audience arrives at an interpretation of an utterance by means of an active process of matching the features of the utterance at various levels with representations they have stored in their long-term memories. When target-text audiences cannot make relevant matches, the communication act is reduced to a futile exercise.

Apart from this sociolinguistic reality as a motivation for a functional approach to translation, one can also argue from a linguistic point of departure and refer to the notion of cognitive synonyms, as defined by Cruse (1986), to counter the criticisms and to argue in favour of a functional text production in translation (see Section 3 above). However, in this context, the concept is dealt with in a broad sense and not limited to the lexical level and linguistic approaches. The extension of the concept includes cognitive synonyms within a contextual relation. It is then possible to draw a distinction between four basic relationships, or congruence relationships, namely:

(a) Identity: A and B have the same members;
(b) Inclusion: Class B is wholly included in class A;
(c) Overlap: Class A and class B have members in common, but each has members not belonging to the other and;
(d) Disjunction: Class A and B have no members in common. (Cruse, 1986: 86–87)

A better approach to classifying semantic relationships between items X and Y (or source-text item X and target-text item Y) is to operate in terms of meaning, and look at the semantic relations between parallel sentences in which X and Y occupy identical structural positions. The most useful primary relations are established by using truth-conditional relations between source-text and target-text sentences. The relations defined by truth-conditional relations are distinguished as cognitive synonyms (not only at the lexical but also at sentence level) and are defined as follows:

X is a cognitive synonym of Y if (i) X and Y are syntactically identical, and (ii) any grammatical declarative sentence S containing X has equivalent truth conditions to another sentence S1, which is identical to S except that X is replaced by Y. (Cruse, 1986: 88)

This can be further complemented by the notion of entailment, which is a useful intuition for translation and semantic analysis (see the Appendix, especially bullets one and two of the basic principles):

A proposition P is said to entail another proposition Q when the truth of Q is a logically necessary consequence of the truth of P (and the falsity of P is a logically necessary consequence of the falsity of Q). (Cruse, 1986: 14)

Entailment can refer to relationships between different items (lexical items, clauses or sentences). The moot point is that the use of a specific lexical item, phrase, or sentence is not an absolute requirement for reconstructing an adequate target-text function as long as there are functional and cognitive synonyms within a given context. A translation may also be effective, in some cases even more effective and functional, when one takes cognisance of the potential audience and keeps in mind that a translation is a proactive activity aimed at a specific target group.

It must be stressed that I am not arguing that a translation should be viewed only in terms of the intelligibility of the translated text. Intelligibility cannot be assessed merely in terms of understandable words and correct grammar, but must be assessed in terms of the impact the message as such has on recipients.

4.4 Norms

First of all, it is worthwhile to look at how Gideon Toury and Andrew Chesterman use the term *norm* in translation and what can be deduced for the purposes of this chapter. It needs to be kept in mind that Toury's terminology is set within a descriptive framework and he attempts to reconstruct the translation process. According to Toury (1980: 53), norms are operative at every stage in the translation process and at every level. Norms can be defined in two ways: either descriptive or prescriptive (see Kramer aus Bochum, 2006: 10–13):

- Descriptive: It defines how a text has been translated and not how it 'could be', 'could have been' or 'should have been' translated. In such a case, a norm is a standard model or pattern regarded as typical.
- Prescriptive: The definition of norms as a prescriptive element: a norm can govern what the translator ought or ought not to do when the task becomes difficult or impossible.

The concept of norms as a 'category for descriptive analysis of translation phenomena' was first put forward by Toury (1980), who defines norms as 'values or ideas shared by a certain community as to what is right and wrong, adequate and inadequate' (1980: 57). Toury (1980: 49–50, 52–62, 115–116, 123–139) describes translation norms as follows:

Translational norms are behavioural constraints with the properties indicated below:

(a) They may be thought of as performance instructions in that they prescribe specific types of translational performance for specific types of translational situations;
(b) They may also be thought of as serving as performance criteria – that is, criteria for the evaluation of instances of translational behaviour;
(c) They belong, like other norms, to the inter-subjective category of constraints regulating behavioural activities and;
(d) They reflect certain (normative) models. (Winckler, 1992: 32)

Toury's (1980: 53–54, 95–96, 123–131) framework starts with *preliminary norms*. These are norms that operate before the translation process itself and concern the choice of the texts that need to be translated or the direction of the translation. He distinguishes between initial norms (aimed at adequacy, adherence to source-system norms or acceptability, adherence to target-system norms) and operational norms, which come into play during the actual translation process and the respective on-the-spot decision-making process. Another distinction he makes is that of textual norms, which are established through a comparison of source and target texts, and extra-textual norms, which are found in explicit, normative statements in the literature about translation (Toury, 1980: 53).

According to Toury (1980: 54), *operational norms* direct actual decisions made during the translation process. These include *textual norms*, which determine the verbal formulation of the texts and the actual selection of target language material; and *matricial norms*, which determine or strongly affect the fullness, location and segmentation of the matrices of target texts. He also states that due to the working of the *initial norm*, the translator has the basic choice between two alternatives where the translator either subjects themselves 'to the original text with its textual relations and norms expressed by it and contained in it [i.e. a weakly adequate translation], or to the linguistic norms active in TL [i.e. an acceptable translation]' (Toury, 1980: 54).

Chesterman (2000: 67) draws a distinction between *expectancy norms* and *professional norms*. The former are primarily orientated towards the product and are 'established by the expectations of the readers of a translation (of a given type) concerning what a translation (of this type) should be like' (2000: 64). These expectations are to a certain extent determined by the current translation tradition in the target culture and, to a certain extent, by the form of similar text types in the target language. The reader(s) of the target text also have expectations about the text type and discourse conventions about the style, register, degree of grammaticality, choice of vocabulary and so on.

The source of the professional norms, according to Chesterman (2000: 67), lies *par excellence* with those 'members of the society who are deemed to be competent professional translators, who the society trusts as having the status, and may further be recognized by others as competent'. Included in the translator's professional norms, lies the accountability norm (i.e. loyalty towards the original author, the commissioner and translator), communication norm (i.e. to optimise communication between the parties concerned) and relation norms (i.e. relevant similarity to be maintained between the source text and target text) (Chesterman, 2000: 68–69). In essence, the professional translator is expected to be a master of the skill, through education and training; accept duties to the broader society, not only to one's clients; be objective and have high-set standards of conduct and professional performance (Feinauer, 2005: 162).

5. Norms for Community Translation

Against the backdrop of 'the cult of the amateur', which, as Keen (2007) argues, has a serious impact on professionalism and makes it more and more difficult to find high-quality material, it is worthwhile to propose norms for community translation practice.

5.1 Initial norm

Norm 1

> *The community translator should subject themselves to the prevailing linguistic and community norms of the target text and the target language polysystem or part thereof and not to those of the source text.*

This is to ensure that an *acceptable* TT is constructed and not a *weakly adequate text*. A weakly adequate translation serves as the *tertium comparationis*. That is, the invariant for the comparison of the ST and TT and provides a 'maximal reconstruction' (Toury, 1980: 108) or 'faithful representation' (Toury, 1980: 141) in the target language of the textual relation and functions within the source text, and of the norms expressed in the source text and contained in it. On the other hand, an acceptable translation is a translation that completely adheres to the norms of the target culture's primary and secondary modelling systems (Toury, 1980: 12, 29, 55, 75 and 116).

5.2 Preliminary norm

Norm 2

> *One should not mention that the text is a translation but should rather ensure that the target text should take the form of a covert translation* (see House, 1981: 194). The translation should be domesticated and take the form of a second original and the reader should not realise that it is a translation.

In a covert translation, socio-cultural differences between the source language and the target language can be overcome. It is for this reason that covert translation assumes the status of a (second) original in the target language, according to House. A covert translation would therefore be a functional equivalent of the source text. According to House (1981: 196), the translator places a cultural filter between the ST and the TT and consequently is able to perceive the ST through the eyes of a member of the target language culture. On the other hand, an overt translation always reads as a translation and only second-level equivalence is possible, e.g. historically linked source texts or timeless source texts (House, 1981: 189).

Within Venuti's (1998) framework this norm entails that a domesticated translation, rather than a foreignised one, needs to be constructed. A domesticated translation is, according to Venuti (1998: 5), '[...] supplemented with features peculiar to the translating language, no longer inscrutably foreign but made comprehensible in a domestic style'. For Munday (2008: 144) the focus in such a case is not only the text itself and invisibility of the style, but also the selection of texts for translation that are open for a domesticated translation strategy. A foreignised translation aims 'to restrain the ethnocentric violence of translation' (Venuti, 2008: 16). Such a translation transcends the target culture and maintains the foreign element of the source text (Shuttleworth & Cowie, 2004). Such a translation succeeds in registering the linguistic and cultural differences between the source text culture and the target text culture.

In addition, within the framework of Nord, an instrumental translation would be preferred as opposed to a documentary translation. A documentary translation presents TT readers with a document of a source culture communication between the author and the ST recipient. Certain aspects of the source text or the whole ST-in-situation are produced for the TT recipient who is conscious of 'observing' a (past) communicative situation of which they are not part (Nord, 1991: 72–73). The TT recipient becomes in this instance a mere observer. On the other hand, an instrumental translation is an instrument for a new communicative interaction between the source culture sender and the target culture audience. It serves as an 'independent message-transmitting instrument in a new communicative action TC and it is intended to fulfil its communicative purpose without the recipient being conscious of reading or hearing a text which, in a different form was used before in a different communicative action' (Nord, 1991: 73).

5.3 Operational norms

As accessible language is paramount for the community, the operational norms should be in accordance with this principle. A balance should be struck between language purism and meaningful innovation.

5.3.1 Encoding norms

Norm 3

The translation should be grammatically sound and the orthography should be correct and in accordance with the grammatical rules of the target language. This is in accordance with the professional norms as portrayed by Chesterman (2000: 67), as a professional product is expected.

To construct a community translation text for the generic reader (as well as the virtual community) does not necessarily mean, in the teleological eye, that the spoken word should be elevated to the level of written language. It also does not mean that grammar and spelling rules should be neglected. The community translator is expected to construct a linguistically sound text where there are no typos, spelling errors or linguistic inconsistencies.

Norm 4

Use informal language and style that is accessible for the mental perception of the reader but regional speech should be used with great care. The language use should be reader-friendly and the reader should be able to identify with it (Fine, 1995: 12–20). In the case of the virtual community, it is really an international community.

Norm 5

Encode information via simple syntactic structures. Use short sentences with clear antecedents in the case where anaphora needs to be established (Fine, 1995: 12–20; Withers-Lancashire, 1995: 37–50). This norm should be read in accordance with norm 4 (see also Holmes' mapping theory again).

One should, however, take note of Cornelius (2010: 175), who points out that the use of short sentences creates the impression that *long sentences* are by definition difficult to understand. As a consequence, the use of readability formulas is encouraged but, as Charrow and Charrow (1979: 1320) point out, sentence length, in itself, does not necessarily lead to reception problems, since 'it is the grammatical, semantic, and contextual complexity of discourse, not sentence length, that determines how difficult it will be for people to understand the discourse'. On the other hand, the use of shorter sentences may lead to vagueness and create obscurity.

Norm 6

Involve the reader by addressing them directly and by asking questions. The reading experience of the translated text should be an active act by the potential reader (Fine, 1995: 23).

Norm 7

Explicate source text information in the target text by using phrases such as: in other words ..., meaning ..., or make use of additions or provide examples. In this manner, certain information will be concretised and the text will be clearer for the reader.

5.3.2 Text layout norms

Norm 8

Condense paragraphs in order to make the TT more accessible. (Withers-Lancashire, 1995: 37–50). For example, long sentences should be shortened, if appropriate (see Norm 5 above), especially in the case of technical information.

Norm 9

Synchronise the text by grouping the information together and reorganising the content if necessary. This is relevant to ensure coherence by means of text structuring mechanisms and the notion of manipulation of segmentation (see Toury, 1980: 54, 102).

Norm 10
  Use headings and subheadings to enhance the reading and understanding of the synchronised material. The reader will immediately recall information by just reading the appropriate heading of a specific paragraph.

6. Conclusion

The overarching aim for developing these community translations norms is to meet the generic reader at whatever level of linguistic competence and social integration. As Fraser (1990: 81) rightly asserts, 'this sensitivity and orientation to the audience makes community translators' approach to translation a more helpful one propounded in translation theory', especially for the generic target text reader. This approach (and norms) is cognisant of the fact that translation cannot exist in a vacuum; it has a purpose and an identity only as far as it is read and used by the target or receptor audience. In order to fulfil the client's and the community's expectations, translators must pay heed to reader variables, context and function. A translation should be judged by the degree to which it meets the recipients' experience and capacity to decode it. This means that it is the audience's background, not prescriptive rules, that determine the strategies to be used for producing the best possible translation. To cite Fraser (1990: 82) once again, the needs of the users are paramount in a community approach and *any* translation will have to start from an analysis of those needs and requirements.

References

Bhatia, V.K. (1993) *Analysing Genre: Language Use in Professional Settings.* London: Longman.

Burns, A. and Kim, M. (2011) Community accessibility of health information and the consequent impact for translation into community languages. *Translation & Interpreting* 3 (1), 58–75.

Campbell, S. (1998) *Translation into the Second Language.* New York: Addison Wesley Longman.

Candido, A., Maziero, E., Gasperin, C., Pardo, T.A.S., Specia, L. and Aluisio, S.M. (2009) *Supporting the Adaptation of Texts for Poor Literacy Readers: A Text Simplification Editor for Brazilian Portuguese.* Proceedings of the NAACL HLT Workshop on Innovative Use of NLP for Building Educational Applications, Boulder, Colorado, June 2009, 34–42.

Census in Brief (2011) See http://www.statssa.gov.za/census/census_2011/census_products/Census_2011_Census_in_brief.pdf (accessed 25 October 2014).

Charrow, R.P. and Charrow, V. (1979) Making legal language understandable: A psycholinguistic study of jury instructions. *Columbia Law Review* 79, 1306–1374.

Chesterman, A. (2000) *Memes of Translation: The Spread of Ideas in Translation Theory.* Amsterdam: John Benjamins.

Cluver, A. (1992) Trends in the changes of translating domains: An overview. In A. Kruger (ed.) *Changes in Translating Domains.* Proceedings of a 'round table' conference held by the Linguistics Department of the University of South Africa on 30 October 1992 (pp. 5–10). Pretoria: University of South Africa.

Collins Cobuild (1990 and 1991). *English Language Dictionary*. London: Collins.

Cornelius. E. (2010) Plain language as alternative textualisation. *Southern African Linguistics and Applied Language Studies* 8 (2), 171–183.

Cruse, D.A. (1986) *Lexical Semantics*. Cambridge: Cambridge University Press.

Eagleson, R.D. (1990) *Writing in Plain English*. Canberra: Australian Government Public Service.

Feinauer, A. (2005) Language practitioners and standards. In M. Boers (ed.) *Rights in Practice: A Compendium on the Rights of Language Practitioners and their Clients* (pp. 162–164). Pretoria: South African Translators' Institute.

Fine, D. (2001) Plain language communication: Approaches and challenges. In F. Viljoen and A. Nienaber (eds) *Plain Legal Language for Democracy* (pp. 17–26). Pretoria: Protea Bookhouse.

Fine, D. (1995) *How to Use Plain Language*. Legal Education Project (LEAP): UCT.

Fraser, J.E. (1990) Tilting the Message: Community Translation in a Reader-Orientated Model of Translation Process. Unpublished master's thesis, Ealing College.

Fourie, J (2003) *The Quality of Translation Regarding Medical Research Questionnaires*. Unpublished Master's thesis. Stellenbosch University.

Gile, D. (1995) *Basic Concepts and Models for Interpreter and Translator Training*. Amsterdam: John Benjamins.

Hermanson, E.A. (1996) Translating for the New South Africa. Problems and perspectives. Paper read at the 23rd Annual Seminar of the South African Translators' Institute – Western Cape. 13 September.

Holmes, J.S. (1988) *Translated! Papers on Literary Translation and Translation Studies*. Amsterdam: Rodopi, B.V.

House, J. (1981) *A Model for Translation Quality Assessment*. Tübingen: Gunter Narr.

Huang, Z. (2002) *Translation Variation Theory* (in Chinese). Beijing: Translation & Publishing Corporation.

Huang, Z. (2000) *Fan Yi Bian Ti Ben Zhi Lun (On the Nature of Translating)*. Beijing: Translation & Publishing Corporation.

Jang, H.T. (2000) Translation quality and the reader's response. http://www.ntu.edu.an/education/csle/student/jang//jang3.html (accessed 20 November 2000).

Jianzhong, X. (2000) Translation variation theory. *Meta: Translators' Journal* 48 (4), 384–397.

Keen, A. (2007) *The Cult of the Amateur*. New York: Doubleday.

Kramer aus Bochum, A. (2006) *Defining the Elusive – Interpreting Quality Research and its Pragmatic Relevance*. Unpublished master's thesis. Fachhochschule Köln, Institut für Translation und Mehrsprachige Kommunikation (ITMK).

Kussmaul, P. (1998) Types of creative translation. In A. Chesterman, N. San Salvador and Y. Gambier (eds) *Translation in Context* (pp. 117–126). Amsterdam: John Benjamins.

Lesch, H.M. (1999) Gemeenskapsvertaling in Suid-Afrika: Die konteks van die ontvanger as normeringsbeginsel. Unpublished Doctoral dissertation, Bellville: University of the Western Cape.

Lesch, H.M. (2005) Societal factors and translation practice. *Perspectives: Studies in Translatology* 12 (4), 256–259.

Lesch, H.M. (2012) *Gemeenskapsvertaling in Suid-Afrika: Die konteks van die ontvanger as normeringsbeginsel*. Stellenbosch: Sunmedia.

Le Roux, W. (1992) Changes in the type of text handled in government offices. In A. Kruger (ed.) *Changes in Translating Domains*. Proceedings of a 'round table' conference held by the Linguistics Department of the University of South Africa on 30 October 1992. (28–32) Pretoria: Unisa.

Marais, K. (2008) Training translators in South Africa: First global questions, *Journal for New Generation Sciences* 6 (3), 48–60.

Marais, K. (2012) Development and translation. In Y. Gambier and Van Doorslaer (eds) *Handbook of Translation Studies*, Volume 3, pp. 26–31.

McMillan, D.W. and D.M. Chavis (1986) Sense of community: A definition and theory. *Journal of Community Psychology* 14, 6–23.

Meintjes, L. (1992) Translation for empowerment and democracy. In A. Kruger (ed.) *Changes in Translating Domains*. Proceedings of a 'round table' conference held by the Linguistics Department of the University of South Africa on 30 October 1992. (pp. 14–18) Pretoria: Unisa.

Munday, J. (2008) *Introducing Translation Studies*. New York: Routledge.

National Language Project (NLP) (1996) Information sheet. Cape Town: NLP printers.

Nida, E.A. (1964) *Towards a Science of Translating*. Leiden: E.J. Brill.

Nord, C. (1991) *Text Analysis in Translation. Theory, Methodology and Didactic Application of a Model for Translation-Oriented Text Analysis*. Translated from German by Nord, C. and Sparrow, P. Amsterdam: Rodopi.

Nord, C. (1992) Text analysis in translator training. In C. Dollerup and A. Loddegaard (eds) *Teaching Translation and Interpreting. Training, Talent and Experience*, (pp. 39–48). Amsterdam: John Benjamins.

Nord, C. (1999) Translating as a text-production activity. Paper presented at the Universitat de Vic, Catalonia Spain.

O'Hagan, M. (2011) Community translation: Translation as a social activity and its possible consequences in the advent of Web 2.0 and beyond. *Linguistica Antverpiensia* 10, 11–23.

Preece, J. (2000) Online communities, designing usability and supporting sociability. In R. Earnshaw, R. Guedj, A. Van Dam and T. Vince (eds) *Frontiers of Human-Centred Computing, Online Communities and Virtual Environments* (pp. 263–277), Springer Verlag: Amsterdam.

Pöchhacker, F. (2004) *Introducing Interpreting Studies*. London: Routledge.

Reiss, K. and Vermeer, H.J. (1984) *Grundelegung einer Allegemeinen Transationtheorie*. Tubingen: Niemeyer.

Rheingold, H. (2000) *The Virtual Community: Homesteading on the Electronic Frontier*. Cambridge: MIT Press.

Schaffner, C. (1997) Translation studies. In J. Verscheuren, J.-O. Ostman, J.B. Blommaert and C. Bulcaen (eds) *Handbook of Pragmatics* (pp. 1–17). Amsterdam and Philadelphia: John Benjamins.

Shuttleworth, M. and Cowie, M. (2004) *Dictionary of Translation Studies*. Shanghai: Shanghai Foreign Language Education Press.

Siegrühn, A. (1992) Community translation. In A. Kruger (ed.) *Changes in Translating Domains*. Proceedings of a 'round table' conference held by the Linguistics Department of the University of South Africa on 30 October 1992 (pp. 14–18). Pretoria: Unisa.

Siegrühn, A. (1991) 'Wie vertaal vir wie en hoe?' *Language Projects Review* 6 (4), 29–31.

Sullivan, R. (2001) The promise of plain language drafting. *McGill Law Journal* 47, 97–128.

Taibi, M. and Ozolins, U. (2016) *Community Translation*. London: Bloomsbury.

Taljaard, P. (1996) *Is kaartgebruikers so dom?* In *SAVI-Bulletin* 6, 9.

Toury, G. (1980) *In Search of a Theory of Translation*. Tel Aviv: Porter Institute for poetics and semiotics.

Vasalikakos, J. (1989) Community interpreting: Translating in Australia. *Jerome Quarterly*. 4 (4), 3–6.

Venuti, L. (2008) *The Translator's Invisibility: A History of Translation* (2nd Edition). New York and London: Routledge.

Venuti, L. (1998) *The Scandals of Translation: Towards an Ethics of Difference*. London: Routledge.

Walker, A.K., Kruger, A. and Andrews, I.C. (1995) Translation as transformation: A process of linguistic and cultural adaptation. In *Die Suid-Afrikaanse Tydskrif vir Taalkunde. Supplement 26*, 99–115.

Winckler, W. (1992) Appendix II: A Draft glossary of some fundamental concepts and principles of Toury's approach to translation studies. Dept. General Linguistics, Stellenbosch University.

Withers-Lancashire, P.J.C. (1995) *Interpretasie en vertaling van 'n regsteks*. Unpublished master's thesis, Johannesburg: University of Johannesburg

Zhang, J. (2007) *On Translation Variation Theory*. Unpublished master's thesis, Beijing: Ningxia University.

Appendix

Brief of commissioner (Translated from Afrikaans)

Dear

Thank you for your interest in translating for INTEC College (International Colleges Group).

Please translate the attached test while keeping in mind the principles of distance education. It involves the following:

- Make the text as accessible as possible;
- Base the text on a grade 8 target reader;
- Use short sentences (one idea per sentence);
- Explain difficult terms;
- Use idiomatic Afrikaans;
- Address the reader directly (use 'jy' and 'jou' (you) instead of 'u', and translate 'a person' and 'one' as 'jy' (you));
- Avoid using sexist language;
- Avoid passive sentences;
- Avoid difficult constructions (e.g. change 'refined sugar products' to 'products with refined sugar'; and
- Use *Die Afrikaanse Woordelys en Spelreëls* as your guide.

Please send the test to me, Nikki Wouterse, at the abovementioned address. We will try to inform you as soon as possible if we can make use of your services.

We wish you success for the test.

Kind Regards

Nikki Wouterse
Editor

How INTEC wants you to translate

Our premise is as follows:

- Our students are on their own, without any educator or help.
- For this reason, our books need to be as simple as possible.
- Take into account that the student will probably not understand complicated words. Explain these words if you have to use them.
- Address the student directly; this makes the text friendlier. See yourself as the educator.
- If you think that something might sound ambiguous, explain exactly what the meaning should be.
- If you think something might be difficult to understand, explain it twice, in different ways.

Use the following basic principles:

- Use short words, rather than long ones.
- Use short sentences, rather than long ones.
- Use short paragraphs that have a logical flow.
- One can only translate something successfully if you understand it completely.
- When you understand something, you can put it simply.
- Our most important requirements are simplicity and successful communication.
- When you're in doubt, look it up.
- Even when you're not in doubt, look it up.
- Die *Afrikaanse Woordelys en Spelreëls* (the new edition with the blue cover) is your most important guide.

5   Volunteers and Public Service Translation

Ignacio García

1. Introduction

Community translation, also called public service translation, generally implies a professional, quality-controlled service *for* linguistic groups with limited access to the mainstream language(s). It gained recognition as a specific field some decades ago, as part of access and equity policies in advanced democracies seeking to address the needs of newly arriving immigrants. However, a quick web search shows that 'community translation' has recently acquired another meaning: the translation of any type of content by volunteer bilinguals, with an emphasis not on *for*, but on *by* the community. In this emerging modern sense, it denotes a web-based (crowdsourced, collaborative, user-generated, wiki, etc.) phenomenon, whereby volunteer bilinguals translate any content type via social media: amateur translation *by* the community. To draw the necessary distinction, some authors (most notably O'Hagan, 2011) have coined the term community translation 2.0. This chapter will follow the same convention, as the 2.0 tag conveniently alludes both to the supporting technological platform (web 2.0) and its broader embedded concept of social media.

Community/public service translation and community translation 2.0 would appear to have little in common. Apart from a passing mention by Lesch (2014) and Taibi and Ozolins (2016), no other author has so far felt the need to unite both concepts. Certainly, social media's impact on professional activities has been the focus of thousands of studies since Locke *et al.* wrote *The Cluetrain Manifesto* in 2000; however, little attention has been paid to how the social media subset of community translation 2.0 impacts on traditional public service translation, hitherto the preserve of professionals.

This chapter attempts to fill that gap by identifying the resultant landscape if both translation concepts (*for* and *by* the community) were to intersect, in the hope that such understanding could help maximise the efficient deployment of perpetually scarce community/public service translation resources. Although mass amateurisation suggests de-skilling and demonetarisation, it need not be wholly negative on professional translators: the entry of bilinguals and social media interaction could also benefit experts in an enhanced role as promoters of standards, trainers/mentors of volunteers and shapers of social perceptions about translation. Such increased influence could conceivably ripple-through into *the long tail* languages, thus far largely inaccessible to public service translation and professionalisation.

2. Translating *for* the Community

Conventional community translation (or, increasingly, public service translation, in clear demarcation of its role) emerged from the sixties and seventies in advanced democracies to cater for the needs of immigrants. The concept has since widened to cover translation for other linguistic minorities, be they transient populations (e.g. pilgrims, as in Taibi, 2011: 215–216) or marginalised local languages in multilingual societies, with South Africa being the oft-mentioned example (Erasmus, 2000).

Until now, most attention in the research literature centred on the more visible modality of community (or public service) interpreting. Nevertheless, community translation is emerging from its cousin's shadow, as this volume attests. It involves facilitating general access to services (health, welfare, justice) by translating and publishing informational material *from* the official language into the languages brought by a society's new entrants, with translation *into* the mainstream language mostly limited to private documents (driving licences, birth or marriage certificates, academic transcripts, police clearances, etc.) for restricted official use in legal, immigration or residency matters.

Given that Australia is considered one of the pioneering countries in the field (Ozolins, 1997), the Australian perspective affords a highly illustrative example. Community translation here emerged in response to the linguistic needs posed by successive waves of assisted immigration after World War Two. Post-war Australia made a gigantic effort in attracting migrants, mostly for economic development although defence figured as well. After the Japanese scare, there was a strong feeling that the country, given its geographical position, was difficult to defend unless its population greatly increased. 'Populate or perish' become the slogan of the moment (Wilton & Bosworth, 1984). The post-war programme was active in every sense, with the government inviting and attracting immigrants, subsidising their travel, providing accommodation on arrival, and funding other settlement services such as English classes. It was a logical extension to implement and fund translation and interpreting services, to assist local authorities and newcomers alike. As old assimilationist policies gave way to multicultural ones, new agencies were set up to promote social cohesion. Part of that cohesive drive was the provision of language services for populations of non-English speaking background (or NESBs in 1980s vernacular), now more commonly referred to as being culturally and linguistically diverse (CALD). Examples include the Community Relations Commission for a Multicultural New South Wales (a government body of the eponymous state) and the Multicultural Health Communication Unit of the Ministry of Health.

Amidst this gradually coalescing system, the creation of the National Accreditation Authority for Translators and Interpreters (NAATI) in 1977 constitutes a significant milestone. NAATI's chartered role was, and remains, that of testing and certifying individuals as competent to translate and/or interpret between English and other languages. Early in the eighties, universities in Sydney and Melbourne began offering NAATI accredited translation and interpreting courses for the languages of greater demand, and governmental bodies and institutions were advised to give preference to certified practitioners when allocating (or receiving) translation or interpreting services.

Ideally then, community translators ought to be university trained and NAATI-certified. In practice, there are simply too many collectives to cater for, and the number continues to grow with *emerging* languages (Australia's most recently settled linguistic groups currently from the Middle East and East Africa). Thus, in the state of New South Wales alone, where 160 languages are spoken, just over one quarter (47, a great achievement even by international standards) fall within the NAATI certification programme; of these, appropriate tertiary training is currently offered for only seven. Moreover, the lag-time between new migrant intakes and corresponding translator certifications makes it more difficult for the system to respond to those who are precisely in most need.

This shortcoming – and shortfall – is by no means specific to Australia. It signals the main limitation of community/public service translation worldwide: professional translation services are not only expensive, but also frequently impossible to provide, particularly at *the long tail* end of the curve. For sorely underserviced languages it may well be a case of somehow tapping directly into one's own community, or getting left behind.

Therefore, let us now turn our attention to community translation 2.0.

3. Translation *by* the Community

Facebook's interface localisation project is the prime example of a successful community translation 2.0 initiative. Bilingual readers of this article who have a Facebook account are warmly encouraged to log in, find the *Translation* tab, and experience the process themselves by contributing some new translations or voting on some existing ones.

Indeed, this is what bilingual users of Facebook keep doing – motivated not by money or curiosity, but by passion. The only potential reward is to be named as a top contributor in a leader board. The intellectual engagement might be akin to doing crosswords, but the outcome goes beyond the solitary satisfaction of a completed puzzle: it enables other users to connect, and the contributor to connect with them too. The success of this scheme, initiated in 2008, must have surprised Facebook itself: the Spanish site went live after only two weeks, French after just 24 hours (European Commission, 2012: 25), and minority languages queued for involvement (Scannell, 2012).

Facebook (or Twitter or other social media platforms) represents one way of harnessing *the wisdom of crowds,* as Surowiecki (2004) would put it. Language is a very sophisticated tool for manipulating complex ideas into discrete units of meaning. These can easily be chunked at various levels: segment (phrase or sentence), paragraph, or entire document, allowing several people to work simultaneously on fragments of various sizes. Consequently, translating such material is well suited for *crowd*sourcing – the process of taking a task that would have traditionally been performed by employees or contractors, and *out*sourcing its constituent chunks for completion via an open call to a loosely defined group (Howe, 2008).

Apart from community translation (and community translation 2.0), this same phenomenon has been tagged in various other ways, depending on the beholder's perspective. The term community translation focuses on the primitive meaning of a group of people (here, bilingual) who have some interest in *common*. Volunteer translation means unpaid work, performed by untrained, non-professionals. Wiki and crowdsourced translation give prominence to the web platform that allows a task to be shared horizontally in real time, facilitating mass collaboration without need of a hierarchical institution at the back-end doing the organising. Open translation harks to the principles of open source software: no one has proprietary rights over the translation, and anyone can seek to improve it. User-generated translation focuses on contributor autonomy in deciding what to translate, and can take on extreme forms such as *fansubbing, romhacking* and *scanlation* whereby volunteers translate a source without the permission – and sometimes against the explicit wishes – of its owner (O'Hagan, 2009).

There is quite abundant literature that describes these phenomena (or manifestations), discusses the merits of the various labels, and examines how they interrelate (Fernandez Costales, 2012; O'Hagan, 2011; Pym, 2011, to mention a few). For the purpose of our discussion, what is of most relevance (echoing Fernandez Costales, 2012) is to distinguish between two types of *community* projects. On the one hand, unsolicited, spontaneous, bottom-up, user-centric collaborative initiatives as exemplified by *fansubbing* or the translations of Wikipedia pages, where only users and their communities benefit. On the other hand, solicited, corporate-initiated, top-down, market-driven collaborative initiatives as exemplified by Facebook, where the commissioner of the task derives benefits by cutting costs, saving time, and engaging with its consumer base.

Facebook's lead has since been followed by Microsoft, Plaxo and Sun (mentioned in De Palma & Kelly, 2008: 9–30), plus Twitter, Linkedin, Google, Symantec (in European Commission, 2012: 24–25), and surely many others that will be awaiting the right application and opportunity. But community translation 2.0 has its limits: it may be easy to find volunteers for the more impactful and exciting sections, but often and even for the most altruistic projects, the community effort falters before the finish line. The obvious incentive for completion is payment. That, however, does not necessarily mean resorting to the relatively small pool of expert professionals (including, where relevant, community/public service translators).

The emerging enterprise solution to unpaid community burnout is a special type of translation which I have referred to elsewhere (García, 2015) as paid crowdsourcing, exemplified by cloud-based translation marketplaces such as Gengo or One Hour Translation. The concept involves using the same technology as community translation 2.0 does, but in a *for-profit* mode. By saving on overheads (file handling, bidding processes) and using admittedly low (but non-zero) remuneration to attract enough amateur or aspiring translators, operators can offer a fast, economical service at – hopefully – a *fit-for-purpose* quality level.

4. Social Inclusion as Shared Ethos

Is there any overlap between community/public service translation and community translation 2.0? On the surface, they seem exact opposites: paid professionals versus unpaid volunteers.

Traditional community/public service translation addresses social policy and minority groups within a given country (in Australia, the CALD populations); someone is in charge, deciding what to translate and how; translators will ideally be trained and certified, and the process operates on a vertical, hierarchical structure (expert-to-community). Community translation 2.0 can reach a worldwide base, whose own members choose what to translate and when; there may be a background institution (as in the case of Facebook) that provides the material and means, and determines who belongs, but it would have no control on who does what: the structure is more horizontal, flexible and egalitarian (peer-to-peer).

The respective translation processes reflect this opposite approach. In the prestige scenario, community/public service translation implements a full translation – editing – proofreading (TEP) sequence, following the *waterfall* template of project management: subsequent steps (i.e. editing) are undertaken only once the previous one (translation) has been completed; community translation 2.0 on the other hand fosters an *agile* project management environment, attempting all steps as simultaneously as possible. Community/public service translation functions within the *print* model: revise first, then publish; community translation 2.0 embodies the *web* model, publish first and then revise if required. With web content, changes are straightforward and inexpensive – assuming it stays relevant long enough to warrant them.

Superficially then, the two are clear opposites, but closer inspection reveals some commonalities and, possibly, scope for cross-fertilisation. Conventional community translation is there to help linguistically disadvantaged minorities gain access to services, and enable them to participate in society on equal footing with prestige-language speakers. Community translation 2.0 is about bypassing the traditional gatekeepers so that everyone can have a public voice. Thus, while their external circumstances are different, both share a core ethos of individual empowerment and social inclusion.

Moreover, social media, in which community translation 2.0 is embedded, are already being used by the newly-arrived to make sense of how a host society works. A web search is an obvious first resort, and will predictably yield peer-to-peer support pages: web rings and forums in the minority language hosted by established fellow migrants and other support groups.

Machine translation (MT) can also help when peer-to-peer support does not suffice. Altavista made MT ubiquitous when releasing free of charge the Babel Fish engine through its browser in the late nineties. Systran-based Babel Fish technology could only do reasonably well for a limited number of major languages for which grammar rules and bilingual dictionaries had been developed. Working not on rules but on massive amounts of monolingual and bilingual corpora, statistical MT could do similarly well for a much greater number of language pairs, over a hundred in Google Translate currently (Google, 2016). At the time of writing (October 2016) a new type of MT technology, neural MT, seems to be leaving the labs and entering beta production with the promise of offering similar, if not better, output with less amount of data required, thus allowing the building of engines into many more language pairs (Wu *et al.*, 2016).

Machine translation will not be perfect but it being immediate and cost-free, and always a right-click away in the browser, will offer migrants another tool to help them make sense of their new world. Limited proficiency in the mainstream language does not mean lack of basic vocabulary and a degree of background knowledge, and MT could help with bootstrapping both.

In this milieu, the web's power and eagerness to respond has challenged the primacy of conventional community/public service translation (expert, vertical). It cannot occupy the same role as it did on inception, over 40 years ago, or even 15 years ago when social media was yet to captivate the planet. In the print age, new migrant groups had to await the publication of material in their language; today's web abhors a vacuum and rushes to fill it.

Corporations and institutions, non-profit and otherwise, are already using social media/community translation 2.0 to good effect. Facebook does it; so too Wikipedia, Global Voices, TED.com, and Microsoft, Symantec… The brief of public service translation agencies is to facilitate communication between linguistic minorities and mainstream society and, on that, social media could assist. Moreover, in something of a *fait accompli*, the 2.0 community may already be pre-empting and influencing them.

The official appropriation of crowdsourced translation solutions is an intriguing possibility that would invert the top-down, expert translation model. It is, however, not without precedent. When Microsoft began localising Windows, it found already entrenched terminology among users in other languages – e.g. Spanish, with (previously) false cognates such as *support/soporte*.

Thus, before exploring these ideas further, we must consider the changes that social media has wrought on translation theory, practice and evaluation. That new landscape will also impinge on the practice of community/public service translation in a modern context.

5. Quality Notions and Web Content

Social media has altered the way communication happens in modern societies. Once there was a clear differentiation between the realms of the *private* and the *public*. Accessing the public space, i.e. to publish, was time-consuming and costly. Filters existed to ensure that published material met received standards of quality: edit first, then publish. In the social media world, publishing and distribution costs are almost zero, it requires just internet host/connection fees, and thus screening for quality can be done later: publish first, then edit.

What is more, things that were formerly kept private can now easily become public through social media. Rather than viewing this new avalanche of content through the lens of Keen (2008) and criticising the harmful effects of *the cult of the amateur*, we will instead side with Shirky (2010) in valuing social media's ability to harness *the cognitive surplus* of our post-industrial society. Bluntly, social media is here to stay, and common-sense advocates making the most of it.

Writing is a cornerstone of educational systems, so there should be every encouragement to do it, and well, without leaving the task solely to professionals. By extension, educated bilinguals should be encouraged to translate, also in the community/public service arena. Volunteer translation is not only about facilitating communication: it is also about *community* engagement. When applied to the empowerment of linguistically disadvantaged communities, it could also constitute an important building block of social capital.

Clearly though, not all content that could benefit from translation has equal value: at one end of the spectrum we have the critical and enduring; at the other, the inconsequential and ephemeral. Community/public service translation was designed for the former; the latter, almost inexistent in pre-digital times, has gained recent prominence with social media.

New and nuanced notions of transcendence mean that translation quality measures have become elastic, or even irrelevant for some web content generally and community translation 2.0 in particular. Facebook, the crowd-sourcer *par excellence*, is unlikely to let its online collaborators loose on legal documents that specify conditions of use. Such applications counsel for a TEP approach involving trusted agencies and proven professional translators – who tend to be perfectionists, willing to deal only with capital-Q quality. Yet, end-users, including consumers of public service translation, may often be satisfied with less. Thus, the canonical TEP process will be too slow for content that has a brief shelf-life or could be edited after upload without significant cost or consequences. A quick *ad hoc* response to a blog or forum post can convey genuine rapport, precisely because it prioritises immediate communication over stylistic pedantry.

Research exists on best practice at the high-quality end of community/public service translation: Melhem (2014) outlines the focus-testing methodology followed by the Translation Service of the Western Sydney Local Health District in the development of multilingual health resources. Similar examples for non-critical content, however, are harder to find.

Nonetheless, a recent survey by a public library in Ottawa, Canada, of its Spanish-speaking community yielded interesting perspectives on optimising website translations. Four versions were presented to respondents: professionally translated, *full* MT post-edited, *light* MT post-edited and *raw* MT. On first viewing, with no mention of budget, conventional translation was the preferred option. On second viewing, where participants were invited to assess quality from a cost/benefit perspective, a significant number changed their mind, with the *light* post-edited solution now considered the best use of taxpayer money (Bowker, 2009). This supports the idea that the most exhaustive approach may not always be the most desirable one for a given context.

For non-critical content, the web has devised alternatives to conventional methods. Be it machine translation (as in the aforesaid study) or community translation 2.0/crowdsourcing, the new, flexible approaches apparently please generators and users. The translation industry is now coming to terms with new evaluation methods that subordinate the *perfect* product ideal to what is *good enough* or *fit for purpose*. Aware of this, new methods to assess quality in translation are being developed around two models, Dynamic Quality Framework, and Multidimensional Quality Metrics. The latter presents an updated version of error deduction by designated experts, the standard translation assessment mechanism (Lommel *et al.*, 2013). The former also includes evaluation based on accuracy and fluency, on ranking, on feedback provided by the community (Facebook) or by the customers (reported usability of machine-translated knowledge base articles), and more (O'Brien, 2012).

These new ways of looking at quality must inevitably affect the community/ public sector space as well.

6. Engaging the Community

Throughout this discussion, a case is emerging for interaction between public service translation and volunteer translators in the community. The literature does not record that this has ever been attempted before. Two potential scenarios are presented here: each complements the other, and neither involves major resources. Both will require ingenuity, though, and there will be challenges to overcome. As we have seen, there are two types of *community* crowdsourced projects: top-down institutional initiatives, and bottom-up grassroots ones. Reflecting this, the first community engagement scenario involves a public service translation agency releasing selected web content for translation by volunteers; the second entails finding and tapping into spontaneous pre-existing community efforts. Each modality offers the potential added value of identifying suitable collaborators for training and advancement.

In the first scenario – agency-instigated community translation 2.0 – whoever owns the collaboration platform controls what is ultimately published. Thus, in the Facebook example, employees at the system back-end have no say in who will participate in the process or what will be translated, but have complete control over what gets published, and can override community-based evaluation results if they wish.

The latest technology now allows even small players to deploy such platforms. Individuals, schools, community centres, sports groups: any person or entity can have a website. Should they wish to engage new foreign-language speakers in their area, then website translation is as simple as adding a link to, e.g. the Microsoft Translator Web Widget. (The translation should, obviously, be clearly identified as computer generated and for gisting only.) Given enough interest, members of responding linguistic communities could be invited to provide crowdsourced alternatives (e.g. via the Microsoft Collaborative Translation Framework) to improve on the *raw* machine translation (see Aikawa *et al.*, 2012). The technology is cost-free. Altruism and enlightened self-interest would remain strong motivators for bilingual contributors within a given community: others will benefit, and potentially recognise and value translators' efforts. Over continued iterations and exchanges, a body of translated community literature emerges – and in a final step, the results could be vetted by a professional translator to check for major bloopers.

More ambitious projects could no doubt be attempted with more resources which, taking into account that collaborative technology platforms are frequently made available at no cost for non-profits, will mainly entail people-power and expertise. The use of Transifex for the translation of Coursera courses by volunteers (Coursera, 2016) offers a good example of how some community information could be translated.

The second scenario should be of relevance for the multiple minority languages. It is precisely this *long tail* that is most neglected under a hierarchical approach, be it conventional community/public service translation or machine translation. By their very nature, public service translation bureaus – and machine translation developers – will always be hard pressed to cater for numerous small populations.

In the information age, truly agile and responsive support for CALD migrants in such groups would first emerge through social media sites, blogs and forums, all written in the respective languages by others who have shared, or who support, their adaptive efforts. It is unlikely to be translation proper, but rather a re-interpretation of arbitrarily collated but potentially relevant mainstream information. The results will predictably run the gamut from useful to harmless to harmful, so any harvesting for broader use requires care.

Connecting with prominent social media writers could provide convenient leverage. By monitoring social media activity, agencies could pinpoint important needs and strategically allocate their resources. This could also sift out talent: individuals with a demonstrably effective understanding of the host society, and the ability to transfer relevant content from the mainstream language into their own.

Both these community engagement scenarios share an important secondary benefit: they bring (literally) on-line new human resources. Once identified, talented people would ideally be trained and eventually certified, thus seeding groups of professional translators in language combinations for which supply sorely lags demand.

7. Extending Public Service Translation

Amateur translation *by* the community is not meant to replace, but rather to extend the reach of professional translation *for* it. As in many other endeavours, volunteering could become a path for the gifted amateur to transition into seasoned expert.

We have long accepted friends, family and interest groups as grassroots language mediators in community interpreting; they may assist when dealing with routine matters at the doctor's or at a social security office interview. There is no reason now to exclude volunteer translators from similar roles. As always, there will be situations that require professionals, and others for which a volunteer approach will suffice. Then there is the diminishing role of text itself: increasingly, product user manuals are pictorial, with written explanations secondary or even irrelevant when the user knows the subject or context. If, as the saying goes, 'a word to the wise is sufficient', then social media, including community translation 2.0, could be a useful stopgap between critical and non-critical domains, and in some cases preferable to conventional translation.

All of this is not to say that the advantages of volunteer, crowd-sourced translation should entice community/public service translation agencies into dismantling their vertical system of checks and balances (which is why Facebook exploited the new reality on its own terms). To do otherwise would regress to the very situation that originated formal community/public service translation in the first place. The idea is to extend the reach of conventional community translation by linking it to community translation 2.0 in a way that addresses the linguistically disenfranchised members of society and allows them to engage more organically with the mainstream – and vice-versa. It is a linkage that could moreover fast track professionalised services for *long tail* languages that the old ways leave chronically neglected.

References

Aikawa, T., Yamamoto, K. and Isahara, H. (2012) The impact of crowdsourcing post-editing with the collaborative translation framework. In *Proceedings of the 8th International Conference on Natural Language Processing*, Kanazawa, Japan.

Bowker, L. (2009) Can machine translation meet the needs of official language minority communities in Canada? A recipient evaluation. *Linguistica Antverpiensia* 8, 123–155.

Coursera (2016) Introduction to the global translator community. See http://www. coursera.community/introduction-to-the-global-translator-community/ (accessed 1 November 2016).

De Palma, D.A. and Kelly, N. (2008, December). Translation of, for and by the people. *Common Sense Advisory*, See http://www.commonsenseadvisory.com/Portals/_default/Knowledgebase/ArticleImages/081218_R_community_trans_Preview.pdf (accessed 1 November 2016).

Erasmus, M. (2000) Community interpreting in South Africa: Current trends and future prospects. In R. Roberts, S.E. Carr, D. Abraham and A. Dufour (eds) *The Critical Link 2: Interpreters in the Community* (pp. 191–206). Amsterdam: John Benjamins.

European Commission (2012) Studies on translation and multilingualism. Crowdsourcing translation, See http://bookshop.europa.eu/en/crowdsourcing-translation-pbHC 3112733/?CatalogCategoryID=luYKABst3IwAAAEjxJEY4e5L (accessed 1 November 2016).

Fernandez Costales, A. (2012) Collaborative translation revisited: Exploring the rationale and the motivation for volunteer translation. *Forum – International Journal of Translation* 10, 1–27.

García, I. (2015) Cloud marketplaces: Procurement of translators in the age of social media. *The Journal of Specialised Translation* 23, 18–38. See http://www.jostrans.org/issue23/art_garcia.php (accessed 1 November 2016).

Google (2016) Languages – Google Translate. See https://translate.google.com/about/intl/en_ALL/languages/ (accessed 1 November 2016).

Howe, J. (2008) *Crowdsourcing: Why the Power of the Crowd is Driving the Future of Business*. New York: Crown Publishing Group.

Keen, A. (2008) *The Cult of the Amateur*. New York: Double Day.

Lesch, H.M. (2014) Vertaalpraktyke in die sosiale media: 'n verbeterde vertaalteks vir 'n virtuele gemeenskap? [Translation practice in the social media: An improved translation text for a virtual community?] *Tydskrif vir Geesteswetenskappe, Jaargang* 54 (1), 129–143.

Locke, C., Levine, R., Searls, D. and Weinberger, D. (2000 [1999]) *The Cluetrain Manifesto: The End of Business as Usual.* Cambridge, MA: Perseus.

Lommel, A., Burchardt, A. and Uszkoreit, H. (2013) Multidimensional Quality Metrics: A flexible system for assessing translation quality. *Aslib.* See http://www.mt-archive. info/10/Aslib-2013-Lommel.pdf (accessed 1 November 2016).

Melhem, E. (2014) Quality assurance: Focus testing of translated text materials at WSLHD. International Conference on Community Translation, University of Western Sydney, 11–13 September.

O'Brien, S. (2012) Towards a dynamic quality evaluation model for translation. *The Journal of Specialised Translation* 17, 55–77.

O'Hagan, M. (2009) Evolution of user-generated translation: Fansubs, translation hacking and crowdsourcing. *Journal of Internationalisation and Localisation* 1 (1), 94–121.

O'Hagan, M. (ed.) (2011) *Translating as a Social Activity: Community Translation 2.0. Linguistica Antverpiensia* 10, 11–23.

Ozolins, U.E. (1997) 'Australia leads the world'... or does it? *Research, Training & Practice.* Proceedings of the Second Macarthur Interpreting and Translation Conference, Sydney, pp. 93–106.

Pym, A. (2011) Translation research terms – a tentative glossary for moments of perplexity and dispute. In A. Pym (ed.) *Translation Research Projects 3* (pp. 75–99). Tarragona, Intercultural Studies Group.

Scannell, K.P. (2012) Translating Facebook into endangered languages. *Proceedings of the 16th Foundation for Endangered Languages Conference* (pp. 106–110). Auckland, Aotearoa/New Zealand.

Shirky, C. (2010) *Cognitive Surplus: Creativity and Generosity in a Connected Age.* New York: Penguin.

Surowiecki, J. (2004) *The Wisdom of Crowds: Why the Many Are Smarter Than the Few and How Collective Wisdom Shapes Business, Economies, Societies, and Nations.* New York: Random House.

Taibi, M. (2011) Public service translation. In K. Malmkjaer and K. Windle (eds) *The Oxford Handbook of Translation Studies* (pp. 214–227). Oxford: Oxford University Press.

Taibi, M. and Ozolins, U. (2016) *Community Translation.* London: Bloomsbury.

Wilton, J. and Bosworth, R. (1984) *Old Words and New Australia. The Post-war Migrant Experience.* Ringwood: Penguin Australia.

Wu, Y., Schuster, M., Chen, Z. Le, Q. V. Norouzi, M. *et al.* (2016) Google's Neural Machine Translation System: Bridging the Gap between Human and Machine Translation. Cornell University Library. See https://arxiv.org/abs/1609.08144 (accessed 1 November 2016).

6 Community Translation in the UK: An Enquiry into Practice

Brooke Townsley

1. Introduction

As a one-time translator of community translation texts into and out of Turkish and lecturer on public service interpreting and translation, I was invited in 2014 to speak about Community Translation (CT) at the 'Translating Cultures: Translation as a Tool of Inclusion/Exclusion in a Multicultural Society conference (Westminster University, London). This invitation led me to reflect both on my own experience of CT and on the state of CT as an activity in the society around me, the United Kingdom. My perception was that, in the UK, the production of translations for non-English speaking communities was an activity in decline, largely due to the financial pressures on public sector spending and a linked turn in the tide of public opinion against the translation of public service documents into so-called community languages. I wondered how far this sense was borne out by the experience of public service based providers of CT. I was also concerned about the quality of the products of CT; past experience suggested variable standards of translation of community texts, and with the advent of automated translation, and invitations to use it on local government authority websites, I was curious to know more about what texts came to be translated and how, how the translations were quality checked and how CT was perceived as an activity among those tasked with delivering the translation products.

It was these questions that led to the enquiry presented in this chapter. In what follows, I report on the results of interviews with five public sector interpreting and translation services based in London and the Midlands of the UK. I approached these providers because personal acquaintance over time offered me access to individuals with experience of managing the processes of CT and of contact with (and within) their local language communities. This familiarity also gave me an understanding of the ethos of the organisations. They are all, at core, guided by principles of public service rather than profit motive; hence their involvement with CT. Our conversations allowed me to build up a picture of the pressures on CT as an activity at these organisations and to reflect on the practices of CT. I start with an overview of the social and political backdrop against which CT is carried out in the UK, before going on to the interviews with individual managers in these services, concluding with a summary of findings and some observations about their implications for the future of CT in the UK.

In recent years, the public discourse in the UK about CT, defined as 'a sub-field of translation covering written translation services needed in a variety of community situations' (Taibi, 2011: 225), has exhibited divergent strands of thought about its functions. One emphasises the role of CT in promoting equality of access and full social participation for non-English speaking communities and is exemplified in a European Union Commissioner's assertion that 'in the civic realm ... translation and interpreting ... become a basic human right that every individual should enjoy' (Vassiliou, 2011). I characterise this as a 'social inclusion' framing of the function of CT and it is this that governs the production of CT at the organisations approached for this enquiry. This model is also implicit in the reasons adduced in a 2007 survey by the UK Commission for Integration and Cohesion (CIC) for why UK local authorities translate documents into community languages. They found that local authorities undertake CT:

- To ensure that non-English speaking residents are able to access essential services, e.g. the police, education services and safety campaigns around fire etc.
- To enable people to access the democratic process, for example enabling people to register to vote or take part in local consultations.
- To support local community groups or intermediaries working directly with new migrants or non-English speaking communities.
- To enable people to function effectively as citizens in society and be able to get along with others, by ensuring that they understand local rules and systems e.g. rubbish disposal or parking restrictions.
- To ensure compliance with the Race Relations (Amendment Act) 2000 and ensure that no-one is disadvantaged in accessing services because of their inability to communicate verbally or non-verbally (Commission for Integration and Cohesion, 2012).

A counter-framing of CT, however, focusses on the potential social dis-benefits of CT. This framing is exemplified in the assertion of the former Communities and Local Government Minister Eric Pickles, that CT, in fact, damages local community cohesion by encouraging segregation (Department for Communities and Local Government, 2012: 11), a theme echoed by Gan, who raises the question of whether providing language services as a whole, including CT, actually increases the segregation of non-English speaking communities (Gan, 2012: 3). This view of CT sees its negative impacts as outweighing any social benefits accrued by increasing access to services for non- or limited English speaking communities and argues for a reduction in the overall volume of both community interpreting and translation. It takes concrete form in the instruction of the Minister to 'Stop translating documents into foreign languages: only publish documents in English' (Department for Communities and Local Government, 2012). This negative framing of CT is supported in parts of the media, which view CT as an unjustifiable burden on the public purse, particularly in a time of financial austerity. A 2015 Freedom of Information request by the *Mail on Sunday* newspaper generated the headline: 'Shock figures reveal huge sums spent on translators by police, councils and hospitals' (Mail Online, 2015), while a BBC report referred to a '£140m bill for public sector translation' (BBC News, 2014). While closer analysis of these reports suggests conflation by the journalists, in their use of the portmanteau word 'translator', of spoken language interpreting with written translation (indicative of a wider ignorance in the media of the details of language work in the public services), they are emblematic of an often-voiced question about the validity of the activity of translating written documents into community languages, given the costs involved and the cuts to public service budgets in other areas.

2. CT Practices at Five Public Sector Language Service Providers (LSPs)

CT at the five organisations contacted for this enquiry takes place against the backdrop of the discourses outlined above, and they were implicit in all the conversations held about practices in the production of CT. The five LSPs contacted have been in existence for more than a decade, providing community translation and interpreting services to their respective local areas and they serve a diverse group of language communities in Greater London and the East and West Midlands. Each LSP has between three and 10 members of staff and commissions community translations from a panel of freelance translators, built up and managed by each organisation. All my respondents had responsibility for the commissioning of translations and all were themselves bi- or trilingual.

My primary aim in the interviews was to investigate the following features of CT as practiced in these LSPs:

(1) Text typologies (what types of texts are translated?).
(2) The reflexive self-perception of these CT providers (how was the activity of community translation viewed by the respondents, given the surrounding discourses?).
(3) The place of theorising about translation in CT practice (what appearance did the academic discourses about translation make in the work of the LSPs and their translators?).

(4) Translation quality (how was translation quality monitored in the pro-
     duction process?).
(5) CT and literacy (how far did first language literacy in the target user
     communities impact on the use of CT products?).

I hoped to gain from the interviews a sense of the health of CT as an activity
and to explore the realities of its day-to-day practice.

In order to explore these features, my interviews were structured around
the hypothesised production cycle of a community translation text (commission, placement with a translator, production, quality control, return to the
client) and were designed to create a conversational space where the views,
perspectives and underlying understandings of these respondents could
emerge. Each interview consisted of a set of main questions (e.g. how do you
receive translations? How are they commissioned and by whom?) followed
by *ad hoc* questions to explore topics as they arose. An opening question
about whom translation jobs were placed with, for example, opened the way
for discussion of the selection of translators, their qualifications and their
understandings of CT, while a question about the procedural steps when a
translation was returned to the LSP opened up discussion of quality control
procedures and how translations were evaluated. A later question about feedback from end users allowed for exploration of the reception of community
translations by target language communities. These questions were posed
during telephone interviews carried out in May 2014, with each interview
lasting approximately one hour, followed up by telephone calls or e-mail correspondence. An additional short online survey was distributed to the same
respondents in late 2015 seeking information about the impact of first language literacy on the use of CT in target communities.

2.1 Text typologies

In response to a question about the types of texts that are presented for
translation into community languages, respondents described a diverse range
of texts of different lengths and levels of complexity, drawn from different
domains and aimed at different target audiences. Examples included a substantial 9000-word translation of an English source text entitled '*What is Post
Traumatic Stress Disorder?*', the translation of a psycho-sexual health questionnaire, minutes of public meetings, housing service leaflets on allocations
policy, annual performance statements of local government bodies, Special
Educational Needs (SEN) statements, Anti-Social Behaviour letters, council
correspondence, and speech and language therapy reports. This underlines a
heterogeneity of text types and target readerships that is characteristic of
CT. In the UK context, they also presuppose a direction of translation out of
English towards a community language, thus supporting Niska's definition
of CT as the translation of texts 'addressed by authorities or institutions to

people who do not understand texts in the language of the text producer' (Niska, 2002: 135). In this respect, three of the five respondents reported that the bulk of their written translation was out of English, with a limited amount from community languages into English. Two respondents, however, offered contrary evidence. One noted a recent increase in translation from Latvian and Lithuanian into English, attributed to recent migration into the local area, while another reported a CT workload generated by a large-scale contract for the supply of interpreting and translation services to a number of regional police forces. This was exclusively into English and required the translation of police interview transcripts, evidential witness statements and large quantities of forensic evidence in written form, including text messages, Facebook posts and letters. Therefore, in practice, as Taibi observes, CT cannot be assumed to be only the translation of texts from the dominant language of service providers into migrant community languages (Taibi, 2011: 214).

2.2 Self-perception: How do the LSPs view their own CT activity?

Although the LSPs approached were chosen because they were providers of CT to their local communities, it was clear that their reflexive view of themselves was that they were primarily providers of spoken language interpreting services rather than written translation. A weighting in favour of spoken language interpreting was implicit in the approach of one LSP to the recruitment of new linguists to their panel: they were recruited to an 'interpreting' panel, or 'list of interpreters' and recruitment was as an interpreter. New candidates were asked at recruitment stage, however, if they 'did translation as well', and if so, this capacity was added to their interpreting profile. The LSPs reported a similar leaning towards spoken interpreting among their language workers. These, I was told, viewed themselves first and foremost as interpreters who sometimes undertook written translation as an extra service. They did not view themselves as community translators per se. One respondent noted that, in fact, in some language pairs, she had 'to beg' these interpreters to do written translation, and that they only undertook CT reluctantly, as a favour to the organisation that offered them interpreting work.

The relative discounting of the significance of CT relative to interpreting is probably a function of the volume of CT work that they receive. One London-based respondent noted the statistic for his service of 2280 interpreting assignments for the month of April (2014) as against 30 CT commissions. Similarly, a West Midlands respondent evaluated the CT workload of his organisation as no more than 5% of its total activity, at around 10–12 translations a week. Even the organisation holding a large-scale contract with local police forces (see above) estimated the ratio of spoken language interpreting to written translations as around 80% to 20%, while a London-based respondent reported that, between 2009 and 2014, the production of community translations had been reduced almost to zero, whereas the spoken language interpreting workload had remained the same or increased. For all these LSPs, CT constituted a small and static, or shrinking, proportion of their total workload.

2.3 Theory and practice: What role does theorising about translation play in the practice of CT?

As a practitioner, the place of theoretical perspectives from Translation Studies in translation practice has always interested me, and I wanted to get a sense of what part theoretical perspectives on translation played in CT. From my experience, community translators generally do not have formal training in translation, and I hypothesised therefore that they worked largely without reference to the theoretical insights of Translation Studies. This hypothesis was partially confirmed by the responses I received; theorising about translation appears to make little or no appearance in the discourse about practice of the LSPs and reportedly of their translators. In other respects, however, regarding the education and training of translators used by the LSP, it turned out to be less accurate.

In answer to my question about the role played by translation theories in their practice of CT, the unanimous response was that theory played no part at all in their production of translated texts. The opinion expressed by one respondent, that translation was a 'common-sense process' and that he expected his translators to exercise the same in their work, is emblematic of a pragmatic bias in their attitude to theorising about translation expressed by all the interviewees. Another suggested that the translators he worked with were probably unaware of the existence of theories of translation at all. Overall, the role accorded by the LSP managers to theory in translation was minor or non-existent and, in their estimation, it was equally unimportant in the practice of the translators they worked with.

This discounting of the significance of translation theory did not equate, however, to a lack of concern for qualification. All five LSPs reported that, wherever possible, they sought formal translation qualifications from those they commissioned. These ranged from the postgraduate level Institute of Linguists Educational Trust (IoLET) Diploma in Translation through the undergraduate level Diploma in Public Service Interpreting, to the Certificate in Bilingual Skills and the Certificate in Community Interpreting. Some respondents reported that prospective translators were also required to produce portfolios of translation work before being accepted on to the LSP's panel.

At first sight, the call for, (in some cases postgraduate) generic translation qualifications such as the Diploma in Translation, or for the Diploma in Public Service Interpreting, with its two 'information translation' (Newmark,

1988) tests might seem contradictory to the overall dismissal of the relevance of theoretical perspectives; holding such qualifications might presuppose at least declarative knowledge on the part of a translator of the body of translation theory. The qualifications cited as desirable, however, measure translation competence solely by evaluation of the production of translated texts under timed conditions, without commentary or annotations and require no declarative knowledge of theory. It is quite possible, therefore, for a translator to hold these qualifications without any grasp of theoretical perspectives on translation or the discourses of translation studies.

In fact, despite their insistence on the importance of qualifications, the respondents' attitude to the relevance of translation qualifications to CT was nuanced; all noted that qualifications on paper were not the only measure of suitability for CT. One reported selecting translators for a task based on their being 'best qualified for the job', but noted that 'best qualified' was based, not on qualifications, but on an assessment of the personal reliability of the translator and the quality of their past work. Another noted that for many community languages, no formal interpreting or translation qualifications existed. Overall, despite citing a range of formal translation qualifications as desirable, it appeared that in practice formal qualification was not a primary consideration when engaging a translator to undertake CT work.

Given that, even where available, respondents seemed ambiguous about the value of qualifications for CT, I wanted to know what criteria the LSPs used to identify a 'good' translator. Respondents offered a range of criteria based mainly on the quality of the translator's personal interaction with the service. One respondent noted that for her, suitability as a translator was a function of being 'responsive, responsible and reliable'. To be deemed a 'good translator', the individual had to return translations on time, word-processed, not handwritten, and that the translation had to reflect the layout of the original. Other respondents also noted a mixture of formal qualification, and personal qualities. Overall, personal qualities were foregrounded over qualification and linguists were judged to be 'good translators' based on their ability to produce translations to deadline, in a useable format and to liaise effectively with the LSP.

If the criteria for the use of particular translators to carry out CT are a mixture of subjective assessments of reliability and formal qualification where available, what then of formal procedures for measuring the quality of target texts? Confidence in the closeness of the relationship of a written translation to a source text is an integral part of the face-value of that text in the receiving community, while more sophisticated translation consumers may want to know how far communicative intentions are reflected in the translation, if the translated text achieves the intended impact on the reader or if the translation meets the requirements of the translation brief. To measure any of these features requires the ability to assess translation quality. The diversity of text types, languages and end users in CT, however, raises a question about how the quality of CT translations is monitored and what quality control measures can, in reality, be exercised.

2.4 How is translation quality monitored in the production process?

A common response from all respondents about quality control was that systematic checking based on source text – target text comparison was, more often than not, beyond the capacity of the organisation. If the language pair in question was available among the in-house staff of the service, a comparison of source and target texts would be undertaken, but the resources required to undertake bilingual reading of all translations returned to the LSP were not available. In these cases, quality control of the translations was confined to identifying whether editorial features of the source text, such as formatting, paragraph structure, names or numerical information were present in the target text. Any assessment of the overall translation quality could only be based on feedback from end users. This, however, was largely non-existent and no formal mechanisms for seeking feedback were reported. One respondent responded that, in 70% of cases, no feedback on written translations was ever received. Another reported that the only feedback on translations ever received was via *ad hoc* remarks made to another language worker, usually an interpreter, and reported back to the LSP. Overall, it seems that an absence of feedback was taken as an indicator of acceptable translation quality.

The advent of freely available automated translation such as Google Translate was also raised in the context of translation quality. All respondents were unanimous that they would not accept translations that they believed had been produced by Google Translate and said that they impressed this prohibition upon their freelance translators. One respondent expressed the opinion that using Google Translate amounted to 'cheating' the LSP. Given the limitations on any meaningful quality control of translation out of English noted above, however, the question remains of how they would be able to identify whether a translation was partially or entirely machine generated. This would only be possible in cases of translation into English, and one respondent did report turning down English target text that had evidently been machine generated. The possibilities for the interplay of human and machine translation to produce CT texts, for example, by human post-editing of a machine translation draft, had not, however, been considered by any of the respondents.

2.5 How far does first language literacy impact on the use of CT translations in the target communities?

The lack of feedback received from end users of CT translations produced by the LSPs noted above also affects the LSP's ability to gauge how far first language literacy in the target language communities impacted on the reception and use of translations. Although all respondents reported the existence of first language literacy deficits among the target language communities they served, particularly among Bengali-, Punjabi- and Urdu-speaking communities, only one of the five could cite empirical research into first language literacy levels that had affected the LSP's policy. This respondent reported that, historically, the delivery of CT by his service had been based on a set of unrealistic assumptions about the capacity of the receiving communities to access information in written form. Research among the largest user community had revealed, however, a first language literacy rate of 78%, and, as a result, the LSP in conjunction with the local authority had moved to a much-reduced level of CT activity, preferring instead to deliver information via interpreters and oral sight translation as required. All other respondents reported a case by case approach where, if the LSP was notified that an intended recipient of a translation might have first language literacy difficulties, they would provide an oral sight translation of text via an interpreter, face-to-face or over the telephone.

3. Conclusions

A summary of the information provided by the LSPs provides the following picture of CT practice.

- CT translations are of both common and heterogeneous text typologies. Although commonly having an informational function, the texts presented for translation come from a wide range of public domains (health, education, social services, local government and administration etc.). Community translators therefore need to have the capacity to manage a diverse workload and terminology, in some cases highly specialised, drawn from a wide range of sub-domains within the field of public services.
- CT is viewed largely as a minor adjunct to interpreting. It forms a relatively small proportion of the workload of the LSPs and is also reportedly a dis-preferred option for the freelancers on their panels. The small proportion of CT activity relative to interpreting is reflected in the self-perception of the LSPs as essentially providers of language interpreting who can undertake CT as a secondary service. Also, there is little or no concept of CT as a discrete profession or of the 'Community Translator', either among the LSPs interviewed or among the freelancers they work with.
- CT is practiced without conscious reference to the discourses of Translation Studies or theoretical insight into translation processes. In many cases, it is practiced without the benefit of formal qualification in CT or general translation.

- Although lip-service is paid to the importance of qualifications in translation, translators are selected for CT work based largely on the quality of their personal interaction with the LSP. Objective measurement of their translation ability is rarely a deciding factor in whether a translator is commissioned for a CT task.
- Systematic quality control of CT products is largely non-existent. Some *ad hoc* solutions to quality control challenges are applied and there are cursory attempts at measurements of target text coherence and accuracy, but there is no capacity for a more systematic approach. Feedback from the end users of translations and/or from the target communities that might shed light on translation quality and appropriacy is also largely non-existent.
- The possibilities for effective use in CT of freely-available machine translation in conjunction with human translation has not so far been considered by the LSPs.
- The impact of first language literacy levels in target communities is recognised but not measured. First language literacy issues are managed on a case-by-case basis, using oral sight translation as a replacement for written text where required.

In conclusion, my investigations with the five CT providers confirmed my impression that CT is an activity in retreat. There has been a shift in the public discourse away from the framing of CT as a tool for promoting equal access and social cohesion, a view that I unquestioningly held during my time as a community translator, and CT struggles to lay claim to being a distinct professional discipline. With such relatively low volumes of work available, there is little incentive for linguists to develop a profile as a community translator, nor for the development of CT specific qualifications. This is reinforced by the current turn, on the part of government, against what is seen as indiscriminate translation of information into community languages. The prognosis for CT in its current form is, therefore, quite poor.

CT faces a major challenge in making a case for its viability and for being a genuine contribution to the life of the dominant and minority language communities. The growth in scholarly interest in CT, however, as evidenced by recent conferences and the appearance of academic volumes devoted to CT, may provide an opportunity for the development of a coherent defense of CT. After all, if equality of access to public services continues to be a guiding principle in public life, then CT will have a role to play in ensuring the rights of individuals to full social, economic and political participation (Taibi, 2011: 226; 2014: 24). Perhaps it falls to the academic community to meet this challenge by suggesting how CT can respond to concerns about the relation between CT and social cohesion, and helping CT adapt to the demands of austerity budgets and to demonstrate measurable benefits from its continuation.

References

BBC News (2014) £140m bill for public sector translation. See http://www.bbc.com/news/uk-england-25933699 (accessed 20 March 2016).

Commission for Integration and Cohesion (2012) Our shared future. See http://collections.europarchive.org/tna/20080726153624/http:/www.integrationandcohesion.org.uk/~/media/assets/www.integrationandcohesion.org.uk/our_shared_future%20pdf.ashx (accessed 25 November 2016).

Department for Communities and Local Government (2012) 50 ways to save. Examples of sensible savings in local government. See https://www.gov.uk/government/publications/50-ways-to-save-examples-of-sensible-savings-in-local-government (accessed 4 December 2015).

Gan, S. (2012) *Lost in Translation*. London: 2020 Health.org. See www.2020health.org (accessed 25 November, 2016).

Mail Online (2015) Shock figures reveal huge sums spent on translators by police, councils and hospitals. See http://www.dailymail.co.uk/news/article-2904814/Shock-figures-reveal-huge-sums-spent-translators-police-councils-hospitals.html (accessed 14 December 2015).

Newmark, P. (1988) *A Textbook of Translation*. Hemel Hempstead: Phoenix ELT.

Niska, H. (2002) Community interpreting training, past, present and future. In G. Garzone and M. Viezzi (eds) *Interpreting in the 21st Century: Challenges and Opportunities:* Selected Papers from the 1st Forlì Conference on Interpreting Studies, 9–11 November 2000 (pp. 133–143). Amsterdam: John Benjamins.

Taibi, M. (2011) Public service translation. In K. Malmkjær and K. Windle (eds) *The Oxford Handbook of Translation Studies* (pp. 214–227). Oxford: Oxford University Press.

Taibi, M. (2014) Community concern. *The Linguist* 53 (3), 24–25.

Vassiliou, A. (2011) Foreword. In *Final Report: Special Interest Group on Translation and Interpreting for Public Services*. Brussels: DG Interpretation.

7 Community Translation in Spanish Penitentiaries: A Coordinated Approach

Carmen Valero Garcés and Raquel Lázaro Gutiérrez

1. Introduction

Successful integration and interaction in prison is usually a first step towards social reinsertion. This process requires a joint effort on the part of both prison staff and offenders. There are many rehabilitation programmes developed by the Spanish Directorate General for Penitentiaries; however, these programmes risk failing because of linguistic barriers, as they are unable to reach foreign prisoners (Baixauli, 2012; Martínez-Gómez Gómez, 2008; Valero-Garcés & Mojica-López, 2014).

The aim of this chapter is to present some of the outcomes of the recent agreement between the University of Alcalá and the Spanish Directorate General for Penitentiaries, signed in 2014. A coordinated research-action project was developed for two years whose main aim was to describe the current communicative needs of foreign offenders in prison and how they are fulfilled. Data were mainly obtained through qualitative methods (interviews and focus groups) and were supported by data from a reduced number of questionnaires. It should be pointed out that, although quantitative data are very difficult to gather in this setting, we were able to grasp useful details from the answers we obtained, and very valuable information concerning the effectiveness of our methodology, which will help us in the near future to design new methodological instruments for data gathering. After data analysis and results were finalised, the action phase was implemented. It consisted of the development of methods to improve communication, which comprised translation and design of multilingual resources such as administrative documents, leaflets, guides, glossaries and pictograms.

Imprisonment occasionally gives rise to traumatic situations, as it entails a notorious lifestyle change for individuals. People entering penitentiary institutions frequently suffer from emotional instability, fear, disorientation, sleep and appetite disorders, and other types of somatisms. This situation can be aggravated for those inmates who have problems expressing themselves and understanding the information they receive in this new environment. In other words, this process is even more difficult in the case of foreign inmates who do not speak the language of the country they are imprisoned in or have very limited knowledge of it.

Effective interaction in this new environment is considered as a first step for subsequent rehabilitation. As research indicates (Baixauli, 2012; De la Cuesta Arzamendi, 2005; Martínez-Gómez Gómez, 2008; Valero-Garcés & Mojica-López, 2014), in the case of Spanish penitentiary institutions, rehabilitation is a process which requires a great effort from both prison staff and inmates. There is a wide array of carefully designed rehabilitation and reintegration schemes offered by the Directorate General for Penitentiaries in Spanish prisons which are illustrative enough. However, these programmes might be doomed to failure if the information does not reach every user as a consequence of language barriers. In addition, these inmates are in many cases highly socially excluded and also unaware of their rights, both as citizens/residents and as prisoners.

In the following pages, part of the results of a coordinated project developed by the Group FITISPos-UAH, in collaboration with the Spanish Directorate General for Penitentiaries, is reported. The main objectives of the whole project are (1) to analyse and describe the measures taken by Spanish prisons to deal with inmates' linguistic diversity and facilitate their social reintegration, (2) to compare these measures to those followed by international and European penitentiary institutions and (3) to propose standards to contribute to the linguistic communication and integration of foreign inmates, which will consequently reinforce the success of rehabilitation and reintegration programmes. However, as this project is still at an early stage and, owing to space and scope considerations, we only deal with community translation and communicative needs of foreign inmates (women, in this case) whose mother tongue is not Spanish (thus excluding foreign inmates from other countries where Spanish is also spoken).

The structure of this chapter is thus articulated around two main sections: (1) an analysis of the communicative needs of foreign offenders in prison (research); and (2) the development of methods to improve communication (action). Different research methods have been used to fulfil the objectives of this exploratory research-action project, among which are interviews, surveys, participant observation and desktop research.

2. Logistic Steps Prior to Research

The main challenge in research in prison settings is obtaining access to research sites and data. Access is often complicated because of bureaucracy: the clearance process involves an excessive amount of paperwork and a long waiting period. This is the reason why we consider it relevant to offer a brief summary of the process that led us to the cooperation agreement between the University of Alcalá and the Spanish Directorate General for Penitentiaries.

In 2011 the University of Alcalá started to establish a partnership with the Spanish Directorate General for Penitentiaries through the University's Master in Intercultural Communication and Public Service Interpreting and Translation. The main aim of the University was to sign an agreement to include the Directorate General in the list of institutions providing placements for our internship programme, so that our students would be able to visit Spanish prisons and practise there as trainee interpreters and translators. After many months, and having realised that the agreement with the Directorate General was going to take even longer, in June 2012 an agreement was signed with one of the prisons located in Madrid (Madrid V – Soto del Real). This agreement made it possible to send one student, who completed her internship there. Some research was also carried out by means of interviews with members of staff, which revealed the need for translation and interpreting services, although we soon felt the necessity to widen the scope of our project.

It was not until late 2012 that the agreement was expanded to include another prison. This time it was a women's prison (Alcalá-Meco Mujeres I) and permission was granted for a wider group of researchers and students to access prisons and carry out internships and research. Most of our research was conducted between 2013 and 2014, when the agreement was extended to cover every Spanish prison. To date, approximately 11 students have completed their internships translating and interpreting for prisons and the research project referred to in this chapter has been initiated.

3. Characteristics of the Study and Research Methods

As mentioned above, this chapter offers some of the results of a pilot research-action project on community interpreting and translation in prison settings. Our point of departure is the hypothetically deficient or, at least, difficult communication with foreign inmates, particularly with those whose mother tongue is not Spanish. A methodology combining qualitative and quantitative instruments was applied, and the methods used comprised interviews with offenders and members of staff, focus groups with offenders, questionnaires distributed among offenders, participant observation, and documental and bibliographical analysis of legislation and existent data elaborated by prison authorities. Given the nature of the research-action project, an important part consists of producing outcomes that can immediately be applied and later tested within the same project.

The aim of the present study is to find out the characteristics of communication with a very specific group of offenders due to restrictions of time and access permit: female offenders who do not master the contact language and culture, in order to, first, determine the quality of communication and linguistic assistance and, secondly, know about the resources used to bridge communication gaps. This piece of research was structured into the following phases:

(1) Documental and bibliographical analysis.
(2) Application for permission to access the penitentiary (which includes the formalization of the above-mentioned agreement between the University of Alcalá and the Spanish Directorate General for Penitentiaries).
(3) Design and elaboration of research methods (interviews, focus groups and questionnaires).
(4) Schedule of visits and implementation of research methods.
(5) Data analysis.
(6) Development of multilingual resources.
(7) Piloting of resources (for a thorough description of phases 1 to 5, please see Valero-Garcés & Mojica-López, 2014: 94–106).

The scope of this chapter is limited as it only focuses on community translation (not interpreting) and part of the research actions carried out within this wider project, although some of the results obtained from other parts of the project (for instance, those which focus on interpreting) will also be offered to support findings. The research methods for the particular research actions described in this paper will be outlined in their respective sections.

4. Analysis of the Communicative Needs of Foreign Offenders in Prison

4.1 Some background: Foreign offenders in Spanish prisons

The presence of foreign inmates in Spanish prisons and public institutions has been increasingly growing in the first decades of the 21st century, as reflected by research, statistics and the media. González García (2006:

161) discusses the growth in the number of foreign inmates pointing out that, while in 1996 this figure was approximately 17.3% of the prison population, it increased to 27.1% in 2003 and in 2006 it reached 30%. Almeida Herrero *et al.* (2006: 23) report that most of these inmates spoke languages other than Spanish, such as Arabic (Moroccans and Algerians were the most numerous groups, with 30.4% and 7.8%, respectively), Romanian and Portuguese.

Statistical research carried out by the Directorate General for Penitentiaries (*Secretaría General de Instituciones Penitenciarias*) shows that the percentage of foreign prisoners was 35.8% in June 2011 (Secretaría General de Instituciones Penitenciarias, 2011) and slightly lower in 2012 (31.3%) (Secretaría General de Instituciones Penitenciarias, 2012). In spite of this decrease, the percentage of foreigners in Spanish prisons is still significant: 1 out of 3 inmates (31.3%) is a foreigner. This percentage is slightly higher for women, as 33.5% of them are foreigners, compared to 31.1% men.

In 2012 the most frequent nationalities of foreign inmates were Romanian and Moroccan, followed by Algerian, Portuguese, Bulgarian and Nigerian, as reported in the most recent General Report of the Directorate General for Penitentiaries (published in 2012). These data suggest potential communication problems, as Romanian and Arabic or any of the other languages spoken by foreign inmates mentioned above are languages which are not usually spoken by members of staff. Most of these inmates do not speak Spanish fluently or do not speak it at all. According to the interviews carried out with members of staff, many had not spent a long time in Spain before they were imprisoned. Moreover, statistics also show that prisons in the region of Madrid register a higher number of foreign inmates when compared to other Spanish Autonomous Communities or regions. It is also worth mentioning that, among the 11 prisons with the highest numbers of foreign inmates, four are in the Autonomous Community of Madrid.

4.2 Survey of foreign inmates at Alcalá-Meco women's penitentiary. Report from a pilot project

In order to verify and update the available data, a pilot study was carried out in one of the prison centres in the Madrid area: Alcalá-Meco women's penitentiary (Alcalá-Meco Mujeres I, also known as C.P. Madrid 1 (Mujeres)). The main objective was to find out about the communicative needs of the foreign inmates and make suggestions for communication improvements. The pilot nature of our project and, consequently, its short length, made it impossible to gather a large number of data, but we hoped that we would be able to obtain enough qualitative information about our object of study as well as about the efficiency of our methodology.

The pilot project was developed from February to June 2013 and some results can be found in Valero-Garcés and Mojica-López (2014: 94–106). The research methodology was based on interviews and surveys to both members of staff and inmates. On the one hand, the aim of the interviews to members of staff was to know the usual activities and procedures that took place in prison as well as how they managed to communicate with foreign inmates. On the other hand, inmates were interviewed and surveyed to know about their life in prison and how they solved communicative difficulties.

A set of interviews was conducted with members of staff to find out about communicative needs and to agree on useful tools and strategies to bridge communication gaps. To design the interviews, information from the Spanish Ministry of the Interior (Directorate General for Penitentiaries) was taken into account. From their website, we knew that inmates are assisted by multidisciplinary professional teams: lawyers, psychologists, sociologists, teachers, social workers and healthcare, security and administration staff work together to assist inmates.

The manager of the centre, the head of the education department, a psychologist and a social worker were interviewed. Questions were open and conversation was encouraged. These professionals shared their detailed vision of the lives of non-Spanish speaking foreign women in prison. We learned that women constituted 8% of the inmate population at a national level. Most of them (80%) were convicted for crimes against public health or prostitution. Inmates from more than 42 nationalities were present in the centre. Although most of them spoke Spanish as their mother tongue (they came from South America), the manager of the prison declared that there were still a large number of women whose mother tongue was not Spanish. When asked whether this caused communication problems, all the professionals interviewed answered that communication was difficult and that they either turned to other inmates who acted as *ad hoc* interpreters or used gestures, but had no translated materials at hand.

On the other hand, the survey of inmates included questions about their age, countries of origin and languages they spoke, and questions aimed at identifying communicative problems. It consisted of seven questions and was presented in English, Chinese, Romanian or Russian. (Those inmates who spoke Arabic insisted on taking the survey in Spanish as their command of the language was very good. Members of the research team checked this was the case.) Furthermore, it was distributed by interpreters who were experts in intercultural communication so that they could help inmates understand and answer the questions. The following paragraphs only report issues concerning the scope of this chapter (further information is available in Valero Garcés & Mojica-López, 2014).

When this piece of research was developed (May 2013), the population of Alcalá-Meco women's penitentiary was at 522 inmates. Of these, 39.08% were Spanish and 60.92% were foreigners, with 45.59% of these being speakers of Spanish as their mother tongue (Spanish General

Administration, *Administración General del Estado*, 2013). For the purpose of our study, only the inmates who did not speak Spanish as their mother tongue were considered. A total number of 15 responses to our survey were gathered (2.87% of the inmates – 9.74% of the foreign inmates – responded), although one of the questionnaires had to be discarded because most of its sections were incomplete. In what follows, some of the main findings are summarised.

The first question was regarding their countries of origin and the languages they spoke. Results reveal that most of the foreign inmates, the target of our study, did not have a good command of Spanish (the institutional language) and thus faced language barriers when they had to communicate with prison staff. Their mother tongues were Romanian (1), Portuguese (4), Moroccan Arabic (2), an unspecified African language (1), Surinamese (1), Chinese (3) and Russian (2). Apart from their mother tongue, eight respondents (53.3%) reported that they had basic knowledge of Spanish as a result of the language classes they receive in prison, whereas three of them (20%) commented that they had a high level of Spanish, although their command of English was self-perceived as being better. Three inmates did not know other languages apart from their mother tongue (Chinese).

Question number 2 aimed to obtain information on the different professionals that the inmates had to interact with. On the one hand, this can provide us with useful information about the context of interactions. Among the professional profiles, we included that of the translator (in Spain it is often the case that translators also act as interpreters or mediators and the other way around). This, on the other hand, allowed us to know how often a linguistic aide was available to them on site.

When asked about the professionals they had been in contact with during the entire criminal procedure, as expected, all of them stated having difficulties when communicating with clerks, social workers, lawyers, police officers, doctors and psychologists. The professional categories with whom the inmates had to interact most frequently were lawyers and doctors, followed by police officers, who registered a notably lower percentage. All the inmates (15) had been assisted by lawyers and almost 100% of them had been seen by doctors, which corroborates the information provided in prison protocols, which establish that inmates must be visited by a doctor before entering prison. Although it seems surprising that in spite of the low or even inexistent command of Spanish, only 5 out of 15 of the respondents reported having been assisted by translators, interpreters or cultural mediators, who registered one of the lowest percentages amongst the different professional categories.

When asked about the way they communicate with professionals the results corroborated the same: most of the inmates (6) had not received any on-site linguistic assistance at all. Three manage to communicate in Spanish and for another three the administration has provided a professional to help with communication. These answers are followed by those who report that it was the administration of the detention centre that provided this professional (usually a member of staff – not a professional interpreter, translator or mediator – who is able to speak the language of the inmate (2)). Finally, the lowest percentage (1) is for the professionals provided by non-governmental organisations (NGOs). Some members of staff also corroborate this information, and also report having contacted embassies or consulates so that they could provide some assistance.

When the inmates were asked about the language service they would like to have in order to efficiently communicate in prison (multiple answers were possible), most of them preferred an on-site interpreter (11), followed by intercultural mediators (2) and translated materials (2).

When asked about the inmates' preferences regarding language assistance services, it was also confirmed that the inmates were aware of the existence of communicative problems, as well as the need for both translations and interpreters. The members of staff who took part in the study also acknowledged existent communicative challenges and signalled that one of the main difficulties was to make higher instances (Penitentiary Administration) understand that the lack of trained and professional translators and interpreters as well as the lack of high-quality translations may involve major (legal) risks, whereas their presence may mean savings in money and time in the long run.

Foreign inmates whose mother tongue is not Spanish reported feeling extremely vulnerable and thought that their situation was worse than that of the inmates who spoke Spanish. We consider that this issue is worth investigating further and we plan to do so in future studies.

5. Measures to Improve Communication with Foreign Offenders

As previously stated, anyone going through an imprisonment process (and especially those who face this situation for the first time) experiences a moment of change when a series of diverse feelings, sensations and thoughts converge. In Martínez-Gómez Gómez's (2008: 493) words, imprisonment is a process entailing a series of physical and emotional challenges for new inmates that require a careful treatment of the situation, especially when inmates are unfamiliar with the system.

Through our documental research we found that not only oral communication is paramount, but written communication is also needed in a variety of settings and procedures. A thorough analysis of legislation and regulations was carried out to ascertain the settings, procedural steps and ways in which communication through the written mode was needed. Our starting hypothesis is that inmates who cannot write or read Spanish will find serious difficulties in a variety of procedures involving written communication if they are not assisted by a translator.

5.1 Prison information and inmate-oriented service system

Prisons provide an information and inmate-oriented service system in order to facilitate inmates' understanding and adaptation to their new situation and also to enhance their social reintegration. Among the services made available in this regard are informative brochures and handbooks, as well as training courses and workshops, which also include written communication. *La Prisión Paso a Paso* (Secretaría General de Instituciones Penitenciarias, 2010) is a guide which has been published in various languages and offers information about the internal organisation and procedures of Spanish prisons. This publication provides valuable insights into the situations in which either oral or written communication is required and, hence, where language barriers may arise.

Throughout the document, there are references to information accessibility. The resources mentioned include bibliographic resources (prison libraries) and human agents (prison staff). Apparently, inmates are granted access to several services by completing written applications or by consulting the penitentiary institution staff. In addition, they can present oral or written complaints or requests and written appeals, which are responded to by the administration in written form. What is more, it can be inferred from this brochure that inmates must communicate details regarding their personal, social and health situation to the different professionals who assist them during their prison term (administrative staff, social workers, health personnel, educators, lawyers, psychologists, teachers, etc.). Likewise, inmates' relatives and friends may request permission to visit them or to use other means of communication (such as telephone calls or videoconferences). Inmates have a duty to participate in training, educational and work activities aimed at preparing them for a future life of freedom. For this purpose, it is equally essential to facilitate appropriate tools and mechanisms to help foreign inmates overcome linguistic barriers when taking part in these activities.

Among the procedures that require written communication, the initiation and following-up of a disciplinary procedure is a remarkable example. Inmates are informed about the opening of the disciplinary record by stating the facts that originated the offence. After this, they are notified in writing of the imposed sanction and they can appeal to the Prison Supervision Court (*Juez de Vigilancia Penitenciaria*). This process is difficult to carry out without the assistance of translators, who restate the information written by the Management Board in a language that can be understood by foreign inmates. Likewise, inmates are likely to prefer using their own language if they wish to modify the record or appeal the sanction.

In addition, foreign inmates may face language barriers in a number of other situations, some of which involve both oral and written communication, e.g. shopping in prison shops, arranging bank transactions (such as bank drafts and transfers), going to the hairdresser's or accessing healthcare facilities. These services are available to all inmates. Nevertheless, inmates with a poor proficiency in Spanish might be unable to access them.

5.2 Spanish legislation concerning communication in penitentiary institutions

It is important to point out that the legislation relevant to penitentiary institutions establishes inmates' right to communicate in their own language, not only with relatives and friends, but also with penitentiary personnel. However, the legal and regulatory instruments do not establish the manner in which messages produced in the mother tongues of inmates are supposed to be conveyed to prison staff. Prison staff do not necessarily have a good command of the inmates' languages.

As previously mentioned, a great number of foreign inmates are admitted to Spanish prisons. This is recognised in the existing legislation, which examines every aspect affecting foreign inmates directly, such as their right to consular access or the possibility of serving their sentences in their countries of origin. Among the services facilitated to foreign inmates, we find training programmes and Spanish language classes. González García (2006) critically states that these programmes, together with the foreign languages classes offered to prison staff, serve as an excuse for concealing communication problems. Apart from general training programmes, there are other types of attention plans specifically aimed at foreign inmates, which stem from their particular needs. An illustrative example is annexed to the Intervention Programme for Perpetrators (*Programa de Intervención para Agresores* – PRIA) about gender-based violence crimes and foreign offenders. Within this subprogram there are a series of recommendations concerning cultural and psychosocial aspects (related to the migration process), as well as other factors addressing possible gaps in the information offered to foreign inmates. At the end of the recommendation list, there is a suggestion that materials involved in the programme should be translated to the languages of foreign inmates in order to facilitate their integration and participation.

As stated above, the resources available for handling linguistic diversity are rather scarce. In the Penitentiary Regulations (*Reglamento Penitenciario*, 1996) there are only three articles that make reference to translation and interpreting services. Article 46[1] refers to written communication and signals that texts written in languages that cannot be translated in the penitentiary institution should be submitted to the General Management authorities. In Article 52[2] the need to provide inmates with informative leaflets written in their own language is acknowledged. In case there are inmates who do not understand any of the languages to which the leaflets are translated, members of staff or other inmates should sight translate for them. If necessary, consulates will be asked for assistance to translate both the leaflets and copies of the General Organic Law for Penitentiaries, the Penitentiary Regulations and the inner rules that govern the prison, which will be at the inmates' disposal at libraries and Admissions Department of Spanish penitentiary institutions. Finally, Article 242[3] states that it is possible to ask a civil servant or inmate to act as an interpreter when foreign inmates do not speak Spanish.

As can be observed, these allusions are mainly focused on the translation of informative documents. With regards to communication in other settings where the translation of administrative documents, for instance, is needed, it is interesting to highlight that this task is usually delegated to civil servants whose jobs are not related to the field or, even worse, it is carried out by the inmates themselves. This practice definitely poses questions regarding the quality of translation and interpreting, which as Martínez-Gómez Gómez (2008) states, '*depende de la disponibilidad y buena voluntad del personal y de los internos con conocimientos de lenguas*', [it depends on the helpfulness and availability of prison staff and foreign inmates who speak different languages. (Authors' translation)]. It also raises questions about the principle of confidentiality. However, there is no reference regarding accessing interpreting or translation services whenever they are needed, even though the website of the Directorate General for Penitentiaries indicates that there is an Arabic translation service available. Apart from providing translation and interpreting services, these translators also offer Arabic lessons to the prison staff. However, they cannot access the prison units. Their task is limited to translating phone conversations and supervising written correspondence following a court order (Gutiérrez *et al.*, 2008: 5–6).

The lack of translation and interpreting services as well as translated documents enormously limits access to the services provided in prisons and also infringes the principles of equality and non-discrimination. The Spanish language classes offered to foreign inmates or the foreign language classes available to staff only offer medium- and long-term solutions. However, they do not guarantee that new foreign inmates, who can speak different languages, will be able to access facilities and programmes in prison.

The scarce measures taken to overcome linguistic difficulties may be explained by security issues (González García, 2006: 162; Martínez-Gómez Gómez, 2008). Nevertheless, the interests and wellbeing of both inmates and prison staff is not afforded sufficient attention. We deem it essential to put in an extra effort to adapt to this situation and the existing European Normative, such as the *European Prison Rules*, adopted by the European Council in January 2006, or the *Green Paper on the application of EU criminal justice legislation in the field of detention* (European Commission, 2011: 11), which devotes one of its chapters to detention conditions and affirms that 'good detention conditions are a prerequisite to the rehabilitation of offenders'.

6. Development of Methods to Improve Communication

6.1 Developing activities to promote access to reintegration and rehabilitation programmes

As can be inferred from the overview above, although there are regulations which acknowledge the right to communication, accessing reintegration and rehabilitation programmes can be a challenge when there are language barriers as there are not effective measures to grant this right. Inmate isolation from the outside world is exacerbated by a lack of involvement with regards to colleagues, supervisors, teachers, doctors, programmes, activities and services. This situation has an impact on the inmates' emotional and psychological stability, which may lead them to repeat the offence. As mentioned by PrisonSMART (one of the most important international initiatives regarding the reintegration of inmates), when inmates are under stress, they react out of fear, anger and false expectations. However, when stress is overcome, inherent principles such as compassion and showing care for others appear:

> When troubled or stressed, then individuals react from anger, fear and misguided notions of how one can be happy. When stress is not dominating an individual, the core human values innate in all human beings become manifest, such as service to others and compassion. (PrisonSMART, 2014)

Reintegration programmes offered by the Directorate General for Penitentiaries are oriented towards the inmates' wellbeing, but we consider that to ensure foreign inmates are able to access any of them, it is essential to eradicate linguistic barriers.

Conclusions from the interviews to members of staff of the Alcalá-Meco women's prison add information worth taking into account when it comes to solving communication problems:

- Members of staff acknowledge that the high number of foreign inmates generates communication problems that are often addressed using foreign inmates as *ad hoc* interpreters and translators, or even with gestures or other strategies that may prevent inmates from exercising their rights to understand and be understood (Valero-Garcés & Mojica-López, 2014: 104).

- Both members of staff and inmates are aware of the need for interpreters and translators, although they did not know the duties and different tasks that these professionals perform.
- The members of staff who participated in this study signalled that one of the major difficulties is making the Penitentiary Administration understand the serious risk of not employing trained professional interpreters and translators. A professional translation and interpreting service may be equivalent to saving time and resources.

In the following section, we would like to suggest some methods and activities to improve communication with imprisoned foreigners with a poor command of the official language. The suggested actions were discussed and agreed on with staff at Alcalá-Meco women's penitentiary through meetings and focus groups. Some of them have already been developed and are being tested, whereas others are still under development.

- Translation of administrative documents (such as detention certificates).
- Translation and revision of informative documents (e.g. leaflets and guides).
- Translation and development of materials for a basic communication in Spanish and other languages.
- Workshops oriented towards developing information-rendering skills by the inmates, thus allowing them to engage in developing a professional career while they are serving their sentence as well as contributing to the new inmates' and their own integration.
- Workshops and courses aimed at training interpreting and translation students to specialise as language providers in this setting.

In this chapter, we focus on the translation activities only.

6.2 Translation and revision of administrative and informative documents

The main need identified by prison staff was the translation of official documents, both those provided by inmates (such as birth certificates) and those issued by penitentiary institutions (such as detention certificates). A reduced number of documents written in languages such as English, Arabic or Romanian were translated into Spanish. These documents were provided by inmates and their translations were commissioned after being received by a member of staff. On the other hand, a set of administrative forms and templates were translated into Arabic, Chinese, English, French, Romanian and Russian to be ready for use in case foreign offenders needed them.

As mentioned earlier, the Spanish Directorate General for Penitentiaries had already published leaflets, brochures and guides in Spanish, Arabic, English, French and Romanian. The revision of these translations as well as the translation of these documents into other languages such as Chinese or Russian was part of the activities developed throughout this project.

6.3 Translation and development of materials for a basic communication

One of the main concerns of staff members was about daily communication. Although a training proposal for foreign offenders who could act as interpreters was put forward, the characteristics of the stay of foreign inmates in prison (usually short detention periods prior to transfers) made prison managers think of potentially faster solutions. Thus, a communication guide was translated from English into Spanish, and then into Arabic, Chinese, French, Romanian and Russian. This guide included vocabulary about people (surveillance officer, governor, inmate education specialist, social worker, doctor, teacher, chief of services, lawyer, judge, etc.) and places (prison, unit, subunit, occupational unit, infirmary, lobby, shop, dining room, classroom, school, sports centre, auditorium, visiting room, library, communications office, bakery, employment office, courtyard, etc.), as well as sentences grouped into the following communication situations: Greetings, Farewell, Personal information, Origin, Profession, Address, Age, Presentations, Telephone communication, Communication skills (Do you speak Spanish?), To locate in time, Dates, Time, During the day, Frequency and habits, Quantities/intensity, Possessions, Describing and comparing things, Shopping, Describing people, Appointments and invitations/free time, Feelings, Weather, Tastes, interests and preferences, Giving an opinion, evaluating, discussing, Consequences, Degrees of certainty, Apologies, Thanking, Congratulations, Places, Travel and transport, Bar and restaurant.

The aim of this guide was twofold. Presented bilingually, it would help foreign offenders to communicate during their first weeks in prison and would also allow them to learn Spanish. Apart from translating both the lists of vocabulary and the communication guide into the above languages, pictograms were also developed to be displayed on walls and used in Spanish classes.

7. Conclusions and Further Research

After the challenging process of establishing cooperation with the Directorate General for Penitentiaries, our aim was to launch a project that would allow us to explore and describe the linguistic diversity found in

Spanish prisons, identify existing solutions to communication problems in accordance with European guidelines and recommendations, and propose solutions to communicative problems that are likely to lead to situations of isolation, social exclusion, insecurity and violation of inmate and staff rights. Among these solutions, we had in mind developing training and reintegration programmes aimed at foreign inmates, organising training programmes for prison staff, translating documents and developing multilingual resources to address communication between prison staff and foreign inmates.

After a year of development of the pilot project, we have not only obtained some data about linguistic diversity and current solutions to communicative problems, but also a greater understanding of the characteristics of the foreign population in Spanish prisons according to the kinds of crimes committed and the administrative processes they go through. However, we are aware that these are just preliminary results and further research is needed. Joint solutions have been proposed in consultation with prison staff, which include translation of documents and development of resources to improve communication.

Some of the translations, particularly those of administrative and informative documents, are already being used. In addition, the translation of the communicative guide, together with a set of pictograms covering key practical concepts, are still being tested. The aim of the translation of this guide and the pictograms is multifaceted, as it is expected to be of help when communicating orally and to serve as a learning tool of the Spanish language. Whether it fulfils these objectives will have to be assessed over a longer period of time.

In the future, we hope that prison authorities acknowledge the usefulness of the translations and opt for increasing the number of translated documents. Although this project has been carried out in Madrid for geographical reasons, it has already been expanded to include other penitentiaries in other provinces, which have their own particularities, and we will soon have further data to continue our research thanks to the project 'Efficient Communication in Penitentiary Centres' funded by the Spanish Ministry of Economy and Competitiveness (ref. REF FFI 2015-69997-R, 2016-2018).

Notes

(1) *Art. 46. Comunicaciones escritas: 'Cuando el idioma utilizado no pueda ser traducido en el establecimiento, se remitirá el escrito al centro directivo para su traducción y curso posterior.' (Reglamento Penitenciario. Art 46).*

[Art. 46. Written communication: 'documents shall be submitted to the General Management for their translation and subsequent processing when the language employed cannot be translated in the penitentiary institution'. Authors' translation].

(2)   *Art. 52. Información:*
'3. A estos efectos, el mencionado Centro Directivo procurará editar folletos de referencia en aquellos idiomas de grupos significativos de internos extranjeros en los Establecimientos españoles. A los extranjeros que desconozcan los idiomas en que se encuentre editado el folleto se les hará una traducción oral de su contenido por los funcionarios o internos que conozcan la lengua del interesado y, si fuese necesario, se recabará la colaboración de los servicios consulares del Estado a que aquél pertenezca.
4. En todo caso, a aquellos internos españoles o extranjeros que no puedan entender la información proporcionada por escrito, les será facilitada la misma por otro medio adecuado.
5. En el departamento de ingresos y en la Biblioteca de cada Establecimiento habrá, a disposición de los internos, varios ejemplares de la Ley Orgánica General Penitenciaria, del Reglamento Penitenciario y de las normas de régimen interior del Centro. La Administración procurará proporcionar a los internos extranjeros textos de la Ley Orgánica General Penitenciaria y de su Reglamento de desarrollo en la lengua propia de su país de origen, a cuyo fin recabará la colaboración de las autoridades diplomáticas correspondientes.' (*Reglamento Penitenciario.* Art 52).

[Art. 52. Information:
'3. For these purposes, the previously mentioned General Management will attempt to edit brochures in those languages spoken by inmates belonging to representative foreign groups found in Spanish penitentiary institutions. Foreign inmates who do not understand the languages these brochures are written in will be facilitated an oral translation by the prison staff or by other inmates who speak the language. If it is deemed necessary, the Consulate of the foreign inmates' countries will be asked for assistance.
4. In any case, when information in written form is inaccessible for Spanish or foreign inmates, it will be provided in another appropriate way.
5. The libraries and Admissions Department of Spanish penitentiary institutions will provide foreign inmates with several copies of the General Organic Law for Penitentiaries, the Penitentiary Regulations and the inner rules that govern the prison. The Management Board will attempt to provide the General Organic Law for Penitentiaries and the Penitentiary Regulations in the inmates' mother tongue. For this purpose, the collaboration of the corresponding diplomatic Authorities will be sought'. Authors' translation.]

(3)   *Art. 242. Nombramiento del Instructor y pliego de cargos (2): 'Posibilidad de asistirse de un funcionario o interno como intérprete si se trata de un interno extranjero que desconozca el castellano.'* (*Reglamento Penitenciario.* Art 242).

[Art. 242. Instructor's appointment and statement of objections. (2) 'It is possible to ask a civil servant or inmate to act as an interpreter when foreign inmates do not speak Spanish'. Authors' translation.]

References

Almeida Herrero, C., Lucena García, M. and Rodríguez Enríquez, F.J. (2006) *Situación de los presos extranjeros en el Centro Penitenciario de Topas (Salamanca).* Salamanca: Cáritas Diocesana de Salamanca.
Baixauli, L. (2012) *La Interpretació als Serveis Públics desde una Perspectiva Ética. La deontologia professional i l'aplicació al context penitenciari.* PhD thesis, Universitat Jaume I.
De la Cuesta Arzamendi, J.L. (2005) Retos principales del sistema penitenciario hoy, in *Jornadas en Homenaje al XXV Aniversario de la Ley Orgánica General Penitenciaria.* Ministerio del Interior, Secretaría General Técnica, DBIIPP.

European Commission (2011) *Green Paper on the Application of EU Criminal Justice Legislation in the Field of Detention*. Brussels: European Commission.

European Council (2006) *European Prison Rules*. Brussels: European Council.

González García, E. (2006) Traducción e interpretación en los servicios públicos de la zona norte. In C. Valero Garcés and F. Raga Gimeno (eds) *Revista Española de Lingüística Aplicada: Retos del siglo XXI en Comunicación Intercultural: Nuevo mapa lingüístico y cultural de España* (pp. 151–174).

Gutiérrez, J. A., Jordán, J. and Trujillo, H. (2008) Prevención de la radicalización yihadista en las prisiones españolas. Situación actual, retos y disfunciones del sistema penitenciario, *Athena Intelligence Journal* 3, 1.

Martínez-Gómez Gómez, A. (2008) La integración lingüística en las instituciones penitenciarias españolas y europeas, in *Actas del IV Congreso Internacional de ESLETRA. El Español, Lengua de Traducción para la Cooperación y el Diálogo*. Toledo (pp. 485–500).

PrisonSMART (2014) Mission statement. See http://www.prisonsmart.org/prisonSmart.htm (accessed 20 December 2015).

Reglamento Penitenciario (1996) Real Decreto 190/1996, de 9 febrero, BOE 15 febrero 1996.

Secretaría General de Instituciones Penitenciarias (2010) *La Prisión Paso a Paso*. Madrid: Ministerio del Interior.

Secretaría General de Instituciones Penitenciarias (2011) *Informe General 2011*. Madrid: Ministerio del Interior.

Secretaría General de Instituciones Penitenciarias (2012) *Informe General 2012*. Madrid: Ministerio del Interior.

Secretaría General de Instituciones Penitenciarias. www.institucionespenitenciarias.es. (accessed 20 December 2015).

Spanish General Administration [Administración General del Estado] (2013). *Informe interno Centro Penitenciario de Alcalá-Meco* (Unpublished report, March 2013).

Valero-Garcés, C. and Mojica-López, E. (2014). La comunicación con mujeres extranjeras en la cárcel. Estudio de caso. In C. Valero-Garcés (ed.) *(Re)considerando Ética e Ideología en Situaciones de Conflicto/(Re)visiting Ethics and Ideology in Situations of Conflict* (pp. 94–106). Alcalá de Henares: Servicio de Publicaciones de la Universidad.

8   Community Translation in the Australian Context

Leong Ko

1. Introduction

Community translation has been in existence for a long time and is referred to by different names in different parts of the world (e.g. Corsellis, 2008; Niska, 1995; Taibi, 2011). Recent developments in translation practice and research suggest that community translation is emerging as a domain in its own right that is attracting growing attention (Burns & Kim, 2011; Taibi, 2011; University of Western Sydney, 2014). Community translation, also known as 'public service translation', 'is emerging as an important, distinct subfield in translation studies' (University of Westminster, 2014).

Australia is a multicultural and multilingual country. According to the Australian Bureau of Statistics (2013), 'Australians come from more than 200 countries, speak over 300 languages at home, belong to more than 100 different religious groups, and work in more than 1000 different occupations'. Translation services are well developed in Australia and a significant portion of translation in the market targets community readers, be they speakers of English or languages other than English (LOTE). As a leading country in the field, Australia offers an appropriate context to explore the nature of community translation, its distinctive features and requirements. This research examines the definitions of community and community translation, the features of community documents and community translation, and the appropriate translation approaches and strategies for community translation in the Australian context, based on data collected from the translation market in Australia. The pair of languages for which community translation is examined is English and Chinese.

The methods employed in this research include a telephone survey with practising translators, a questionnaire for translation students and case studies of real examples of community translation.

2. Community and Community Translation

In English, the word 'community' has been used to such an extent that its definition and boundaries have become blurred. For instance, if one is asked 'What is the community of the University of Queensland?', the answer may be 'It is teachers and students of the university' or 'It is teachers, students and administrative staff'. However, what about the parents of students? What about the area where the university is located? What about people who live in this area? In a way, all of these can be included in the community of the University of Queensland. It seems that different people may have different opinions about what the term 'community' refers to.

Dictionaries provide the following definitions of 'community':

A social group of any size whose members reside in a specific locality, share government, and have a cultural and historical heritage. The community, the public. (*Macquarie Dictionary*, 1987)

A social group of any size whose members reside in a specific locality, share government, and have a cultural and historical heritage. A social, religious, occupational, or other group sharing common characteristics or interests: the business community; the community of scholars. The community, the public; society. (*Random House College Dictionary*, 1979)

Organized political, municipal, or social body; body of people living in same locality; body of people having religion, profession, etc., in common, (the immigrant community; the mercantile community; the Jewish community); *the* public; monastic, socialistic, etc., body practising community of goods; body of nations unified by common interests. (*Concise Oxford Dictionary*, 1976)

Although the three definitions all give 'locality' as a feature of community, they also mention common 'religion', 'profession', 'characteristics' or 'interests' and so on as other features of community. As such, it is natural to assume that people who share those common characteristics or interests may or may not live in the same place. So, based on the above definitions, 'community' is a term that is broadly used to refer to any group of people who share common characteristics or interests, and who may or may not reside in the same locality. In this sense, the translation of materials produced out of or for such a community may be considered community translation, in spite of the fact that community translation has also been referred to as public service translation in some parts of the world (e.g. Corsellis, 2008; Niska, 1995; Taibi, 2011).

To find out what practising translators understand by the term 'community', the author of this chapter randomly selected ten practising Chinese translators in Australia from NAATI's Online Directory of Professional

Translators (NAATI, 2014) and conducted a brief telephone survey. A specific question was asked in the survey: What do you think 'community' refers to in the Australian context? Their responses are summed up as follows:

- People who speak the same dialect or language.
- People from the same country or region.
- People of similar background.
- People of similar age.
- People who live in the same area.

Their understanding of 'community' shares some common ground with the features listed by dictionaries, such as common culture and characteristics and residing in the same locality. However, their perception is more specifically related to factors associated with their translation work, such as the same dialect or language, the same country or region and similar background.

Whether we use the definitions provided by dictionaries, or the concept as it is perceived by practising translators based on their work experience, it can be assumed that in the Australian context, 'community' is a very broadly defined term. From the perspective of translation, translation of documents or materials produced by the community and/or for the community, including its individual members, can be referred to as community translation, and these documents or materials encompass government reports, policies, legal documents, community newsletters, public notices, various certificates and testimonials, and official letters, to name just a few. It is based on this understanding that community translation is discussed in this chapter.

3. Community Translation vs Translating Communities

When discussing 'community translation', it is necessary to distinguish it from 'translating community' in order to avoid confusion. This is because these two terms look similar but have very different meanings. The following are some descriptions of translating communities found on the internet:

> While Google tries to solve the problem of machine translation, online communities have formed to take the task of translating content into their own hands. Translating communities have sprung up all over the Web dedicated to translating movie and t.v. show subtitles and popular novels ... While the idea of community translation closely resembles crowd sourcing, it differs crucially in that these communities are entirely

volunteer-based and open source and, while some larger sites might have some ad revenue, they do not work in the service of a larger money-making entity. (Smith, 2014)

Anyone can apply to translate for Adobe TV. We are looking for translators who are fluent in more than one language and can translate the content of Adobe TV videos while maintaining the tone and personality of the speaker ... Adobe TV translators are volunteers, so there is no payment for completing translations. For every minute of video you translate, you will earn 50 Adobe TV points. (Adobe Translation Center, 2014)

Community translation enables your own readers and customers to contribute and edit translations to your site. If you have a passionate user community, quite often people will volunteer time to help improve translations, for example by correcting machine translations. People do this for many reasons whether it is to help a friend or relative read in their language, for public service, or to practise their own language skills. (Speaklike, 2014)

The term 'translating community' therefore refers to a group of volunteers who work together in a specific area or for a specific project for their own interest and free of charge. It is different from 'community translation' as discussed in this chapter and volume.

4. Community Translation in Australia

In the above sections, we have broadly discussed definitions and understandings of community and community translation. This section addresses specific aspects of community translation in the Australian context, including types of materials encountered in community translation, features of texts, terminologies that may appear in community translation, readerships and clients' needs to be considered in translation, and finally appropriate strategies to be adopted in community translation to suit its specific needs. The discussion is based on the analysis of real examples collected from the translation market in Australia.

4.1 Types of materials for translation

Australia is a multilingual and multicultural country, where there are many communities of migrants from different countries and regions as well as indigenous Australians. Here, it is worth examining the kinds of materials that are translated in Australia. The following are some examples encountered in the translation market.

Example 1

> Living in Brisbane
> A message from Lord Mayor Graham Quirk
>
> If you are heading to the Ekka, don't forget to drop by Council's stand in the Woolworths Pavilion.
> .....
> Other dates to note this month include the Valley Fiesta on 23–24 August, which extends this year to include a daytime program of live street art, markets and pop-up bars. From 16–24 August we celebrate Seniors Week with a whole host of events such as the Lord Mayor's Seniors Gala Cabaret on 17 August. (Quirk, 2014)

This example contains localised terms such as 'Ekka', 'Valley Fiesta' and 'Seniors Gala Cabaret', some of which would require a degree of local knowledge and culture to understand. For instance, the 'Ekka' was originally established to 'promote and encourage the agricultural and industrial development of Queensland; as well as provide a unique opportunity for country and urban residents to come together in a celebration of Queensland lifestyle' (Ekka Royal Queensland Show, 2014). It is now a popular carnival in Brisbane that attracts children, adults and tourists alike. So far, there is no ready translation in Chinese, and ethnic Chinese people in Brisbane merely use the English term in their communications.

Example 2

> My Queensland Community Newsletter
> C'mon, Get in the Game!
>
> In an effort to encourage active participation in sports and recreation at the grassroots level, the Queensland Government is offering access to funds through the latest round of Get in the Game funding.
>
> Get in the Game consists of three funding programs run over a period of three years.
>
> The *Get Started* program assists children and young people .... The *Get Going* program offers local sport and recreation organisations funding of up to $10,000 ... The *Get Playing* program offers local sport and recreation organisations funding of up to $100,000... (My Queensland Community Newsletter, 2014)

The text in this example does not contain much information concerning local culture. However, there are a number of specific colloquial expressions such as 'C'mon', 'Get Started', 'Get Going' and 'Get Playing' that do present some challenges in terms of translating them into appropriate Chinese words as concise as their English counterparts.

Example 3

Electric Motor Research: Environmental issues

US Analysis of the replacement of old motor technology including financial analysis.

- 12.4 million motors of more than 1 hp in service in U.S. manufacturing facilities
- CEE reports that about 2.9 million of these motors fail each year, of which 600,000 are replaced
- Industrial electric motor driven systems used in production account for about 679 billion kWh, or about 23% of all the electricity sold in the USA. Motors used in industrial space heating, cooling and ventilation systems use an additional 68 billion kWh
- NEMA Premium motor program could save over 5800 GWh (5.8 billion kWh) of electricity and prevent the release of nearly 80 million metric tons of carbon into the atmosphere over the next 10 years. That would be the equivalent of keeping 16 million cars off the road. (NEMA – National Electrical Manufacturers' Association)

This example encountered in the Australian translation market indicates that community translation in Australia can extend well beyond the public service sector and national boundaries. This argument is also supported by Corsellis, who states that 'translation in the public service sector can also include an international dimension' (Corsellis, 2008: 32).

With regard to translation from Chinese into English, materials encountered in the translation market in Australia include driver's licences, birth certificates, graduation certificates, marriage certificates, medical reports, immunisation records, herbal medicine, personal statements for various purposes, restaurant menus, business proposals, various agreements, letters, police reports, detention notices, silicon test reports, receipts and invoices. Some of these types of documents – e.g. driving licences, birth certificates, graduation certificates, and marriage certificates – rarely appear in English-Chinese translation.

Materials similar to the above examples, as well as other examples provided in this chapter, are very often encountered in the Australian translation market for the broad community. They appear in both the public service and other sectors and are largely of a non-literary nature.

4.2 Features of texts and challenges for translation

Due to the fact that materials for community translation are often of a local nature and contain colloquial expressions, and that the translation of such materials may be targeting specific readerships from certain backgrounds, all such factors present challenges for translation. The following subsections are therefore devoted to the investigation of challenges for community translation from the perspective of terminologies, language expressions, readerships and clients' needs.

4.2.1 Terminologies in community translation

Correct understanding of terms and translating them into appropriate target language terms are essential in community translation. They ensure that messages in the source text are accurately conveyed and correctly perceived. It has been found that texts in community translation often contain terms of a local or domestic nature, which may not have equivalents in a LOTE, hence posing a challenge to translators.

Example 4

Now you can claim your Medicare rebate here.
...
If you're bulk billed, nothing changes. (Medicare Australia)

'Medicare' is the Australian public health system, in which the government covers a certain proportion of medical costs for Australian citizens. 'Bulk Billing' is Medicare's claim system in which doctors charge Medicare directly without requiring patients to pay for medical costs. So far, there is no satisfactory Chinese translation for 'Bulk Billing'. One suggestion has been to translate it as 'Card Swiping System', which does not convey the exact meaning of bulk billing, but merely refers to the process of swiping a patient's Medicare card in the machine provided for billing purposes.

Example 5

Slip Slop Slap Seek Slide

One of the most successful health campaigns in Australia's history was launched by Cancer Council Australia in 1980.
....

The Slip Slop Slap slogan has become institutionalised as the core message of the Cancer Council's SunSmart program. The campaign is widely credited as playing a key role in the dramatic shift in sun protection attitudes and behaviour over the past two decades. In 2007, the slogan was updated to Slip Slop Slap Seek Slide to reflect the importance of seeking shade and sliding on wraparound sunglasses to prevent sun damage.

LiveSmart. Be SunSmart. (Cancer Council Australia, 2014)

The most challenging part of this passage seems to be the comprehension and translation of the five words 'Slip Slop Slap Seek Slide', which mean 'slip on a shirt, slop on sunscreen and slap on a hat, seek shade and slide on wrap-around sunglasses to prevent sun damage' (Cancer Council Australia, 2014). Without this knowledge, it would be extremely difficult to translate this expression.

From the above examples, it can be seen that texts for community translation in the Australian context tend to be localised, context-specific and culture-specific. The challenges for translators mostly lie in the correct understanding of terminology in the source language and natural expression in the target language. Indeed, these twin challenges are so significant that many translators and would-be translators find it difficult to either understand such terms or express them appropriately in the target language.

The following is an extract from a questionnaire administered in 2013 to a group of translation students from various disciplines (90% of whom were overseas students and had not lived in Australia before), who had just commenced undertaking the Master of Arts in Chinese Translation and Interpreting in the University of Queensland, Australia.

Please explain the meaning of the following terms and answer questions in either English or Chinese, without using dictionaries. If you don't know, leave it blank or write 'don't know'.

		Don't know or wrong answer % (total 27 students)
1	Neighbourhood Watch	96.3
2	Garage sale	85.2
3	Industrial Award	100
4	Holiday loading	100
5	Industrial relations	100
6	Ombudsman	100
7	Statutory declaration	100
8	Trade certificate	100
9	Group Certificate (for taxation purposes)	96.3
10	Bulk Billing	100
11	Formal (in secondary school)	96.3
12	Affidavit	88.9
13	Centrelink	100
14	Medicare	59.3
15	Hung parliament	96.3
16	What are the Council Rates?	100
17	What is the difference between 'salary' and 'wage'?	92.6
18	Tradesmen	100

These terms are not technical jargon. Rather, they are common terms that are used in people's daily lives in Australia. The responses to the questionnaire indicate that students who are new to this country have very little understanding of the meaning of these terms. Without a clear understanding, it is obviously difficult to translate them correctly.

4.2.2 Language expressions

It has been observed from the examples in Section 4.1 that language expressions in the materials for community translation could be colloquial. This is another challenge for translation in terms of finding possible equivalents in the target language, or otherwise resorting to other solutions.

Example 6

Line up a retirement where you can live well.
Inspect this Sat & Sun 10am–12pm or call for an appointment. (Aveo Durack, 2014)

This is a marketing advertisement for properties in a retirement village, which depicts a group of retirees playing lawn bowls. The sentence 'Line up a retirement where you can live well' is grammatically simple, but is difficult to translate. Based on a correct understanding of its meaning, the translator would need to adopt a creative approach in order to reproduce a translation that is both meaningful and natural.

Another challenge encountered in community translation in Australia is ambiguous, unclear or poor expressions sometimes encountered in the source text. In the following examples, the ambiguous part is underlined.

Example 7

The Work Capacity Decision(s)

- Under subsection 43 (1) (a), I have determined that you have a current work capacity of 20 hours per week (4 hours per day, 5 days per week) …
- Under subsection 43 (1) (b), I have determined the following role(s) constitute suitable employment for you: laundry worker.
- Under subsection 43 (1) (f), any other decision of an insurer that affects a worker's entitlement to weekly payments of compensation, including a decision to suspend, discontinue or reduce the amount of the weekly payments of compensation payable to a worker on the basis of any decision referred to in paragraphs (a)–(b). (QBE Workers Compensation (NSW) Limited, 2014)

Grammatically, the last paragraph does not flow well from the previous two paragraphs, and therefore the meaning is unclear.

Example 8

This is an important meeting to understand how the reforms affect the care services you will be receiving. Please speak to your case manager (3275 3688) to book a seat. <u>If you need assistance with transport from home or someone to look after the person you are caring for while you come for the meeting</u>. (Cathay Community Association Inc., 2014)

The last sentence is incomplete, and therefore the meaning is unclear.

This kind of ungrammatical and unclear language expressions sometimes appear in materials for community translation in both English and Chinese. In the process of translation, it would require translators to work out the intended meaning from the context or check with the clients or commissioners for the correct meaning.

4.2.3 Readerships and clients' needs and their implications in translation

In community translation, readerships and clients' needs are another important factor to be considered. For instance, when assigning a translation task, the client may instruct that the translated text is for newly arrived migrants who are not well-educated and therefore a simple and straightforward language should be used. Considerations associated with readerships and clients' needs have a direct bearing on the translation output and often require translators to adopt translation strategies relevant to specific translation tasks in order to meet client expectations.

Example 9

English: How do I get to Specialist Clinics?

By car

A patient drop-off zone is located at the front entrance, at Daly Wing, 35 Victoria Parade, Fitzroy. There is limited paid street parking. The nearest car parks are in Fitzroy St (off Victoria Parade) and at Melbourne Museum (enter from Nicholson St or Rathdowne St). (St Vincent's Hospital, 2014)

Chinese: 我怎么去专科门诊?

汽车

在 Daly Wing, 35 Victoria Parade, Fitzroy 前门处有患者下客区。路边 收费停车位有限。最近的停车场位于Fitzroy St（在Victoria Parade 附近）和 Melbourne Museum（从Nicholson St 或Rathdowne St进 入。）

In the above Chinese translation, parts of the English text – specifically the address, street and place names – have been left in English. The reasons for this are twofold. Firstly, the translation is for readers who live locally. They know the English names for these streets and places and use them in their daily lives. When translating such proper nouns, the common practice is to use transliteration, or translation according to the pronunciation. However, because an English word can have different pronunciations in Chinese, which can result in the choice of different Chinese characters, transliteration would therefore result in the same English word having different Chinese versions. This would be confusing to local Chinese residents. It is much easier to leave such words in English. Secondly, if a Chinese reader of the above translation lost his/her way, he/she could use the translated Chinese document containing place and street names in English to ask the police for assistance, and the police would be able to give them directions. If all of the text was translated into Chinese, the police (or other English-speaking people) would not be able to help in this way.

Example 10

English: To request a review complete the attached WorkCover *Application to insurer for internal review* form and forward this to QBE to PO BOX 1588, Sydney 2001 or email: internalreview@qbe.com, together with any further information you may have to support your claim.

The review of the decision will be done by an Independent Review Team at QBE. If they do not overturn the decision in your favour, you would then need to ask for a review by the Merit Team at WorkCover NSW within 30 days. (QBE Workers Compensation (NSW) Ltd, 2013)

Chinese: 如果您要求复审，请完成附件中的 WorkCover 保险公司内部复审申请 （WorkCover *Application to insurer for internal review*） 表，并连同可用来支持您索赔要求的信息寄给 QBE，地址是 PO BOX 1588，Sydney 2001，或者发送电邮: internalreview@qbe.com。

复审工作将由 QBE 的独立复审小组进行。如果他们没有推翻决定，您可以在 30 天内要求新南威尔士州工作保护 (WorkCover NSW) 的绩效小组 (Merit Team) 进行复审。

In this translation, apart from the mailing address, which has been left in English for the reason discussed above, the special terms 'WorkCover *Application to insurer for internal review*' and 'WorkCover NSW' have been translated, but their English terms have been provided in brackets. There are two objectives in adopting this practice. Firstly, the Chinese translation will provide Chinese readers who do not understand English with the necessary information. Secondly, the English terms are provided in case it is necessary for someone to check or refer to the original terms for some reason. However, the reason for giving 'Merit Team' in brackets is a little unclear. Since its meaning can be clearly translated and the need for cross-reference is not well established, it does not seem necessary to provide the English term here.

The translator probably thought that it was an institutional name and therefore that it was safer to retain the English term in brackets. Indeed, translators' discretion sometimes plays a part in whether an English term is provided in brackets.

Example 11

In some cases, the English text must be left in English. For example,

English: If you would like a survey in Simplified Chinese please fill the box below with the password from your questionnaire. This password can be found on the back page of the questionnaire you received with this letter. The password is beneath the barcode, where we have written 'password' in this image. (Department of Health of Victoria, 2014)

Chinese: 如果您希望获得简体中文的调查，请把问卷中的密码填入以下的方框内。您可以在随函问卷的背面找到这个密码。密码位于条形码之下，如图所示 "password" （即密码）。

In this case, when translating the passage into Chinese, the word 'password' has to be kept in English. Very likely, this is because the persons processing the questionnaire speak English only and need this reference for identification and processing. However, in order to assist Chinese readers, the Chinese meaning of 'password' is provided in brackets.

Example 12

In the following example, the names of interest are underlined.

English: The Best Site on <u>Doncaster Hill</u>

A high profile and elevated development site with excellent exposure, three street frontages and a Planning Permit for 273 apartments plus ground floor retail over 12 levels. This rare offering directly opposite <u>Westfield Doncaster Shopping Centre</u> consists of 3964 m² (approx.) of prime developable land across two separate titles. The plans have been designed by renowned <u>Peddle Thorp</u> Architects and provide the opportunity to construct a modern landmark development with a stunning architectural design.
- Commanding & strategic location opposite <u>Westfield Doncaster</u>
- 14km east of the Melbourne CBD
- 1.1km to the <u>Eastern Freeway</u> and close to public transport
- Positioned within the '<u>Doncaster Hill Activity Centre</u>' and identified within the '<u>Doncaster Hill Strategy</u>' (Colliers International, 2014)

Chinese: 唐卡斯特山最佳地段

高档开发区，环境优良，三面临街。计划许可证批准建造 273 间公寓和底楼零售商店，共 12 层楼。这个难得的开发区位于唐卡斯特西田购物中心正对面，面积 3,964 平方米（大约），位于可开发的黄金地段，包括两个产权地块，由著名佩德尔．托尔建筑公司设计。这是一个具有绝佳建筑设计的标志性现代开发项目。

- 绝佳地点，面对唐卡斯特西田购物中心
- 位于墨尔本中央商务区以东 14 公里
- 距东区高速公路 1.1 公里，位于公共交通附近
- 位于 "唐卡斯特山活动中心" 范围之内，并被确定为 "唐卡斯特西山规划" 的一部分

Although the source text contains many proper nouns such as place names, a person's name and the name of a project, none of these has been left in English or provided in brackets. The author of this research was contracted to translate this document. He was specifically advised that the translation was for Chinese readers in China and that all proper nouns should be translated. This request is understandable and justified, because readers in China who do not understand English and do not live in Australia would have little familiarity with these proper nouns, which would therefore mean very little to them if left in English or provided in brackets. Instead, such a practice might confuse them. A full translation of every proper noun would better communicate the message of this property marketing advertisement.

One interesting point to note is that the practice of providing source text terms in brackets is much more common in translations from English into Chinese than the other way around. Very often English terms are found in a Chinese translated document in Australia. However, almost no Chinese terms are found in translations from Chinese into English. The same is true in newspapers. In Chinese newspapers published in Australia, English terms can be found every now and then, mostly in the form of proper nouns concerning people, places and institutions; but no English newspapers include Chinese terms, even when an event specifically relating to China is being reported. According to this author's observations, it was only in the early 2000s that some English newspapers in Hong Kong began to include Chinese terms in their reports about China, and these terms were limited to a few prominent people's names, such as the president, premier, deputy premiers, ministers and deputy ministers. The reasons for such a practice are yet to be explored. In Australia, one probable reason is that English is regarded as the mainstream language, so the inclusion of English proper nouns in a Chinese translation may provide a convenient reference if needed.

Example 13
English: Spotlight on UQ in China

The concept of 同舟共济, or tong zhou gong ji, translated from Mandarin as 'people on the same boat should assist each other', reflecting a mutual commitment to research and education that underpins UQ's relationship with China. (UQ Contact Summer, 2014)

Chinese: 中国：聚焦昆士兰大学

"同舟共济"这一理念的意思是 "在同一只船上的人应互相帮助"，这反映出昆士兰大学与中国的关系是建立在研究和教育的相互承诺 之上。

This is an interesting case. Firstly, the Chinese idiom appears in both Chinese characters and *pinyin* (Mandarin pronunciation) in the English text, as it is not a common practice to include a Chinese phrase in an English text; secondly, when it was translated into Chinese, both *pinyin* and the message about 'translated from Mandarin' were omitted. It is apparent that the English text was intended for English readers, so the *pinyin* for the Chinese characters was provided to aid pronunciation and a note about translation from Mandarin was provided to help readers understand the meaning of the idiom. However, when it was translated into Chinese, it became unnecessary and inappropriate to tell Chinese readers about the pronunciation and provide the information that it was 'translated from Mandarin'. Although the translator translated 'people on the same boat should assist each other', even this may be considered unnecessary, because all Chinese readers would know the meaning of the idiom.

Based on the above findings on community translation in Australia, it can be seen that effective and appropriate community translation would require translators to have a good command of contextual knowledge, professional practices, local practices, cultural knowledge and relevant jargon. In addition, they should have a correct understanding of their client's needs, the target readership and the intended purposes of the translated documents. This means that it is essential for them to involve clients in the translation process. Finally, it is important that community translators should be locally trained.

4.4 Appropriate translation approaches and strategies

Translation is a text-based linguistic practice. In an attempt to classify texts in translation, Reiss developed a diagram that classified texts as 'informative', 'expressive' or 'operative', in which texts such as reference works, reports, lectures, and operating instructions are included in the 'informative' category (quoted in Munday, 2001: 74). From the examples presented in previous sections, it has been found that materials for community translation in Australia largely fall into the 'informative' category. Reiss further states that in the translation of informative materials, the target text should 'transmit referential content' and the translation method should consist of '[p]lain prose', without redundancy and with the use of explicitation when required" (Munday, 2001: 75). This basically suggests that in the translation of informative texts, the source language content should be conveyed accurately and the expression in the target language should be plain and easy to understand. This principle coincides with the expectations in community translation.

Furthermore, it has been observed in the above discussion that various factors need to be considered when practising community translation, including the exact meaning of the source text, appropriate expressions in the target text, the needs of both source language and target language readers, the functions of the translated text, and the intentions of the clients who provide the source text for translation. It is therefore necessary to consider appropriate translation approaches and strategies.

Newmark (1982) proposes two types of translation: semantic translation and communicative translation. Semantic translation focuses primarily on the semantic content of the source text, whereas communicative translation focuses essentially on the comprehension and response of receptors. Newmark points out that:

> Semantic translation attempts to render as closely as the semantic and syntactic structures of the second language allow the exact contextual meaning of the original. Communicative translation attempts to produce on its readers an effect as close as possible to that obtained on the readers of the original. (Newmark, 1982: 39)

Venuti also proposes dual approaches to translation – namely, foreignisation and domestication (Venuti, 1995: 19–20) – which is a reflection of Schleiermacher's argument that '[e]ither the translator leaves the writer in peace as much as possible and moves the reader toward him; or he leaves the reader in peace as much as possible and moves the writer toward him' (Schleiermacher, 1813/1992: 41–42). Based on these two approaches, in a translation practice where the foreignisation approach is used, the translated text should maintain some features of the source language such as culture, style, forms of expression, and other elements, in such a way that readers may feel as if they were living in the country of the source language; in a translation practice where the domestication approach is employed, the translated text should be produced in such a way that readers do not experience much foreignness when they read the translation. The approaches proposed by Newmark and Venuti are of referential value because when undertaking community translation, both the content of the source language and appropriate expressions in the target language need to be considered.

With regard to factors that relate to the needs of the clients commissioning the translation and the end users of the translation, Hönig (1997, quoted in Adab, 2001: 135) argues that clients may have a preconceived notion of what translation products should look like. Pinto (2001) points out that user satisfaction should be regarded as the basic principle and means of measuring quality, and that it is important to 'ensure the complete satisfaction of users, personnel, business managers, and society in general' (Pinto, 2001: 290). Indeed, the requirements of clients are pragmatic and should not be ignored. Such factors have a bearing on translation strategies. Some researchers such as Holz-Manttari (1986, quoted in Munday 2001), Vermeer (1989) and Venuti (1992, 1998) have developed 'translational action' and 'skopos' theories, which point out that translation is driven by its outcomes and/or purposes and is controlled by factors such as the needs of the receivers, clients, publishers, readers and translation agents (Munday, 2001: 79–80, 153–154). This is particularly true in the case of community translation.

The above views, coupled with the findings from the examples and case studies presented in this research, confirm that, depending on the needs of individual cases and based on the requirements of clients and end users, a mixture of semantic and communicative translation, domestication and foreignisation may be employed to achieve different purposes in community translation. In order to achieve these purposes, a range of specific translation strategies may need to be used, including adaptation, modulation, borrowing, paraphrasing, keeping source texts untranslated or providing them in brackets, and using explanatory notes.

5. Conclusion

Community translation in Australia is a localised translation practice that is intended to serve different communities within this country and their members. The materials for translation are generally non-literary, of a local nature, and are mostly generated within the country and translated for local residents. There are a number of specific challenges for translation, particularly in terms of localised terminologies, colloquial language expressions, types of readerships and clients' needs. In order to produce a satisfactory translation, translators are expected to have a good knowledge of local institutions and their practices, and employ a combination of semantic and communicative translation, domestication and foreignisation approaches, along with various case-specific strategies, in order to achieve the intended communication purposes and functions of the translation. Finally, it would be ideal if translators could be locally trained or have extensive translation practice in this country.

References

Adab, B. (2001) The translation of advertising: a framework of evaluation. *Babel*, 47 (2), 133–157.

Adobe Translation Center (2014) Community translation. See http://tv.adobe.com/translations/learnmore/ (accessed 9 August 2014).

Australian Bureau of Statistics (2013) Australian social trends, April 2013. See http://www.abs.gov.au/AUSSTATS/abs@.nsf/Lookup/4102.0Main+Features30April+2013 (accessed 20 November 2014).

Aveo Durack (2014) Line up a retirement where you can live well (mimeo).

Burns, A. and Kim, M. (2011) Community accessibility of health information and the consequent impact for translation into community languages. *Translation & Interpreting* 3 (1), 58–75.

Cancer Council Australia (2014) Slip slop slap seek slide. See http://www.cancer.org.au/preventing-cancer/sun-protection/campaigns-and-events/slip-slop-slap-seek-slide.html (accessed 3 September 2014).

Cathay Community Association Inc (2014) Invitation to home care packages on consumer-directed care information session (mimeo).

Colliers International (2014) Take the title and the crown – Doncaster Hill (mimeo).

Concise Oxford Dictionary, 6th Edition (1976) Oxford: Oxford University Press.

Corsellis, A. (2008) *Public Service Interpreting: The First Steps*. Hampshire: Palgrave Macmillan.

Department of Health of Victoria (2014) Important information for people who prefer to read and write simplified Chinese (mimeo).

Ekka Royal Queensland Show (2014) See http://www.ekka.com.au/about-ekka/history.aspx (accessed 3 September 2014).

Kilcoy Pastoral Company (2013) Welcome to Kilcoy Pastoral Company. See http://www.kpc.com.au/index.php/en/ (accessed 24 January 2013).

Macquarie Dictionary, 2nd Revised Edition (1987) NSW: Macquarie Library Pty Ltd.

Medicare Australia. Now you can claim your Medicare rebate here (mimeo).

Munday, J. (2001) *Introducing Translation Studies: Theories and Applications*. London and New York: Routledge.

My Queensland Community Newsletter (2014) C'mon, Get in the Game! Issue 13 July 2014 (mimeo).

National Accreditation Authority for Translators and Interpreters (NAATI) See https://www.naati.com.au/ (accessed on 26 August 2014).

NEMA – National Electrical Manufacturers Association. See http://www.nema.org/Policy/Energy/Efficiency/Pages/NEMA-Premium-Motors.aspx (accessed 16 November 2012).

Newmark, P. (1982) *Approaches to Translation*. Oxford: Pergamon Press Ltd.

Niska, H. (1995) Just Interpreting: role conflicts and discourse types in court interpreting. In M. Morris (ed.) *Translation and the Law* (pp. 293–317). Amsterdam: Benjamins.

Pinto, M. (2001) Quality factors in documentary translation. *Meta*, XLVI, 2, 288–300.

Prime Minister's Science, Engineering and Innovation Council, PMSEIC Expert Working Group on Food Security (2014) Australia and Food Security in a Changing World. See http://www.chiefscientist.gov.au/wpcontent/uploads/FoodSecurity_web.pdf (accessed on 30 August 2014).

QBE Workers Compensation (NSW) Ltd (2013) Workers compensation claim (mimeo).

QBE Workers Compensation (NSW) Ltd (2014) The work capacity decision(s) (mimeo).

Quirk, G. (2014) A Message from Lord Mayor Graham Quirk – Living in Brisbane, August Edition 2014. Brisbane City (mimeo).

Random House College Dictionary, Revised Edition (1979) New York: Random House Inc.

Schleiermacher, F. (1992 [1813]) On the different methods of translating. In R. Schulte and J. Biguenet (eds) *Theories of Translation*. Chicago and London: University of Chicago Press.

Smith, B. (2014) Community translation for fun and ... well, just fun. See http://people. ischool.berkeley.edu/~bailey/bsite/projects/Hive_Translation_Smith.pdf (accessed 9 August 2014).

Speaklike (2014) How to implement community translation. See http://www.speaklike. com/how-to-implement-community-translation/ (accessed 9 August 2014).

St Vincent's Hospital (2014) Information for new patients (mimeo).

Taibi, M. (2011) Public service translation. In K. Malmkjær and K. Windle (eds) *The Oxford Handbook of Translation Studies* (pp. 214–227). Oxford: Oxford University Press.

University of Western Sydney (2014) Call for papers for the International Conference on Community Translation. See http://www.uws.edu.au/communitytranslation/ home/call_for_papers (accessed 11 August 2014).

University of Westminster (2014) Call for papers – translating cultures: translation as a tool for inclusion/exclusion in a multicultural society. See http://www.westminster. ac.uk/aboutus/faculties/humanities/departments/languages/Documents/?a=279546 (accessed 4 December 2014).

UQ Contact Summer (2014) Spotlight on UQ in China (mimeo).

Vermeer, H.J. (1989) Skopos and commission in translational action. In L. Venuti (ed.) (2000) *The Translation Studies Reader* (pp. 221–232). London and New York: Routledge.

Venuti, L. (ed.) (1992) *Rethinking Translation: Discourse, Subjectivity, Ideology*. London and New York: Routledge.

Venuti, L. (1995) *The Translator's Invisibility: A History of Translation*. London: Routledge.

Venuti, L. (1998) *The Scandal of Translation: Towards an Ethics of Difference*. London and New York: Routledge.

9 Linguistic Diversity Among Swahili-Speakers: A Challenge for Translation in Australia

Jean Burke

1. Introduction

The demand for translation into Swahili has increased markedly over the last decade due to its emergence as one of the fastest growing languages in Australia. In large part this is related to a policy shift in 2001 to the planned acceptance and settlement of more refugees from Africa, until 2007 when accepted numbers were reduced. Swahili-speaking refugees from Central and East Africa come from multiethnic and multilingual communities. On migration to Australia these small communities are located within a larger multicultural system where the official language is English. There can be a tendency to see language and ethnicity as conflated and to see ethnic and language groups as homogenous without recognising cultural and linguistic variety within these groups.

Community translation facilitates communication from and to the authorities and aims to promote inclusiveness and participation of the minority language groups in society (Lesch, 1999). This is important when considering that African refugees have been identified as one of the most disadvantaged migrant groups in Australia (Department of Immigration and Multicultural Affairs [DIMIA] cited in Harte *et al.*, 2011: 326). Language issues are part of the questions about identify faced by migrants, both forced and voluntary (Martin cited in Musgrave & Hajek, 2013). This chapter aims to increase understanding among language service providers, policy makers and the general community of the linguistic and cultural diversity of Africans in Australia. It aims to understand the needs and strengths of communities who speak Swahili as one of their languages. Motivation to address this topic arose from the author's experiences in interpreting and translating Swahili. The curiosity of language service providers seeking to understand their linguistic diverse readers and how to provide the most appropriate services was another inspiration.

This chapter presents a community profile around language, rather than ethnicity or country of birth. It reviews relevant literature and presents statistical analysis of data from the Settlement database of the Department of Immigration and Border Protection and the Australian Bureau of Statistics census. It also discusses the status of Swahili translation in Australia and strategies to adapt translation processes within its linguistically diverse context, which may also apply to similar linguistic situations, such as other lingua franca. This chapter describes the case of Swahili-speaking communities in the sociocultural context of Australia. It is situated within the scope of pragmatics, emphasising 'the study of language in use' (Baker, 1992: 217) and its translation as a communicative act.

2. The Global Spread of Swahili

Swahili is a widely spoken language in Africa, second only to Arabic. Over 100 million people (Ogwana, 2001) from an area covering 14 countries speak Swahili. It is an important lingua franca for communication throughout much of East Africa and the Democratic Republic of Congo (DRC). Swahili is a national language, used orally in parliament, administration, media, education, and/or official language in which laws of the country are made and publicised (Lodhi, 1993: 81), of five nations. These nations are the United Republic of Tanzania, Kenya, Uganda, Rwanda and the Congo (DRC). It is also spoken in many of the countries bordering these: in Burundi, Rwanda, Northern Zambia, Malawi, Mozambique, Southern Somalia, Southern Sudan, the Comoros as well as Oman, Madagascar (Amidu, 1995; Lodhi, 1993; Ogwana, 2001) Mayotte and South Africa. Swahili is now one of the working languages of the Organization of African Union (Kiango, 2005).

The word Swahili derives from the Arabic word *sahel/sawahil* meaning coasts (Amidu, 1995). Many factors have contributed to the development of Swahili as a lingua franca along and beyond the East African coast. Its spread has been facilitated by African and foreign influence through trade, slavery, colonial rule and administration, religious movements, independence struggles, national identity and globalisation (Amidu, 1995; Moshi, 2006; Ogwana, 2001). Swahili has thrived in the context of linguistic diversity, which prevents interethnic communication, the similarity among Bantu languages in vocabulary and structure (Ogwana, 2001) and its lack of identification with any specific ethnic group. The movement of soldiers and refugees due to political instability and war and with it 'disruption of ethnic cohesion' (Ogwana, 2001: 4) has also favoured the spread of Swahili.

Swahili has expanded beyond Africa to Europe, the Americas and Australia through returning expatriates (such as the author), migration and the movement of refugees (Moshi, 2006: 171). In particular, refugees who have fled civil war and unrest in Central Africa (Rwanda, Burundi and DRC) originate from countries where Swahili is spoken. Many have often also spent considerable time encamped in East Africa (Tanzania, Kenya or Uganda) where Swahili is even more prevalent. Hence Swahili functions as a lingua franca both in refugee-sending countries of Central Africa, in host countries of first asylum in East Africa, such as Kenya (Odhiambo-Abuya, 2004) and in new communities where refugees settle, such as Australia.

3. Swahili and Linguistic Diversity

The most standardised form of Swahili, known as Standard Swahili (*Kiswahili Sanifu*) is particularly spoken throughout Tanzania and into Kenya. Standardisation was driven by British colonial policy in the 1930s to have an African lingua franca for their East African territories (Casco, 2007). It was largely based on the coastal dialect *Ki-unguja*, spoken in Zanzibar, which was the centre of culture and trade at that time (Legere, 2006). The influence of the Inter-Territorial Language Committee, which was tasked with standardisation, was limited to areas under British colonial administration. Conversely, countries such as Congo, under Belgian administration, had no influence on the committee (Casco, 2007). After independence, the Institute of Kiswahili Research (IKR), as part of the University of Dar es Salaam (Legere, 2006) continued the standardisation process. Later Kenya created its own regulatory council. Currently the National Council of Swahili, known as BAKITA (Baraza ya Kiswahili ya Taifa), supervises terminology development (Legere, 2006).

Swahili is more often spoken as a lingua franca (language of communication) across tribes and national borders, than as a mother tongue, and hence takes various forms, according to the geography and the language policy of relevant African countries. As a lingua franca, Swahili has assimilated many loan words from language contact: the largest contributor being Arabic through trade (Petzell, 2005), but also Persian, Portuguese, German and English. Of the major dialects, Congolese Swahili is particularly relevant to understand for Australian professionals, government departments and interpreting and translation agencies because of the new settlers from the regions where it is prevalent. In analysing Burundian Swahili, Der-Houssikian (2009) found dialect-specific deviations from the coastal Swahili of Tanzania and Kenya. Well-known dialects of Swahili include Kiunguja (Zanzibar), Kimvita (Mombasa), Kiamu (Lamu), Kipate (Pate), Kisiu (Siu), Kingazija (Comoros Islands) (Amidu, 1995; UCLA, n.d.). More recent (simplified) dialects include Kingwana (Congo and Democratic Republic of Congo) (UCLA, n.d.) and Sheng (Nairobi) (Githiora, 2002).

Linguistic diversity among Swahili-speakers is complex and results from a variety of factors, such as ethnic background, linguistic background of communities, patterns of migration, colonial and post-colonial policies. The language policies of the countries where Swahili-speakers come from affect the domains in which Swahili is used and the fluency of its speakers. Within Swahili-speaking communities, situated in multilingual contexts, there are differing levels of proficiency, literacy and competency in passive under-standing and active use of Standard Swahili and Swahili dialects. Factors influencing the varying proficiencies include lack of formal education, differ-ent policies in language-in-education between different regimes and coun-tries and disruption in refugee life (Borland & Mphande, 2009: 345). For example, Borland and Mphande (2008:12) found that most Sudanese, Burundians, Ugandans, Somalians, Ethiopians and Congolese surveyed in Victoria had learnt Swahili through their community interaction rather than formal schooling.

Swahili is spoken in countries with an abundance of languages, a typi-cally African situation (Lodhi, 1993) which produces both multilingual societies and multilingual individuals. For instance, in Tanzania 131 ethnic languages are spoken alongside Swahili and English. There are about 61 languages in Kenya (Kishe, 2003) and 47 in Uganda. DRC surpasses all these with about 221 ethnic languages as well as French, Lingala, Swahili, Kongo and Chiluba (Kishe, 2003). The resultant multilingualism of many individuals can lead to the use of different languages in specific domains as well as variability in fluency and proficiency. Woods (1994) describes the situation in the Republic of Congo as one where 'residents are likely to be exposed to three layers of language; an inner, ethnic language; the outer, official language, French and an intermediate national language' (Woods, 1994: 19). Schneider (1999) describes this phenomenon, evident also in Tanzania, as 'triglossia'. This is encouraged by language policies, such as those in Tanzania, where Swahili is the language of instruction in primary schools but English is the language of instruction in secondary and tertiary education. Furthermore, refugees especially may experience a number of stages in migration. They may therefore increase their language repertoire in each stage (Musgrave & Hajek, 2013). This can be more accentuated for those from a minority language group in their homeland (Musgrave & Hajek, 2013).

Swahili often functions as a lingua franca in Australia. Swahili can have symbolic status related to national or African identity that transcends tribal-ism. In Victoria, Africans surveyed saw Swahili as a 'neutral' lingua franca that avoids tribal associations (Borland & Mphande, 2008: 12). Swahili does not constitute ethnicity, and so is ethnically neutral as an *African* language, meaning diverse groups can identify with it (Russell, 1990). Massamba (1990: 4) stated Swahili is a lingua franca because it is a 'language which has no borders or areas or nationality' (translation from Swahili). Swahili is a medium of communication between groups of refugees in their new com-munities (Moshi, 2006) despite the differences between them, in terms of ethnicity, country of origin and birth.

4. The Profile of Swahili-Speakers in Australia

Community profiles as developed by government departments or community agencies tend to focus on ethnic groups or countries of birth as the central characteristic of communities (DIMIA, 2006; Lucas *et al.*, 2011; Service for the Treatment and Rehabilitation of Torture and Trauma Survivors [STARTTS], 2013). However, language is also an identity marker and an aspect of culture around which communities organise themselves and access services and support. This chapter has reviewed relevant literature in order to present a community profile around language, rather than ethnicity or country of birth. This is complemented by a statistical analysis of the Settlement Reporting Facility of the Department of Immigration and Border Protection (DIBP) and Australia Bureau of Statistics (ABS, 2013) census data using Tablebuilder software. This analysis has been modelled on a statistical profile of the Sudanese-born in Australia conducted by Lucas *et al.* (2011).

4.1 The census and settlement data

The census is a national collection of self-reported data from households conducted every five years that provides information useful for understanding communities and planning services (ABS, 2013). It records individual characteristics including country of birth, ancestry, language spoken at home, English language proficiency and educational level. The language question in the census asks about (one) language spoken at home, yet many Africans are multilingual and use different languages in various domains. Moreover, many who speak African languages that are not listed by the census are collapsed into 'not elsewhere classified' (nec) or 'not further defined' (nfd) (Lucas *et al.*, 2011: 17). Hence, the census does not allow for recording information about complex language use typical in African communities. This may in part explain the lack of preparedness amongst Australian government and other agencies for the linguistic complexity and diversity of the recent migrant settlement from Africa (Borland & Mphande, 2009).

The settlement database documents the records of settler arrivals on entry to Australia since 1991. It regularly updates from sources such as Medicare and Adult Migrant Education Scheme (AMES), making it probably a more accurate dataset than the census (Harte *et al.*, 2011). It records country of birth, age, gender, migration stream, main language spoken, English language proficiency and residence. Data from the census, government agencies and service providers give an incomplete picture (Borland & Mphande, 2006, 2009). Official records give restricted choices, and it may be that people identify the lingua franca, such as Swahili, as their main language because it is listed among the choices, whereas their mother tongues may not be listed. Ndhlovu (2009) also cautions that generic terms such as 'Swahili speakers' can erroneously suggest homogeneity and overshadow micro-level forms of diversity. Despite these limitations, national data can provide useful, though incomplete, information about the landscape of a community that can contribute to building a sociolinguistic profile.

4.2 The data on Swahili speakers

In the 2011 census, 6885 Australian residents indicated that Swahili was their main language spoken at home (see Figure 9.1). This is a significant increase from 1996, when 826 persons reported speaking Swahili at home, 1404 persons in the 2001 census and 3051 in the 2006 census (ABS, 2013). The percentage increase of 70%, 117% and 126%, respectively, placed Swahili as the 14th and 8th fastest growing language in 2001 and 2006.

The growth in Swahili use is linked to the increasing numbers of settler arrivals from DRC, Burundi, Rwanda, Kenya and Tanzania (DIAC, 2008). East African-born arrivals to Australia increased in the early 2000s, due to policy changes in Australia that resulted in increased numbers of African humanitarian entrants, which make up the majority of Swahili settlers. These entrants are from two categories, either granted visas on humanitarian grounds or entering under the Special Humanitarian Program, sponsored and supported by proposers. Smaller numbers enter on Family Reunion visas, while very few enter as skilled migrants (see Table 9.1).

Settlers speaking Swahili have been born in diverse African countries, with the majority originating from the DRC, with significant numbers from Burundi, Tanzania, Congo Republic and Kenya (see Table 9.2). These are either refugee-sending countries or host countries, such as Tanzania and Kenya, where children have been born in refugee camps. Hence, the country of birth of settlers may differ from their ancestry or country of origin. For example, the birth of babies to Congolese parents in Tanzanian refugee camps will be registered in Tanzania. Fewer numbers of Swahili-speakers come from neighbouring countries.

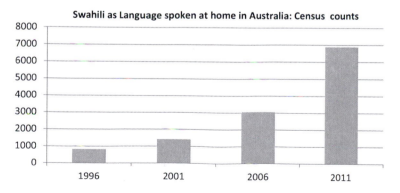

Figure 9.1 Census counts of Swahili as language spoken at home

Table 9.1 Migration stream of settlers with Swahili as main language, 1991–2014 (Department of Immigration and Border Protection [DIBP], 2014)

Migration streams	Numbers
Humanitarian	3612
Family	248
Unknown	112
Skilled	37
Other	1
Total	4010

Australian residents who speak Swahili are geographically dispersed widely throughout Australia with the largest numbers in Western Australia and Victoria. They have predominantly settled in significant urban areas (see Figure 9.2). They are also relatively dispersed within the states themselves. This geographical dispersion creates challenges for the provision of accessible interpreting and translation services.

English language proficiency is self-assessed and self-reported in settlement data. Amongst speakers of Swahili the number of those with poor or nil English proficiency is proportionally much higher than those whose English is reported as good or very good (see Figure 9.3). Such large numbers

Table 9.2 Country of Birth with Swahili as main language, 1991–2014 (DIBP, 2014)

Country of birth	Numbers
Democratic Republic of Congo	1891
Burundi	505
Tanzania	477
Congo Republic	429
Kenya	243
Malawi	126
Rwanda	81
Zambia	64
Uganda	61
Sudan	32
Zimbabwe	32
Mozambique	15
Somalia	14
Combined (<10)	40
Total arrivals	4010

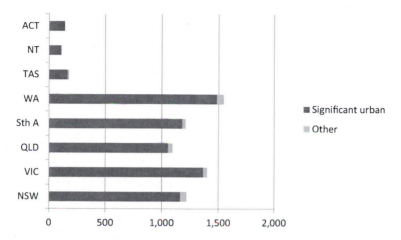

Figure 9.2 Distribution of Swahili-speakers by State, 2011 (ABS, 2013)

of those who rate their English Language poorly or non-existent has significant implications for the provision of language services.

This is consistent with the data on educational background. Significant numbers of Swahili-speakers have not completed either primary school or high school, with smaller portions having completed these levels (see Figure 9.4).

The majority of Swahili-speakers in Australia are from DRC. Likewise, Swahili is the language most spoken by Congolese from the DRC, with less speaking French and other African tribal languages (see Table 9.3). A report on Victorian speakers of African languages found that amongst agencies

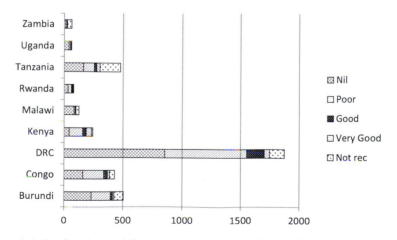

Figure 9.3 Settlers by Swahili as main language by English Proficiency, 1991–2013 (DIBP, 2014)

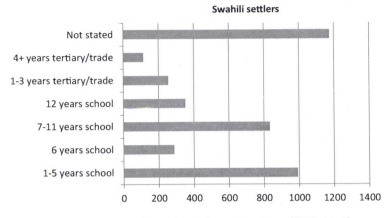

Figure 9.4 Years of Education of Swahili settlers, 1991–2014 (DIBP, 2014)

surveyed, their databases recorded English, French, Lingala, Nyanga and Swahili as the languages spoken by people from the Democratic Republic of Congo (Borland & Mphande, 2006). Some Congolese indicated that Swahili is their first language (Borland & Mphande, 2006). These data clearly show that although Swahili is commonly spoken by Congolese, it is not the only language spoken by this heterogeneous community.

There are fewer Swahili-speakers from Burundi than those who stated that Kirundi is their main language at home. However, Swahili is reported more than French and African tribal languages (see Table 9.4). More settlers from Tanzania report speaking a variety of African languages at home, which are likely to be their tribal languages, though it is possible that they also speak Swahili (see Table 9.5). Speakers of Kirundi who were born in Tanzania are likely to have been born in refugee camps to Burundian parents, illustrating the heterogeneity of members of African communities (see Table 9.5).

Table 9.3 Main language spoken by settlers from DRC, 1991–2013 (DIBP)

Languages spoken at home	Numbers
Swahili	**1872**
French	642
African languages, nfd	301
African languages, nec	141
Lingala	162
Kinyarwanda	108
Kirundi	48

Table 9.4 Main language spoken at home by settlers from Burundi, 1991–2013 (DIBP)

Languages spoken at home	Numbers
Kirundi	846
Swahili	**505**
African languages, nfd	339
French	124
African languages, nec	45

Table 9.5 Main language spoken by settlers from Tanzania, 1991–2013 (DIBP)

Languages spoken at home	Numbers
African languages, nfd	533
Swahili	**477**
Kirundi	324
English	206

The settlement data provide a picture of a diversity of languages being spoken at home by Australian settlers born in DRC, Burundi and Tanzania. These are Swahili, tribal languages, languages specific to Congolese, Rwandans and Burundians and the official languages of French and English.

4.3 Swahili variations

Variations in vocabulary between Swahili dialects or Swahili as spoken in different regions and countries can be significant and cause confusion and misunderstanding in interpreting and translation. Common discrepancies between (Tanzanian) Standard Swahili and the Swahili most familiar to many Congolese refugees are evident in weekdays and numbers (Casco, 2007; Kihore, 1997). Congolese Swahili uses a simplified numbering system, equivalent to 'three tens', 'four tens', for example, instead of the unique Arabic-based numbering of Standard Swahili for 30, 40, (that is, *makumi matatu, makumi manne* instead of *thelathini, arobaini*) (Casco, 2007) (see Table 9.6).

In Standard Swahili, the weekdays follow the Islamic/Arabic calendar naming in the case of *Alhamisi* (from the Arabic Al-Khamis) and *Ijumaa* (Aj-Jumaa, meaning the day of congregation), while the rest follow the numerical system using *juma* (Arabic for week) (Kihore, 1997). Congolese Swahili, however, names Sunday as *Siku ya Mungu* (God's day) for the day of rest with most of the following days counted numerically, beginning the days from the Christian Sabbath, rather than the Arabic/Muslim system used in Standard Swahili (see Table 9.6).

Table 9.6 Examples of variations between Standard Swahili and Congolese Swahili

English	Standard Swahili	Congolese Swahili
thirty	Thelathini (Arabic loan word)	Makumi matatu (three tens)
forty	Arobaini (Arabic loan word)	Makumi manne (four tens)
Sunday	Jumapili (the second of the week)	Siku ya Mungu (the Lord's day)
Monday	Jumatatu (the third of the week)	Siku ya Kwanza (the first day)

Table 9.7 Examples of variations between Standard Swahili and Kenyan Swahili

English	Standard Swahili	Kenyan Swahili
brother	kaka	ndugu
relative	ndugu	jamaa
wife	mke	bibi
grandmother	bibi	nyanya
tomato	nyanya	tunguja

Variations in Swahili as spoken in Kenya and Tanzania can also cause confusion (see Table 9.7). These include *ndugu*, meaning '(elder) brother' in Kenya, which mostly means 'relative' in Tanzania. *Bibi* can mean 'wife' in Kenya and Congo but 'grandmother' in Tanzania, which could lead to unfortunate misunderstandings when taken out of context.

Variations in pronunciation and writing exist also at the level of phonemes and letters. For example, often words beginning with two consonants CC (consonant, consonant) in Standard Swahili are pronounced CvC (consonant, vowel, consonant) in Congolese Swahili. Table 9.8 lists some examples as documented by de Lany (1967) and Luffin (2007: 23).

Pronunciation between Standard and Congolese Swahili is different in important ways. De Lany (1967: 45–46) noted the following differences: /dh/ becomes /z/ e.g. dharau becomes zarau, /kh/ becomes /h/, /gh/ becomes /g/, /th/ becomes /s/, /d/ or /z/, /j/ becomes the y consonant e.g. moja becomes moya. Final double vowels may be split by /l/ or /r/ (de Lany, 1967).

People naturally consider their own dialect as most appropriate and valuable. Strong attitudes are often held about the adequacy of various dialects and forms of Swahili, with debates about whether coast or inland Swahili is more pure or proper. The coast is considered more 'arabised', whereas the inland is more bantuised and African (Casco, 2007). More extreme can be attitudes that such dialects as Kingwana are not 'proper', are corrupted, or simplified to such an extent to be called 'kitchen' Swahili, while Standard Swahili may be viewed as 'dictionary' language irrelevant to daily life. This lingual diversity and the multilingualism of Swahili-speakers create

Table 9.8 Examples of variations in spelling between Standard Swahili and Congolese Swahili

English	Standard Swahili	Congo Swahili
person	mtu	mutu
child	mtoto	mutoto
tree	mti	muti
hand	mkono	mkono
son	mwana	muwana

challenges in providing interpreting and translation and other services for them in Australia.

5. Swahili Translation

Numerous agencies and government departments in Australia have recognised the demand for Swahili as an emerging language and the need for more translators and interpreters (Borland & Mphande, 2006; National Accreditation Authority for Translators and Interpreters [NAATI], 2006; Parliament of NSW, 2005). Demand tends to outstrip supply and recruitment of Swahili interpreters continues to be required. Encouragement and assistance has been given through the New Interpreters Project (NAATI, 2008). In May 2005, NAATI (2006: 20) identified Swahili as one of five languages in greatest demand and shortest supply. Hence, they began recruiting for a Swahili examiners panel. Testing and accreditation at paraprofessional level became available by 2009, which is the highest possible level that Swahili translators and interpreters can attain. As yet there is neither Swahili nor non-language specific translator or interpreter training available at tertiary level.

Most translators and interpreters in Australia are employed where there is the greatest demand, that being in the community sector, by various government departments concerned with health, immigration, social security, legal issues and education (Rogers, 2006). Community translation is bidirectional and crucial for minority language speakers to participate in society and access information. Hence, informative and instructive texts from authorities are complemented by translations of letters for immigration purposes and certificates of birth, marriage, national service and driving licenses as residents and citizens communicate to public services.

Swahili translators and interpreters are generally engaged as contractors on a casual basis. Swahili is regarded as a rare language in Australia as it is only spoken by relatively small numbers of people and there is not enough translation and interpreting work to sustain full-time employment

(The Australian Institute of Interpreters and Translators [AUSIT], 2005). For this reason, many Swahili translators and interpreters do both translating and interpreting work. The increased demand for Swahili services is likely to be due to its status as a 'preferred and/or available option' for communication with requests for Swahili made in the absence of interpreters and translators in a person's own language (Borland & Mphande, 2006: 37) (such as Kirundi or Kinyrwanda). Fortunately, more of these mother tongues are being recognised as in demand and recruitment and support of appropriate translators and interpreters is taking place.

The variations within Swahili as understood and used by Swahili-speakers in Australia is a challenge for translation of documents that aim to be understood by *all* Swahili-speakers. Standard Swahili is likely to be the most appropriate choice for translated material given its neutral status and its high status as a 'language of culture, education and communication' (de Lany, 1967). It is also a lingua franca for inter-ethnic communication as used in mass media, education and government in relevant African countries. Using standard Swahili may be the best approach for certain situations such as official documents or government material outlining legal information for national readership, even if some of the vocabulary is not entirely understood by all Swahili readers.

A Standard Swahili translation, however, may not be understandable to every Swahili reader, depending on their schooling background, dialect and literacy. Translators should be prepared to adapt their translations in order to communicate optimally with the diverse Swahili readership. In line with government and agency clients' aims to achieve receptive understanding of their communications by a broadly targeted audience, translators can carefully select vocabulary to avoid common misunderstandings among the variety of Swahili readers. One strategy is to retain some English in the Swahili translation to facilitate understanding. This is particularly crucial in the case of times and weekdays for Congolese readers who may be more familiar with these in English or French than Standard Swahili (Burke, 2012).

Selection of more Bantu-based words over Arabic-based words is likely to lead to greater understanding by more Swahili-readers from the inland regions and Central Africa, while still being understood by those from coastal regions and East Africa. Simplification of vocabulary and grammar is also likely to maximise readers' understanding. Similar strategies to keep text 'simple, readable, clear, easy to understand, free of ambiguities, readily available to anyone from different social and educational backgrounds' has been recommended by Pita (2014) in relation to translating Spanish language varieties, and would also be relevant for Arabic variants. All these strategies align with perceiving translation as a means to communication, requiring consideration of 'the target audience in a heterogenous community' (Lesch, 2014) while aiming for accurate *and* communicative translations (Ozolins, 2014).

Translators of rare languages, such as Swahili, often work alone in translating, checking and proofreading documents. However, an optimal translation may be achieved when several translators from different countries are involved in translating and checking a document, allowing variants to be considered (Burke, 2012). Pita (2014) suggests that 'language varieties can sometimes interfere in the interpreting process' and this is just as applicable in the translation process, when the translator or (future) reader does not (fully) understand a text. Newmark (1981) compares the art of semantic translation, which is usually the work of one translator to the craft of 'communicative translation, sometimes the product of a translator's team' (p. 63), which requires specific skills, knowledge, creativity and 'above all, common sense'. A diversity of linguistic backgrounds in a translation team of translator, checker and/or proofreader may produce a translation most likely to be understood by the widest range of readers, or at least, less likely to be misunderstood. This team process may best facilitate the reviser to be absolutely reader-focused (Ozolins, 2014). This may result in an obvious translation rather than a covert translation which appears to be an original (House cited in Lesch, 2014). A covert translation using pure Standard Swahili may not be possible when prioritising communicability and accommodating a mix of language varieties and explanations. Choices may be made to compromise consistency and fluency for acceptability and communicability.

Code-switching by Swahili writers is a phenomenon which presents issues for translators. In the author's experience this is commonly encountered in letters from asylum seekers or family members of refugees from Central Africa which require translation into English for immigration purposes. Such letters may consist of a combination of Standard Swahili and/or Congolese Swahili with French and/or English and possibly peppered with words from Kirundi, Kinyrwanda, Swahili slang, Sheng or tribal language expressions. In such cases, translators need to use creative strategies to produce an approved document. These include consultation with peer translators and with clients themselves about non-standard words, complemented at times with confirmation checks using online translation tools or internet searching to investigate word usage.

Service providers are beginning to carefully consider the best means for communicating to African Australians, including Swahili-speakers (Burke, 2012). Research conducted by Borland and Mphande (2008: 12) indicated that female and older Swahili speakers stated preferences for face-to-face communication. Applying these known preferences, some service providers are using audio and visual technologies such as CDs, DVDs and video clips and story-telling approaches for informative and instructive texts which are appropriate for those with lower literacy levels or who have cultural preferences for oral means of receiving information (Burke, 2012: 10).

6. Conclusion

Multilingualism and ethnic diversity are striking characteristics of communities in which people nominate Swahili as a language that they speak. Hence, caution needs to be exercised in profiling Swahili speakers in Australia, and other African groupings. Moreover, their linguistic diversity, in terms of variations in Swahili spoken and read, educational background, and variations in proficiency creates needs for community translation which prioritises communication and understanding in flexible ways. Keeping text simple, using standard Swahili for official documents, and retaining some English for clear communications exemplify such accommodation, as does the use of audio and video communications and story-telling approaches. Community translation in the context of linguistic diversity requires the development of multiple strategies based on better understandings of language in context and the role of community translation in complex situations.

Language diversity is a challenge for community translation. Pita (2014), writing from her experience of Spanish translation, argues that 'language diversity provides translators the opportunity to develop models that can contribute to translation research'. An implication of linguistic diversity is to suggest caution in judging translator's abilities based only on client feedback when an issue of clarity may be related to a mismatch of language variation. Instead, translators can harness their diverse linguistic backgrounds within mixed translating and checking teams to produce a more widely understood translation. Translators can discuss variations with clients and peer translators, and investigate frequency of online word usage. The strategies recommended in this chapter aim to take account of and work with language variations in order to provide minority language groups with equitable access to information, ability to communicate effectively with authorities and empowerment to participate in society.

References

Australian Bureau of Statistics [ABS] (2013) *Census home> data & analysis*. See http://www.abs.gov.au/websitedbs/censushome.nsf/home/data (accessed December 2013).

Amidu, A.A. (1995) Kiswahili, a continental language: How possible is it? (Part 1). *Nordic Journal of African Studies* 4 (2), 50–70.

Australian Institute of Interpreters and Translators [AUSIT] (2005) *Translating and interpreting terminology*. See http://www.ausit.org/eng/showpage.php3?id=851 (accessed 22 September 2009).

Baker, M. (1992) *In Other Words: A coursebook on translation*. London: Routledge.

Borland, H. and Mphande, C. (2006) *The Number of Speakers of African Languages Emerging in Victoria*. Report for the Victorian Office of Multicultural Affairs. Department for Victorian Communities.

Borland, H. and Mphande, C. (2008) *Communicating with Victoria's Emerging African Language Communities: Issues and responses*. Open Road: Exploring diversity. See http://www.openroad.net.au/conferences/2008/borland.html (accessed 23 August 2010).

Borland, H. and Mphande, C. (2009) Linguistic diversity and language service provision: Emerging African language communities in Victoria. In H. Chen and K. Cruickshank (eds) *Making a Difference: Challenges for Applied Linguistics* (pp. 341–358). Newcastle: Cambridge Scholars Publishing.

Burke, J. (2012) Translating Swahili: Adapting for diverse audiences. *AUSIT- In Touch* Spring, 9–10.

Casco, J.A.S. (2007) *Standard Swahili: Is it still a prevailing category?* Cuadernos de Trabajo del Centreo de Estudios de Asia y Africa Num. 12. Centre for Asian and African Studies. El Colegio de Mexico. Presentation at the 8th African Language Teachers Association Conference. April 29–May 1, 2004. Madison Wisconsin. Expanding our vision for African Language Pedagogy: A priority for the 21st century. See http://ceaa.colmex.mx/nuevositioceaa/imagenessitioceaa/cuadernosdetrabajo/cuaderno12.pdf (accessed 24 December 2009).

de Lany, M. (1967) A phonological contrastive analysis: North American English-Standard Swahili. *Swahili: Journal of the Institute of Swahili Research* 37 (1), 27–46, accessed 26 December 2009. http://www.eric.ed.gov/ERICDocs/data/ericdocs2sql/content_storage_01/0000019b/80/37/c3/3e.pdf

Der-Houssikian, H. (2009) Innovations on the fringes of the Kiswahili-speaking world. In F. McLaughlin (ed.) *The Languages of Urban Africa* (pp. 178–190), London: Continuum.

Department of Immigration and Border Protection [DIBP] (2014) *Settlement reporting: Providing statistical data on permanent arrivals to Australia*. See http://www.immi.gov.au/settlement/srf/ (accessed 24 June 2014).

Department of Immigration and Citizenship [DIAC] (2008) *The people of Australia: Statistics from the 2006 census*. Canberra: Commonwealth of Australia.

Department of Immigration and Citizenship [DIAC] (2013) *Settlement Reporting Facility*. See http://www.immi.gov.au/living-in-australia/delivering-assistance/settlement-reporting-facility/ (accessed 3 December 2013).

Department of Immigration and Multicultural Affairs [DIMIA] (2006) *Congolese community profile*. Canberra: Commonwealth of Australia.

Githiora, C. (2002) Sheng: Peer language, Swahili dialect or emerging Creole? *Journal of African Cultural Studies* 15 (2), 159–181.

Harte, W., Childs, I. and Hastings, P. (2011) African refugee communities in Southeast Queensland. *Australian Geographer* 42 (3), 325–342.

Kiango, J. (2005) Tanzanian's historical contribution to the recognition and promotion of Swahili. *Africa & Asia* 5, 157–166.

Kishe, A. (2003) Kiswahili as vehicle of unity and development in the Great Lakes region. *Language, Culture and Curriculum* 16 (2), 218–230.

Kihore, Y.M. (1997) Kiswahili naming of the days of the week: what went wrong? *Afrikanistische Arbeitspapiere (AAP)* 51 (1997), 151–156. See http://www.ifeas.uni-mainz.de/SwaFo/swafo4/4_11_kihore.pdf (accessed 24 December 2009).

Legere, K. (2006) Formal and informal development of the Swahili language: focus on Tanzania. In O. Arasanyin and M. Pemberton (eds) *Selected Proceedings of the 36th Annual Conference on African Linguistics* (pp. 176–184). Somerville, MA. Cascadilla Proceedings Project. See http://www.lingref.com/cpp/acal/36/paper1422.pdf (accessed 16 December 2009).

Lesch, H. (1999) Community Translation: Right or privilege? In M. Erasmus (ed.) *Liaison Interpreting in the Community* (pp. 90–98). Pretoria: Van Schaik.

Lesch, H. (2014) From practice to theory: societal factors as a norm governing principle for community translation. *International Conference on Community Translation*, University of Western Sydney, 11–13 September 2014.

Lodhi, A.Y. (1993) The language situation in Africa today. *Nordic Journal of African Studies* 2 (1), 79–86.

Lucas, D., Jamali, M. and Edgar, B. (2011) The Sudan-born in Australia: A statistical profile. *Australasian Review of African Studies* 34 (1), 82–102.

Luffin, X. (2007) On the Swahili documents in Arabic script from the Congo (19th Century). *Swahili Forum* 14, 17–26. See http://www.ifeas.uni-mainz.de/SwaFo/SF_14_03%20Luffin.pdf (accessed 24 December 2009).

Massamba, D. (1990) Kiswahili kama lugha ya Mawasiliano na matumizi yake katika Vyombo vya Habari. *Zonal Seminar on Policy and Planning incorporating Media Institutions in the Development and Spread of Swahili in countries using Swahili.*

Moshi, L. (2006) The globalized world languages: The case of Kiswahili. In O. Arasanyin and PM. Emberton (eds) *Selected Proceedings of the 36th Annual Conference on African Linguistics* (pp. 166–173). Cascadilla Proceedings Project: Somerville, MA. See http://www.lingref.com/cpp/acal/36/paper1421.pdf (accessed 14 December 2009).

Musgrave, S. and Hajek, J. (2013) Minority language speakers as migrants: some preliminary observation on the Sudanese community in Melbourne. *International Journal of Multilingualism* 10 (4), 394–410.

National Accreditation Authority for Translators and Interpreters [NAATI] (2006) *NAATI 27th Annual Report 2005–2006.* See http://www.naati.com.au_pdf annual-reports_2005–2006_27th_Annual_Report.pdf (accessed 16 May 2007).

National Accreditation Authority for Translators and Interpreters [NAATI] (2008) *New Interpreters Project.* See http://www.naati.com.au (accessed 14 August 2008).

Ndhlovu, F. (2009) The limitations of language and nationality as prime markers of African Diaspora identities in the state of Victoria. *African Identities* 7 (1), 17–32.

Newmark, P. (1981) *Approaches to Translation.* Oxford: Pergamon Press.

Odhiambo-Abuya, E. (2004) Parlez-vous l'anglais ou le Swahili? The role of interpreters in Refugee Status Determination interviews in Kenya. *Forced Migration Review 19.* Refugee Studies Centre, Oxford Department of International Development, University of Oxford,. See http://www.fmreview.org/FMRpdfs/FMR19/FMR1922.pdf (accessed 28 August 2010).

Ogwana, J. (2001) Swahili yesterday, today and tomorrow: Factors of its development and expansion. *Trans. Internet-Zeitschrift fur Kulturwissenschaften* 11. See http://www.inst.at/trans/11Nr/ogwana11.htm (accessed 16 December 2009).

Ozolins, U. (2014) Revision and quality assurance in community translation. *International Conference on Community Translation,* University of Western Sydney, 11–13 September 2014.

Parliament of NSW (2005) *Report of Proceedings before Standing Committee on Law and Justice Inquiry into Community Based Sentencing Options,* 1 September 2005. See www.parliament.nsw.gov.au/.../$FILE/050901%20hearing%20corrected%20Sydney.pdf (accessed 16 May 2007).

Petzell, M. (2005) Expanding the Swahili vocabulary. *Africa & Asia 5,* 85–107.

Pita, A. (2014) Translation and language ideologies. *International Conference on Community Translation,* University of Western Sydney, 11–13 September 2014.

Rogers, S. (2006) *T & I Labour Market in Australia.* Macquarie University Faculty of Human Sciences. See http://www.ling.mq.eduau/translation/lmtip_australia.htm (accessed 6 August 2010).

Russell, J. (1990) Success as a source of conflict in language-planning: The Tanzanian case. *Journal of Multilingual and Multicultural Development* 11 (5), 363–375.

Scheiderer, S. (1999) *Triglossia in Tanzania.* Se http://home.columbus.rr.com/sciences/tanzania.html (accessed 6 May 2005).

Service for the Treatment and Rehabilitation of Torture and Trauma Survivors [STARTTS] (2013) *Community consultation reports.* See http://startss.org.au/resources/community-consultation-reports/ (accessed 3 December 2013).

UCLA International Institute (no date) *Language Profile: Swahili.* UCLA Language Materials Project. UCLA International Institute. Centre for World Languages. See http://www.lmp.ucla.edu/Profile.aspx?LangID=17&menu=004 (accessed 16 December 2009).

Woods, D.R. (1994) Changing patterns of language utilization in the Republic of Congo. *African Languages and Cultures* 7 (1), 19–35.

Concluding Remarks

Mustapha Taibi

This collection of chapters has outlined some of the main issues in community translation. From migrant and refugee populations requiring translated information on public services in Australia, to incarcerated migrants in Spain who need both written and oral communication facilitators, or native South Africans who are now able to receive institutional information in their local languages after decades of Apartheid and marginalisation, the situations depicted and the problems discussed pose a number of serious questions, not only for community translators, but also for translation scholars, policymakers, public services and tertiary education providers.

Community translation is by definition a written language service that enables members of the community – usually disempowered minority language speakers – to have access to information and social participation. As such, it would be expected that community translation should be recognised and operationalised as 'a basic human right that every individual should enjoy', as European Union Commissioner Androulla Vassiliou asserts (cited in Brooke Townsley's chapter). As the same politician adds, 'in the multicultural, multi-ethnic and multilingual Europe of tomorrow, translation will play a fundamental role in ensuring peace and prosperity'. In Europe as elsewhere, ensuring the right to information and communication, especially in multilingual situations where there are significant socio-economic gaps, is key to social justice, social cohesion and mutual understanding.

However, as is clear from some of the contributions in this book, the level of recognition of community translation as a societal obligation towards disempowered language groups is not at its best. Budgetary constraints are often cited to justify lack of optimal translation services or a low volume of multilingual resources available to speakers of non-mainstream languages. Community translation in some cases is also caught up in broader debates about national unity, multiculturalism, integration and social cohesion. Unfavourable attitudes towards migrants, refugees, local ethnic minorities or marginalised majorities (e.g. South Africa) are then framed either in an economic or patriotic discourse. Opponents to multiculturalism and multilingual communication generally claim (1) that community translation is costly and resources are limited, and/or (2) that providing translations into other languages undermines social cohesion. Eric Pickles, the former UK

Communities and Local Government Secretary, uses both arguments: community translation, in his opinion, is 'very expensive and poor use of taxpayers' money' and has an 'unintentional, adverse impact on integration by reducing the incentive for some migrant communities to learn English' (*The Telegraph*, 2013).

In the words of Tony Judt, the historian and cultural commentator, 'We know what things cost but we have no idea what they are worth' (Judt, 2010: 1, cited in Cronin, 2013: 43). Applying this to community translation (and interpreting), it can be sustained that policymakers who oppose or do not sufficiently promote language services look at the cost and either fail to see or turn a blind eye towards the added value of multilingualism and professional language activities. Community translation and other language services do not only assist in making use of the valuable human capital of multilingual societies, but also contribute to sustaining key societal values such as democracy, equity and engagement. To use Harold Lesch's country as an example, democratisation in South Africa would not have been effective or credible without recognising African languages as official languages and providing multilingual resources for speakers of languages other than English and Afrikaans.

Closely related to democracy, social equity and participation is the issue of accessibility, a theme that runs through the entire volume. Policymakers and public service managers decide how many resources are to be made available in different languages and what languages are to be included, thus determining accessibility in terms of whether information is multilingual and, if so, the languages and formats in which it is disseminated. Further to such decisions being made, accessibility becomes a matter for community translators to deal with. A central question that arises at this point is whether community translators translate in order to mirror the content and stylistic features of the original text or to ensure their translations are accessible and comprehensible. This is a serious dilemma for translators working for linguistically diverse 'speech communities' (e.g. Swahili speakers in Australia in Burke's chapter) or target readerships with relatively lower socio-educational levels (e.g. the South African case in Lesch's chapter). With influential functionalist approaches to translation such as Skopos Theory, such questions should in principle be things of the past: translation is not an act of imitation or mirroring, but a reproduction of the source text which is in line with the new communicative purpose and situation, including the sociocultural background, knowledge, expectations and needs of the reader (Reiss & Vermeer, 1984: 101). However, accessibility continues to be debatable and understood in different senses.

Another central question in this book is the quality of community translations and how to ensure it. Taibi (Chapter 1 in this volume) suggests a quality framework that involves the participation of different stakeholders at different stages: before translation (e.g. policymaking, training, selection and briefing of translators), during translation (e.g. appropriate functionalist approach, language appropriateness, consultation with community members) and after translation (e.g. translation checking, seeking community feedback, etc.). Running through these stages is an overarching or transversal value that stems from the nature of community translation: the fact that it aims to empower certain social groups by facilitating access to public service information. As such, the framework is nothing but a number of guiding principles, with a central criterion or *macro-skopos*. It would be desirable for other scholars or community translation teachers to take it further and develop a more detailed assessment tool. An anticipated challenge is how to keep a balance between holistic and excessively analytic approaches to translation quality assessment.

Given the real-life interests at stake and the human lives affected by its availability and quality, community translation cannot be left to *ad hoc* approaches and measures. And a key element to ensuring professional services is adequate training. As is made clear in Dorothy Kelly's chapter, this is an area where the current state of affairs is far from what is desirable; not only in terms of specific community translation education, but also as far as relevant language combinations are concerned. Although Kelly believes that the skills required for community translation can be subsumed under existing generalist translation programmes and reinforced through specialised modules, the main problem in many countries is that the languages needed for community translation are not covered by generalist programmes (Taibi, 2011: 221–223). In some societies, this can lead to quality standards that vary according to translation setting and working languages: (1) scientific, literary and business translations, for instance, conducted by professionals, and community translations produced through ad hoc alternatives; or (2) community translations in some (major) languages achieving higher quality standards than translations into other (minority or emerging) languages.

Like other aspects of community translation, training has its challenges and constraints (e.g. large number of small language groups, lack of qualified trainers in some languages, cost for trainees and for training providers, etc.). However, provided there is sufficient interest and social commitment among translation scholars, educators, higher education leaders and institutional decision makers, innovative and collaborative ways can be found to overcome these issues. As Kelly (this volume) suggests, universities can collaborate to create expertise pools and shared teaching resources, facilitate mobility arrangements for students and staff, reach out for local communities to create opportunities for community service learning (as Rueda-Acedo's chapter shows), and use innovative online technologies to offer distance education for future community translators.

Reference to innovative technologies leads us to the last point in this closing overview of issues facing community translation: the interface between human and machine translation, and between 'community translation' in the sense of public service translation and 'community trans-lation' in the sense of amateur or collaborative translation for communities of interest on the internet, as is discussed in García's chapter. Due to funding cuts, some public services around the world are turning to machine transla-tion services available on the internet as a makeshift solution to language barriers between them and their target users who do not speak the official language(s) of the country or local community in question. If published unedited, 'translations' produced in this manner are likely to be more harm-ful than helpful; not only to the public service users but also to the transla-tion profession. Similarly, the practice of 'community translation' as an amateur service to online communities (O'Hagan, 2011: 14) may be an appealing model for some, to the extent that they could envisage it as trans-ferable to the area of public service translation. García (this volume) argues that community translation and 'community translation 2.0' can comple-ment each other: one undertaken by professionals for critical or sensitive materials, and the other by amateurs for non-critical matters, especially those requiring immediate or fast translation. Time will tell whether García's proposal is workable. However, apart from raising a serious question about who will assess the risk involved in each translation task and how it would be assessed, the proposal, like machine translation, might involve a shot in the foot of professionalisation efforts.

Looking forward, a final word is due on what is not covered (or not addressed sufficiently) in this volume and, therefore, where future publica-tions would make valuable contributions to research on community trans-lation and communication between public services and minority-language speakers in general. One area where further research is needed is the per-spectives of the target communities of community translation, and their views on communication needs, translation quality, translator role, dis-semination methods and the different means to empowerment. Another is the interface between community translation and other professions (e.g. community interpreting, cultural mediation or social work) and disciplines (e.g. social marketing, human rights or public health). Interdisciplinary research is likely to shed more light on – and, hopefully, provide solutions for – many of the issues pertaining to community translation and language services in multicultural and multilingual contexts. To close on a positive note, it is worth mentioning that some colleagues in the International Community Translation Research Group are currently working on a few research projects that would contribute to filling both gaps. Focusing mainly on community translation reception in healthcare settings, the projects place the perspectives and feedback of the intended readership at the centre of their focus, and bring together interdisciplinary expertise, including social marketing, public health, counselling, psychology, cross-cultural research, research with vulnerable populations and, naturally, community translation.

References

Cronin, M. (2013) *Translation in the Digital Age*. London and New York: Routledge.

O'Hagan, M. (2011) Introduction: Community translation: Translation as a social activity and its possible consequences in the advent of Web 2.0 and beyond'. In M. O'Hagan (ed.) *Linguistica Antverpiensia: Special Issue on Translation as a Social Activity* 10, 11–23.

Reiss, K. and Vermeer H.J. (1984) *Grundlegung einer allgemeinen Translationstheorie*. Tübingen: Niemeyer.

Taibi, M. (2011) Public service translation. In K. Malmkjær and K. Windle (eds) *The Oxford Handbook of Translation Studies* (pp. 214–227). Oxford: Oxford University Press.

The Telegraph (2013) Stop wasting millions translating leaflets into foreign languages, Eric Pickles tells councils. See http://www.telegraph.co.uk/news/politics/9924577/Stop-wasting-millions-translating-leaflets-into-foreign-languages-Eric-Pickles-tells-councils.html (accessed 10 March 2016).

Index